PENGUIN

THE BE

Geoffrey Boycott first played for Yorkshire in 1962. He played his first Test match for England just two years later. In an eighteen-year career he played in 108 Test matches, scored 22 Test centuries, including a highest score of 246, and ended with a Test average of 47.73. Since retiring as a player he has enjoyed a hugely successful career as a commentator. He lives in Jersey and South Africa.

The Best XI

GEOFFREY BOYCOTT

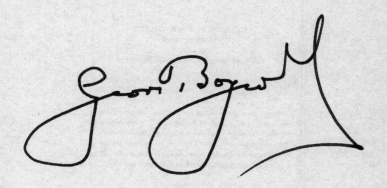

PENGUIN BOOKS

PENGUIN BOOKS

Published by the Penguin Group
Penguin Books Ltd, 80 Strand, London WC2R 0RL, England
Penguin Group (USA) Inc., 375 Hudson Street, New York, New York 10014, USA
Penguin Group (Canada), 90 Eglinton Avenue East, Suite 700, Toronto, Ontario, Canada M4P 2Y3
(a division of Pearson Penguin Canada Inc.)
Penguin Ireland, 25 St Stephen's Green, Dublin 2, Ireland (a division of Penguin Books Ltd)
Penguin Group (Australia), 250 Camberwell Road, Camberwell, Victoria 3124, Australia
(a division of Pearson Australia Group Pty Ltd)
Penguin Books India Pvt Ltd, 11 Community Centre,
Panchsheel Park, New Delhi – 110 017, India
Penguin Group (NZ), 67 Apollo Drive, Rosedale, North Shore 0632, New Zealand
(a division of Pearson New Zealand Ltd)
Penguin Books (South Africa) (Pty) Ltd, 24 Sturdee Avenue,
Rosebank, Johannesburg 2196, South Africa

Penguin Books Ltd, Registered Offices: 80 Strand, London WC2R 0RL, England

www.penguin.com

First published by Michael Joseph 2008
Published in Penguin Books 2009
1

Copyright © Geoffrey Boycott, 2008
All rights reserved

The moral right of the author has been asserted

Typeset by Rowland Phototypesetting Ltd, Bury St Edmunds, Suffolk
Printed in England by Clays Ltd, St Ives plc

ISBN: 978–0–141–03721–9

www.greenpenguin.co.uk

Penguin Books is committed to a sustainable future
for our business, our readers and our planet.
The book in your hands is made from paper
certified by the Forest Stewardship Council.

Mixed Sources
Product group from well-managed
forests and other controlled sources
www.fsc.org Cert no. SA-COC-1592
© 1996 Forest Stewardship Council
FSC

Contents

Illustrations

14. Sir Donald Bradman. Setting traps for him was a waste of time. © Offside

15. Bill O'Reilly. One of the three best leg spinners Australia ever produced and 'The Don' thought he was the best. © Getty Images

16. Ray Lindwall. A lot of English batsmen wished he had stuck with rugby league. © Getty Images

17. Dennis Lillee. He said of me: 'Like a good red wine, he got better with age.' He did, too. © Patrick Eagar

18. Shane Warne captured the public's imagination as very few have done. © Patrick Eagar

19. Adam Gilchrist, one ball short of the fastest Test hundred of all time. © Patrick Eagar

20. Graeme Pollock. The first name you write down when picking any South African side. © Patrick Eagar

21. Barry Richards: only four Tests before the curtain came down. © Patrick Eagar

22. Mike Proctor, a real match winner wherever he played. © Patrick Eagar

23. Vijay Hazare. Not much of a stylist but he didn't give up easily. © Getty Images

24. The young Sachin Tendulkar, who went on to make a bigger impact on the world stage than any other cricketer. © Patrick Eagar

25. Sunil Gavaskar, one of the two best openers of my time, consistent and run hungry. © Patrick Eagar

26. Chandrasekhar. He might have had a withered right arm, but crikey, he could bowl all right. © Patrick Eagar

27. Bishen Bedi. Poetry in motion, perfectly balanced and a joy to watch. © Patrick Eagar

28. Kapil Dev. Far and away the best pace bowler India has ever produced. © Patrick Eagar

29. Prasanna, a little fellow who could spin and had subtleties of flight. © Patrick Eagar

30. Imran Khan. He's number one, it, Mr Pakistan to cricketers all over the world. © Patrick Eagar

31. Javed Miandad. A tough, spiky individual who loved getting up the opposition's noses. © Patrick Eagar

32. Wasim Akram. Aggression and the ability to swing it and seam it from left arm over the wicket made him special. © Patrick Eagar

33. Waqar Younis. The other half of a lethal partnership with Wasim Akram. © Patrick Eagar

34. Sir Garfield Sobers, the greatest cricketer there has ever been, blessed with so much natural talent. © Patrick Eagar

35. Sir Viv Richards. The swagger, the chewing gum, the faint smile; enough to give bowlers the jitters. © Patrick Eagar

36. George Headley. They called him 'The Black Bradman' after his mastery of Clarrie Grimmett. © Getty Images

37. Malcolm Marshall, one of the three best fast bowlers I ever faced. © Offside

38. Lance Gibbs. The ideal foil to fiddle a few out, 309 of them! © Patrick Eagar

39. Curtly Ambrose. Terrific stamina brought him 405 wickets at 20.99 each. © Patrick Eagar

40. Martin Donnelly. Only appeared in seven Tests but remains a legend in New Zealand. © Getty Images

41. Bert Sutcliffe and Jack Cowie. Bert became an iconic figure in New Zealand and was rated by Wally Hammond, while Jack's nine Tests were spread over 12 years. © Getty Images

42. Sir Richard Hadlee. He kept you under pressure all the time with hardly anything to hit. © Offside

Preface

We all like picking our best ever teams. It's a lot of fun, but in the end it all comes down to opinion – there's no right or wrong, and cricket lovers the world over will always disagree. It's fairly obvious that half the players in anyone's best team would be everybody's choice; it's the other half which causes debate and divides opinion because in most countries it's possible to select *two* great sides. So how do you make a judgement on the best team ever? There are players we've never seen, some we've never heard of, and our opinions are bound to be coloured by what we've seen or read. So present day players or those of the recent past have a big advantage. Since the advent of television in the 1960s images of players and teams have made a huge impression on people. But what about those who went before: do we rely just on their statistics?

I've always believed that statistics don't lie but nor do they tell the whole story. You can't be a great player without great figures but some of the biggest names of the past only played a handful of Tests; in the early years there were only the England–Australia games, then two world wars interrupted many careers and South Africa because of apartheid was excluded for 20 years. Then there are the runs made and wickets taken against weak opposition like New Zealand, India and Pakistan when they first became Test-playing nations, the equivalent to Zimbabwe, Bangladesh and the West Indies at the moment. Yes, figures are a vital part of the assessment but I think you have to study them and it's how we interpret them that's important.

In the early years the pitches were very poor with stones on them for heaven's sake, and even when they improved they were still open to the elements so batting was much more difficult; as the number of low-scoring games proves, bowlers controlled situations and dominated. Then we have to look at the leg-before law which prior to 1937 dictated that the ball had to pitch in line from wicket to wicket and be going on to hit the stumps. So automatically batsmen went back and across which negated a lot of offspin, the nip-back seamers and the inswinger.

Fast bowlers were pretty toothless up until the Bodyline tour of 1932–33 because they were expected to pitch it up outside or on off stump. It was just not the done thing to bowl at a batsman's ribs – 'not cricket', as the Aussies whinged. There was no systematic attempt to intimidate or put batsmen under pressure by making them think they were going to get hurt. All that was to change.

Then we have the difficulties of playing on two different surfaces, turf and the matting used in India, Pakistan and South Africa. The Springboks favoured the mat until S. F. Barnes's side annihilated them and then they quickly switched to turf, although it was 1930–31 before the first turf pitch was laid at Newlands and 1935 at the Wanderers. In Australia uncovered pitches didn't matter too much because they didn't get a lot of rain, but when it did come down you ended up with a 'sticky dog' and the pitch was unplayable. That didn't change until 1954–55 when full covering was introduced at the start of Len Hutton's tour, but in England it didn't happen until 1979. The Test and County Cricket Board (forerunner of the England and Wales Cricket Board, ECB) said: 'At the behest of overseas boards and in fairness to the paying public, pitches for Test matches in England will be fully covered at all times.' Thank you very much. I had 15 years on uncovered pitches and some of them were very juicy, let me tell you. In my first Test at Trent Bridge against Australia in 1964 I was 23 not out overnight when it rained and next morning Garth McKenzie broke my finger. That's the difference between uncovered and covered pitches.

There's a difference in equipment too. No helmets, not even batting gloves in WG's day and when they were introduced they were only flimsy cotton affairs with little rubber spikes on the back right up until the 1940s when the horsehair glove came in. Bats are now heavier and better and hit the ball harder and further and have evolved like golf clubs and tennis racquets. Even the wickets increased in size to 28in tall by 9in wide in 1931. In 1969, after experimental seasons in England, the no-ball law changed in all Test cricket from a bowler being required to keep his *back* foot behind the return crease to keeping his *front* foot behind the popping crease (the front line where the batsman stands). Sir Donald Bradman said the alteration was 'the worst thing that has happened to cricket' and other illustrious commentators like Richie Benaud agree. So do I.

Overarm bowling wasn't legalized until 1864 although it was still permitted to bowl underarm and roundarm. By the time of the first official Test bowling as we know it today was standard although WG stuck to roundarm for a while. We've also had four-ball, six-ball and eight-ball overs around the world at various times and one ball for the whole of an innings, however long. Bradman's 1948 team in England were allowed a new ball at 65 overs; I wouldn't have fancied facing Lindwall, Miller and big Bill Johnston with a new cherry that often. There were also timeless Tests which meant that batsmen were never under pressure to score quickly; one of them, in South Africa at Durban in March 1939, lasted ten days and was only abandoned as a draw because the MCC team had to catch the last train to Cape Town or miss the boat home. Another, the fourth Test in Jamaica in 1930, went on for nine days before they called it off as a draw.

I feel cricket always mirrors the times we live in and the world has changed since those days. The pace of life is quicker, everything has to be easier, faster, there's a desire for instant gratification. Cricket in England kept pace by introducing the Gillette Cup in 1963 with 65 overs a side; then came the one-day John Player League in 1969 with 40 overs a side and the Benson & Hedges Cup followed with, initially, 55 overs a side. Now the Twenty20 competition which started in England in 2003 has become a money-spinner worldwide.

Market research by the ECB showed that the public wanted quickfire, all-action games. Twenty20 delivers; it's all over in three hours and it's taken off like a rocket, even in India where there was resistance because they couldn't get enough TV adverts in the shortened version compared to 50 overs a side. Vast sums of money are being invested and suddenly this concertina cricket is taking over the game.

Meanwhile administrators do nothing to help Test cricket. It's 90 overs a day and in most matches teams can't even bowl them in six and a half hours – and financial penalties don't work. I'd have four-day Tests with 65 eight-ball overs a day and do away with the constant time-wasting that goes on.

In 2007, of the 31 Tests played, 12 finished in under four days while bowlers managed a paltry 13 six-ball overs an hour. Batsmen are playing more shots and we need to get the bowlers moving. It doesn't matter whether you play three-, four-, five-day or timeless Tests, there are always going to be draws. Like football, they're part of the game, but all over the world Test match cricket is struggling except in England and in Australia for the Ashes series.

In hot countries like South Africa, Australia, India and Pakistan we have to try day–night Tests. People aren't going to take their holidays to see games like they once did so we've got to play when they have the time to watch. I know all the arguments against: the white ball doesn't last, the dew causes a problem, but that's rubbish. We can put a man on the moon but we can't develop a white ball which retains its shape and colour? Then use a new ball at each end – it's been done before: I played in Australia in 1979–80 when Lillee and Thomson had a new ball each! The dew only has an effect on one-day games at certain times of the year so you avoid those periods. Not too difficult to work out, is it? The diehards and stick-in-the-muds never want to change anything so that performances can be judged against those of the past. But, as we've seen, that's nonsense because the game has changed so much over the years. There was a time when we all had outside lavatories and washed in a tin bath in front of the fire; now it's en suite bathrooms and hot and cold running water. It will be different again in the next 30 or 40 years. Cricket has to keep pace and administrators, who appear to have forgotten about the paying public in their pursuit of TV money, have got to do something to help Test cricket to flourish. For my tournament I'll make the changes needed. For a start I'd have a 10-run fine for every over in a day not completed so that time-wasting would affect the result of the game. Fines are a joke: they are so piffling compared to earnings and allow teams to get away with murder. The free hit for a no ball in one-day cricket worked wonders and overstepping is rare now. That's because three or four no balls could cost you the game. The same thinking should be applied to slow over rates. We've got to get the public back into watching Test matches – speeding up the game with innovation is one way forward.

Nobody wants to play in front of two men and a dog; you want big crowds, atmosphere, the big stage. Cricket is dying through poor administrators who rely too much on TV cash to keep the game afloat and I want to see a regeneration.

The conditions, playing regulations and laws have all evolved, equipment has improved and in this book I've taken all these things into account as well as judging a player's statistics against his contemporaries. If it was a simple matter of figures any schoolboy could just go through *Wisden* and it wouldn't take too long because current players would win most of the arguments. But if a player was perceived by the public as a legend or an icon against others of his era then that must be a factor. If they've captured the imagination of the people it's important, in my view, to take into consideration what rules they played under and what sort of pitches they played on. The difficulty is in comparing a man who has played only 20 or so Tests with someone who's played 150.

I think that today's batsmen with extra equipment and better pitches have records which are five to 10 runs better than those of their predecessors while it's harder for the bowlers to get wickets on flat, dry pitches with much shorter boundaries. The pitches themselves are better prepared, can start in pristine condition and the covering has improved no end. In the old days the covers stood off the ground and when the rain lashed down it got underneath them. At Lord's where there is an 8ft 8in fall from one side to another the water ran down the slope and on to the pitch. Today they have a space age thing that looks like a hydrofoil but does its job. Other grounds used tarpaulins which although they kept the rain off made the pitch sweat. To see what happens, try this: take a plastic bag, tie a knot in it and leave it overnight. Next morning you'll have water in it and that's just like the condensation caused by tarpaulins. Now they put coir matting on the pitch and tarpaulins on top so there's no sweating.

Currently there's a lack of genuinely great players. Today's batsmen are having a field day against mediocre bowling and the Aussies are miles above the rest.

My idea is to pick a group of 13 or 14 players for each country who will play each other at home and away, in all conditions. If it's on the subcontinent there will be turning pitches so it's important to have quality spinners. We've also seen that on good, covered pitches whoever has the class fast bowling holds all the aces. It's simple; on good pitches spinners don't hurt you, fast men put you in hospital. So fast bowlers dominate my selections.

I'd love to see pitches start very dry all over the world, which is good for batting but means there will be turn – a cricket match without spinners is like a chess match without two important pieces, a less interesting game. Many groundsmen, or curators as the Aussies call them, want the pitch to last a full five days so it doesn't start as dry as it should, but really you want to see some turn after the third day which would force teams to go back to picking two spinners. When there's bounce and turn spinners win matches, when it's flat they don't worry anybody.

If I had my way games would be played under the old back foot no-ball law that Bradman and Benaud advocated. Most players today aren't old enough to have seen it, let alone played under it, but it was better for the umpires because they had more time to look up and focus on the batsman and better for bowlers because they could get their heads up earlier and look where they were bowling.

I go along with the LBW law as it is now, I'd take a new ball at 65 eight-ball overs and use the English Duke's ball, which did for the Aussies in 2005, rather than the Kookaburra because it swings more (as they found out) and swing bowling is becoming a lost art.

I want the boundary ropes right back to use the full size of the ground which would cut out the half-hit shots that go for six. Why do I want eight-ball overs? Because if the batsman gets on top and is handing out a bit of stick I think it's more fun for the spectators and, conversely, if the bowler is weaving a web he's got two more deliveries to spring the trap. That's the sort of stuff which has people on the edge of their seats.

I'd go back to the old bouncer rule and do away with the current nonsensical two-an-over limit. A quick bowler is entitled to have a go at a new batsman, to let him have a few round his ears. It's a test of his courage, character and ability and perfectly legitimate. But I would empower umpires to say 'enough is enough'. Dickie Bird was a prime example of doing it the right way: he'd let the bowler have a bit of latitude and then say 'that's it' and if the bowler didn't take any notice he'd let him have a warning. Two warnings and he's off. I've seen Dickie do it and it's the way short-pitched bowling should be handled by strong umpires. I expected the short stuff, it's part of being an opener and separates the timid, those who lack bottle, from the others and asks the question: 'Have you got the stomach for a fight?'

In making my selections I know I could set out a case for many others from all the countries but to misquote

Abraham Lincoln: 'You may please all of the people some of the time, you can even please some of the people all the time; but you can't please all of the people all the time.' I hope my best XI pleases you, and at the very least provokes some lively debate wherever this great game is followed.

England

Dr William Gilbert Grace (1880–99)

Dr W. G. Grace just has to be in the team. He was the first sporting superstar, a legend in his own lifetime and still one today. Show that photo of him in coloured cap, big belly, big beard to anyone all over the world and they will know who it is. Certainly he was cricket's first icon.

If you look at his Test match figures they are very modest if not downright ordinary by present day standards but what he achieved in the first class game was mind boggling. Batsmen didn't score as highly in those days and there were lower totals in most matches and although I wouldn't say bowlers dominated they had a much bigger say on pitches which were not always the best.

In his biography of WG, published in 1934, Bernard Darwin quoted the doctor as saying:

Many of the principal grounds were so rough as to be positively dangerous to players and batsmen were constantly damaged by the fast bowling. When wickets were in this condition you had to look out for the shooters and leave the bumping balls [bouncers] to look after themselves. At this time the Marylebone ground [Lord's] was in a very unsatisfactory condition, so unsatisfactory that in 1864 Sussex refused to play owing to roughness.

WG also played in an era where bowling evolved from underarm to roundarm to overarm on these poor pitches and it wasn't plain sailing. George Freeman, the Yorkshire fast bowler of the period, said after the doctor made 66 in 1870 on a ropey old pitch: 'A more wonderful innings was never played. Tom Emmett and I have often said it was a marvel the doctor was not either maimed, unnerved for the rest of his days or killed outright. I often think of his pluck when I watch a modern batsman, scared if a medium ball hits him on the hand.'

If the doctor's Test results were only on a par with his contemporaries, in the domestic game he was in a world of his own, making an astronomical number of runs. He also took nearly 3,000 wickets with an extraordinary strike rate of one every 44 balls and he was miles in front of any other English player of the time.

That famous picture of him hides the fact that in his youth he was a natural athlete and in 1866 won the national 440 yards title and two days later made 244 not out for Gloucestershire against Surrey at The Oval. That's just phenomenal.

He was the first man to score 100 hundreds, he got 2,000 runs in a season five times, in 28 summers passed the 1,000-run mark and he did the 1,000-runs, 100-wickets double eight times. In 1896 he exceeded 2,000 runs and 100 wickets and a year earlier made 1,000 runs in the month of May, not by the end of May which includes matches in April, but just in the 31-day period. This guy was exceptional, make no mistake about that, and was a hugely popular figure. It was reckoned that along with William Gladstone, the prime minister, he was the most recognized man in England and when the MCC team sailed to Australia he went first class while the rest of the players were in steerage!

He finally fell out with the Gloucestershire committee; it was said at the time that 'He loved playing for the county but as regards the Gloucestershire committee he had the greatest contempt.' Words I wish I had heard about 20 years ago when I had similar feelings about the Yorkshire committees!

So he left and in 1899 founded his own club, London County, who were really mercenaries playing for a purse of guineas against all-comers (sometimes 22 in a team), and the prize was always bigger if the doctor was playing because they charged twice as much for admission if he was in the side.

While his reputation grew and grew on the cricket field he still had the time to found the English Bowls Association and practise as a GP in the winter although it took him 11 years to pass his medical exams, starting as a 19-year-old and finally becoming an MD when he was married with three children. An amazing man.

The public readily recognized his feats and in 1879 at Gloucestershire he had a testimonial which, based purely on subscriptions, raised £1,500. Fifteen years later a newspaper raised £5,000 in one-shilling (5p) subscriptions from readers, the MCC raised £2,000 and Gloucestershire £1,500, and the total came to £9,073 8s 3d. In today's money that's over £720,000 in pure donations; no fancy dinners, golf days or auctions, just the public putting their hands in their pockets. There was no TV or radio and newspapers were more local than national. All a far cry from today when nonentities become stars through reality television and celebrity is rarely based on achievement. With none of that shallow hype the doctor was a huge superstar. Just think what he would have become today.

It's impossible to ignore his stature in the game. At London County between the ages of 51 and 60 he made 26 hundreds and although there was talk of gamesmanship – one story recounts how he had his bails clipped early on in a game in front of a big crowd at The Oval, and, replacing them, told the astonished bowler, 'These people have paid to watch me bat, not you bowl, so please carry on bowling, young man' – does it matter? People are still talking about him 100 years later and telling the same stories. Pure legend.

The most influential club in the world, Marylebone Cricket Club, which is still responsible for framing the laws of the game, honoured him by erecting the Grace Gates at Lord's in June 1922, a tribute to the game's most iconic figure. W. G. Grace and Old Father Time together at cricket's spiritual home.

Sir John Berry Hobbs (1908–30)

The more I read and hear about Jack Hobbs the more astonished I am, not just at his sensational statistics or the fact he was the first professional cricketer to be knighted, but by the dedication and method he used to become such an icon of English cricket.

The eldest of 12 children, he taught himself the game by using a stump and a tennis ball in the fives courts (very like a squash court) at Jesus College, Cambridge, where his father was the groundsman and umpire. With no formal coaching he practised on his own through the long vacations and the hand–eye coordination and footwork, he said in his autobiography, were responsible for his ability to play predominantly off the back foot and place the ball accurately.

This simple practice laid a wonderful foundation, giving me a keen eye and developing the wrist strokes which I had seen in college matches. Boy as I was, I tried to emulate the same strokes and I was surprised at the number of successful strokes I managed to make. That was the way I became a natural batsman. The footwork came automatically and the practice became a great source of enjoyment when I recognised how important everything was.

This, to me, is the real key as to what made him a great player and it's fascinating that the great Don Bradman used a similar method as a child when he was growing up in

Bowral on the other side of the world a few years later. When he was 12 years old or so he played schoolboy cricket on Parker's Piece, Cambridge, where Ranjitsinhji practised, and Hobbs saw his beautiful wrist-play, but the hero of Jack's boyhood was Tom Hayward, son of Dan Hayward who looked after the nets and marquees on the ground. Tom was instrumental in taking him to Surrey after Essex refused to give him a trial. They must have felt real twerps a couple of years later when he made his first championship century against them.

Like WG, he gave a new twist or direction to the game. Grace was the first to cope with overarm fast bowling, the first to mix forward and back play. Hobbs was brought up on principles more or less laid down by WG and his contemporaries, left leg forward to the length ball, right foot back to the ball a shade short, but the leg hadn't to be moved over the wicket to the off. Pad-play among the Victorians was just not the done thing, oh no, they thought it was unsporting.

Hobbs made his first-class debut for Surrey on a bitterly cold Easter Monday in 1905 against The Gentlemen of England, led by the doctor himself. Hobbs, then 22 years and 4 months old, scored 18 and then took only two hours over 88 in the second innings. Grace contemplated the youth from his position at point, stroked the beard and said, 'He's goin' to be a good 'un.' He could not have dreamed that 20 years later Hobbs would beat his own record of 126 centuries.

Jack learned to bat in circumstances of technique and environment much the same as those in which Grace made his runs. Bowlers concentrated their line of attack, by and large, on the off stump. Pace and length on good pitches, with varied flight. On sticky pitches the fast bowlers were often rested, the damage done by slow left-arm spin or right-hand off breaks. In those days only one ball was used throughout a team's innings, no matter how long, and the seam was not as prominent as it is now. In 1907, two summers after Hobbs's baptism of first-class cricket, the South Africans came to England, bringing a company of wrist-spinners in Vogler, White, Faulkner and Schwarz the like of which hadn't been seen before. Hobbs faced them only twice, scoring 18 and 41 for Surrey and 78 and 5 for C. I. Thornton's XI at Scarborough. But two years later, when the MCC visited South Africa, Hobbs demonstrated that he had found the answer to the problems of the back-of-the-hand spinners. He'd never seen the matting wickets then used in South Africa on which they turned the ball prodigiously, but in the five Tests of 1909–10 he scored 539 runs at an average of 67.37, double the averages of England's next best four run-makers, Thompson (33.77), Woolley (32.00), Denton (26.66) and Rhodes (25.11).

I find it fascinating that his career was divided into two periods, each different from the other in style and tempo. Before the First World War he was Trumperesque, quick to attack on spring-heeled feet, strokes all over the field, deadly but never brutal, all executed by the wrists.

When cricket resumed in 1919, Hobbs, who served in the Royal Flying Corps as a mechanic after a short spell in a munitions factory, was heading towards his 37th birthday and regarded as a veteran. But in this second phase he did away with some of the daring shots and ripened into a serene, classic stylist with a poise that was only ever approached by Wally Hammond.

In the three years from his forty-third birthday Hobbs scored some 11,000 runs, averaging round about the sixties. Yet he once said that he preferred to be remembered for the way he batted before 1914. 'But, Jack,' his friends protested, 'you got bags of runs after 1919!' 'Maybe,' replied Hobbs, 'but they were nearly all made off the back foot.'

In those later years some people said that Hobbs took advantage of the leg-before-wicket law which, prior to 1937, allowed batsmen to pad up against offspin pitched outside the off stump. It's true that Hobbs and Sutcliffe brought the second line of defence to a fine art and on two sticky pitches made marvellous opening stands against Australia at The Oval in 1926 and at Melbourne two years later. But Hobbs believed the bat was the first line of defence, not the pads.

Sir Alec Bedser told me he saw Hobbs bat in a charity match well after he had retired and said it struck him how Jack held the bat with his left hand further round towards the back of the bat, much further round than the modern player or the coaching manuals tell you. They said that if you held the bat like that you wouldn't be able to drive fluently through the off side. Well, that's a load of rubbish, it didn't stop Bradman or Hutton, did it?

You can't fail to be impressed by some of the tributes to him from some of the greatest players of all time. Andrew Sandham, who shared 66 opening stands of over 100 with Hobbs, said, 'I don't think I ever saw a ball beat him and get him out. It was usually an unforced error that accounted for his wicket. He appeared to have all the time in the world to place the ball exactly where he wanted.'

Wilfred Rhodes said, 'He was the greatest batsman of my time. I learned a lot from him when we went in first together for England. He had a cricket brain and the position of his feet as he met the ball was always perfect. He could have scored thousands more runs, but often he was content to throw his wicket away when he had reached his hundred and give someone else a chance.' (I don't know if I agree with the last bit!)

Herbert Sutcliffe said, 'I was his partner on many occasions on extremely bad wickets, and I can say this without any doubt that he was the most brilliant exponent of all time, and quite the best batsman of my generation on all types of wickets. On good wickets I do believe that pride of place should be given to Sir Don Bradman.'

Jack Fingleton, the Aussie batsman and author, wrote, 'Although figures indicate the greatness of Hobbs, they don't convey the grandeur of his batting, his faultless technique and the manner in which he captivated those who could recognise and analyse style. Australians who played against him believe cricket never produced a more correct batsman. But, it is well to note Hobbs' claim that he never had an hour's coaching in his life. He was a self-taught cricketer, observing, thinking and executing for himself.'

Neville Cardus wrote, 'Immediately the bowler began his run, Hobbs seemed to have some instinct of what manner of ball is on the way; rarely does he move his feet to an incorrect position. His footwork is so quick, that even from behind the nets it is not always possible to follow its movement in detail.'

Mouth-watering stuff, eh? What a player he must have been and to read tributes like that just makes me wish all the more I had seen him bat.

In 1914 he was awarded a testimonial but The Oval had been taken over by the army at the start of the Great War and his benefit game was moved to Lord's. Although he was allowed to keep the gate money the MCC refused to allow a collection from the huge crowd! Later tributes brought him £1,671 2s 7d and he opened a very successful sports shop in Fleet Street, one of the first, where he regularly served behind the counter.

It was fitting that in 1934, his last season, Surrey opened the Hobbs Gates at their famous ground, unusual that. Most times you have to be dead before such an honour is given.

Sir Leonard Hutton (1937–55)

Len was one of the most complete batsmen ever to play the game and I meet many, many people who say he was their boyhood idol. There's not much of an argument that he was England's best since the Second World War. I never actually saw him play in a first class match. I was twice taken to Park Avenue, Bradford to see the great man but both times rain set in and, as it is apt to do in Bradford, never gave up all day. Apparently he had great technique, on uncovered pitches he was the master, and that was allied to wonderful elegance when conditions were more favourable. He played all his life under the LBW law which changed in 1937 and made batting much harder, so his considerable achievements are all the more worthy.

He was run out for a duck on his Yorkshire debut and failed to score in his first match for England against New Zealand at Lord's in 1937 but only a year later when he was 22 years of age he made the then world record Test score of 364 against the Australians at The Oval, beating Wally Hammond's 336 in 1933. His batting after 1945 was still of the highest quality which is all the more remarkable because after an accident in the gym while in the Services during the war he had to have an operation which shortened his left arm. Looking at his figures it didn't seem to make much difference, but when the Yorkshire middle order bats-man Ted Lester remarked on what a player he was, Arthur

'Ticker' Mitchell, the county coach, replied, 'You should have seen him before the war.'

In 1950 Hutton made the first double century in a home Test by an England player, 202 against the West Indies, and in the winter followed it with 156 out of 272 in the fourth Test against Australia in Adelaide and became the only England batsman to carry his bat through an innings twice. An oddity in his CV is the dismissal for 'obstructing the field' in the Test against South Africa at The Oval when he instinctively swatted an edged delivery away and was deemed to have prevented Russell Endean making a catch.

Some say his greatest innings came on an infamous sticky dog in Brisbane in December 1950 when, batting at number six to accommodate an opening pairing of Cyril Washbrook and Reg Simpson, he made 62 out of 122. Others claim his 30 out of England's 52 all out at The Oval against Australia in 1948 to have been his finest hour. In that series a new ball was due after every 65 overs and Ray Lindwall, Keith Miller and Bill Johnston, the Aussie pace bowlers, must have thought all their Christmases had come at once. Twenty overs apiece and a new cherry? That would be hard work for any batsman anywhere.

England broke with the amateur tradition when they made him captain against India in 1952, incidentally Fred Trueman's explosive debut, and he made the first double hundred by an England captain overseas with 205 in Jamaica in 1954.

He was the sort of man who kept his cards close to his chest and was very wary and guarded unless he knew you well. I went to him for advice in 1965 when I was in my third season to ask how he coped with swing and suchlike but he never really said anything and I find it strange that such a legend should have been so reticent.

He did, however, have a very waspish sense of humour. Bill Bowes told me that during the Manchester Test against South Africa in 1951 Cuan McCarthy, their pace man, bowled a testing spell at the end of the day mainly to Jack Ikin who opened with Len. Bill remarked to him at the close of play that in Ikin 'we seem to have found a good 'un'. Len replied, 'Good player was at the other end.'

In his last eight Test matches he made 1,109 runs and was knighted shortly after his retirement in 1956. It was some 10 years or so later when I played in a benefit match with him. He hadn't played for such a long time that we only bowled spinners to him but, fielding at short leg, I was impressed by the way he released the bottom hand so that the ball could be played softly.

Len was so highly thought of by the Yorkshire public that his benefit in 1950 raised a then record of £9,712 and in 2001 the county club erected gates at the Kirkstall Lane end of the Headingley ground in his memory.

Perhaps his retirement was a little premature; he felt very keenly that although he was good enough to captain England he wasn't considered good enough to captain Yorkshire who were the last county to do away with the amateur tradition. Although he made the vast proportion of his runs at the top of the innings, he's number three in my side because I want three openers against the new ball.

Walter Reginald Hammond (1927–47)

This man has to be my number four, there's no doubt at all about that. Every person you speak to who saw Wally Hammond play or played against him say he was simply the best, top of the shop.

Len Hutton didn't have a lot to say about many people, but he simply rolled his eyes and shook his head in awe whenever Wally's name was mentioned. He was the doyen of his era and the superlatives have flowed down the ages about his batting.

He had an odd start in life, learning most of the basics in China where his dad was based in the army, and when they moved back to England he was already in his early teens. In a house match at Cirencester Grammar School he made 365 not out and Gloucestershire immediately wanted to pick him up. But he was born in Dover and after Hammond had played a couple of games as a 17-year-old, Kent, through the hugely influential and autocratic Lord Harris, kicked up such a fuss about him not being Gloucestershire born that MCC ruled he had to spend two years obtaining residential qualification. During that time he could only turn out in a handful of non-competitive games in the summer while playing football for Bristol Rovers in the off season. He was 20 before his full-time career resumed and then he had to miss the 1926 season after suffering a debilitating tropical disease picked up the previous winter on MCC's goodwill tour of the West Indies prior to their admission as a Test nation. He'd already made 732 runs and taken 22 wickets before coming back to a Bristol hospital where he was at death's door for months and he was hardly recognizable when as a haggard figure he was able to return to the county ground at the back end of the summer. But a winter coaching in South Africa restored his health and he was back with a big bang, scoring 1,000 runs in May 1927, the first since WG.

There was no denying his genius on the MCC trip to Australia in 1928–29 when he out-Bradmanned Bradman with 905 runs in the series at an average of over 113, making 251 in Sydney, 200 in Melbourne and 119 and 177 at the Adelaide Oval in the second, third and fourth Tests. He will always be remembered for the then world record score of 336 not out in Auckland against New Zealand, made in just 318 minutes, not even a full day's play, the third hundred coming in just 47 minutes! He was clearly awesome when he was firing, like Bradman and Viv Richards put together.

He had an arrogance, like all great players, that sometimes upset his fellow professionals. The story goes that he did not think much of Monty Cranfield, a Gloucestershire offspinner, said he could play him with a stump and duly took the hapless bowler back into the middle and proceeded to do just that. After Tom Goddard bowled Gloucestershire to victory, among the joyful celebrations of a win bonus Wally poured on the cold water and said, 'You're not *that* good – I could play you with the edge of the bat.' He went out on to the square and again showed his tremendous powers much to Goddard's humiliation. But if that was the dark side of him he could also be generous. When the same Goddard – a wonderful bowler with nearly 3,000 wickets at under 20 apiece – was worried that his benefit match in his home city of Gloucester wouldn't last into three days,

Hammond told him not to worry, he'd see to it and did, by batting the whole of the second day for a triple hundred. Cyril Washbrook was another who would never speak ill of him and often recounted Wally's kindness to him on his first tour. But if there were character flaws, what of it? I'm picking a team that would perform on the field, not because they were good to their mum.

Hammond was also a more than useful medium pacer with more than 700 wickets at 30 and a great slip fielder. His 167 hundreds put him third in the all time list behind Hobbs and Patsy Hendren and who knows, he might have been top if not for missing those three seasons. In 1938 he reverted to amateur status which allowed him to captain England in the series against Australia including the comprehensive win at The Oval where Len Hutton overtook his world record and he led MCC on the first postwar tour Down Under. But, suffering from arthritis, he had a poor time of it in the Tests and retired immediately on his return.

I met him in South Africa on the 1964–65 tour when he came to watch the practice day in Durban. Nobody recognized him except for the BBC commentator Brian Johnston who spotted him behind the nets, went up and introduced himself by saying he once interviewed him on the old radio programme *In Town Tonight*. Brian invited him to meet the players and he spent the whole of the Test match as a guest in our dressing room. I believe that by then he'd fallen on hard times and that the MCC management put up the money to fly him down to Port Elizabeth for the fifth and final Test.

At six feet tall and with the build of a heavyweight boxer, Wally Hammond lorded it over the cricket fields of the world. There was none better.

Denis Charles Scott Compton
(1937–57)

My fifth batsman just has to be Denis, the golden boy of the postwar era. Those who saw him bat are knocking on a bit now but they still talk about being thrilled and mesmerized by his performances and he holds a special place in their memories. He had flair and inventiveness at the crease and that devil-may-care attitude of so many players who lived through the Second World War and lost so many of their pals. Compton was intent on savouring every moment of life and brought huge enjoyment to cricket followers everywhere as he went about his business. With Bill Edrich he formed a partnership which thrilled the country and in 1947 the pair made 7,355 runs between them, Compton making 18 centuries in his aggregate of 3,816 and his partner 12 hundreds. Some going is that. It was a well-deserved and rare honour that MCC named the two stands at the Nursery end of the ground after them.

But Compton wasn't just a cavalier strokemaker. He could buckle down when the going was tough, then, having battled through the hard times, he could change gear and take an attack apart. To have someone in the late middle order who can take the bowling by the scruff of the neck is why he gets my vote.

Quick on his feet against spin, and sometimes the seamers too, he could be flamboyant and play outrageous shots because he had marvellous hand–eye coordination.

Good looking, a charmer and popular with the ladies,

Denis was the darling of the London set and became known throughout the land as the Brylcreem boy when his sleek head appeared on advertising hoardings all over Britain. He enjoyed a playboy lifestyle but underlying the carefree persona was a steeliness never better shown than when in the Manchester Test of 1948 he went to hook the very quick Ray Lindwall and was hit over the eye. He retired hurt for stitches, returned with his head swathed in bandages and made 145 not out in five and a half hours. That's the sort of raw courage which lay at the heart of the man.

He was every boy's idol and not only as a cricketer. He played outside left for Arsenal and appeared in the FA Cup final at Wembley when they beat Liverpool 2–0 in 1950, as well as winning a league championship medal and playing for England in 14 wartime internationals. Not just a two-bit second division player but a top drawer star at one of the biggest clubs in football. A naturally gifted athlete who was one of the last genuine dual sportsmen who excelled at both games.

The long hot summer of 1947 really saw him at his peak as a batsman, averaging 94.12 in the five Tests against the touring South Africans and making a record 3,816 runs in the season at an average of 90.85, racking up 18 centuries. In 78 Test matches he averaged 50.06 and if that wasn't enough he took 622 first class wickets with his left arm chinamen and googlies. Among a catalogue of extraordinary feats came 300 in three hours for MCC against Northern Transvaal in Benoni on the 1948–49 tour of South Africa.

It was football, however, which laid him low when an old knee injury became a real handicap and he had a disastrous tour of Australia in 1950–51 averaging only 7.57 in four Tests. The Compton Knee became a running story in the newspapers, but he showed he was no dilettante by fighting injury and scoring the winning runs when England regained the Ashes after 20 years at The Oval in 1953, his highest Test score, 278 in 290 minutes against Pakistan in 1954 and making 94 in his final Test in 1956.

If there was a flaw in his *Boy's Own Paper* story it was in his running between the wickets. Trevor Bailey, an England colleague, said, 'A call from Denis was merely the basis for negotiation.' And he even managed to run out his brother, the Middlesex wicketkeeper and Arsenal centre half, in Leslie's benefit match. But that apart he just has to be in my side over other major players who on figures alone demand consideration.

Herbert William Sutcliffe made 149 centuries, averaged 60 in Test matches and had the ability to play on all types of pitches. His partnership with Jack Hobbs was legendary and in a 27-year career he made 38,558 runs for Yorkshire alone at an average of 50.2 and is one of only two men to make 100 hundreds (112) for the county. Always immaculately turned out with his black hair slicked down, he was a stickler for having everything just right. Bill Bowes told me that when he was a young kid he went straight from the field into the lunch room because he was starving. He felt a hand on his shoulder and Herbert said quietly, 'Bill, be a good chap and go and put your blazer on.'

He had a supreme belief in his own ability and after heavy overnight rain at The Oval in the fifth Test of 1926 there was high anxiety in the England camp that they would be caught on a real sticky dog. Asked what he thought, Herbert said he slept beautifully, didn't hear the rain and added, 'We shall be all right as long as Jack doesn't get out!' They made 172 together, Herbert finishing with 161 and Hobbs 100.

He once stopped me on the stairs at Park Avenue,

Bradford, in 1971 when I was having a pretty good time of it with the bat and said, 'Geoffrey, you could be the first Englishman to average 100 in a season and you should do it.' He was the first person to mention that to me and, as things turned out, I did it.

No doubt he was a wonderful player but I can't put him in front of Grace, Hutton and Hobbs among the openers.

The other man I considered for the middle order was **Kenneth Frank Barrington**. He averaged 58.67 in Tests, with 20 centuries and, as Wally Grout the Australian wicket-keeper put it, 'walked out to bat with a Union Jack stitched to his back'. If you were in trouble Kenny was *the* man, a big heart and tremendous determination. He was a great late cutter and he had two sweep shots, one hard at square leg, the other more dainty and much finer. With his open, two-eyed stance bowlers thought he would be vulnerable outside off stump but oh no. He could drive and hit over the top but he had to be sure the ball was there to be hit and took few chances. I don't think he could change gear and savage bowlers as Compton did and although everybody loved Kenny, a fine man, he didn't capture the imagination like Denis.

Elias Henry 'Patsy' Hendren demands consideration on his sheer weight of runs. Second only to Hobbs with 170 centuries, the short, stocky Hendren was a tremendous cutter and puller of the ball, a great character and one of the first men in the game to wear a helmet of sorts. In 1933 Hendren caused something of a sensation at Lord's by batting against the West Indies' fast bowlers wearing a special cap made by his wife. It had three peaks, two of which covered the ears and temples, and was lined with sponge rubber. Hendren said he needed protection after being struck on the head two years earlier by the new-fashioned persistent short pitched bouncers. He averaged over 47 from 51 Tests, which is pretty good. Another with a great record is Frank Woolley, the Kent left hander. Although he averaged only 36 in Tests he made 1,000 runs in a season 28 times, a figure equalled only by WG. Peter May, Colin Cowdrey, Ted Dexter and David Gower were all fine middle order players but I believe that Denis was the daddy of them all and he gets my vote for the fifth batting place.

The All-Rounder

It comes down to just three really: Tony Greig, Trevor Bailey and Ian Botham.

The contribution of **Anthony William Greig** to English cricket has been underestimated because of his allegiance to Kerry Packer and *his* choice to recruit players for World Series Cricket while still the England captain. His critics hold that as a black mark against him which rules out anything else he may have done. But whatever the argument it should not detract from his performances for England.

He wasn't given sufficient credit for his ability to bat under pressure against either pace or spin, in many cases better than the specialist batsmen, and, bowling from a great height with swing, he was deceptive. If his seam bowling wasn't that penetrative he learned quickly how to adapt to conditions and had a good cricket brain. An example came in 1974 in the West Indies where we played on flat pitches in the first four Tests. There was no swing once the shine had gone, no movement off the seam and the West Indian batsmen were simply hitting through the line of the ball. That's when Greig with his big hands was smart enough to turn to offcutters and with four left handers in the top six he was able to exploit the rough outside their off stump. In Port of Spain, Trinidad, he had eight for 85 and five for 70 as we won by 26 runs.

He was a great catcher anywhere in the field but at slip he was exceptional for a man of 6ft 7in. It's very difficult to hold the low ones with that height but he did and he was the best tall man I've ever seen in that postion. Add to those abilities his hugely competitive nature and a cheerful disposition and you had one hell of a cricketer.

Trevor Edward Bailey was mainly a fine bowler with a lovely action and extremely accurate while also being a defensive batsman who earned his nickname of 'Barnacle' for his rearguard actions for England.

His best bowling performance came on the West Indies tour of 1954 when he took the new ball with Fred Trueman and in Kingston, Jamaica, in the fifth Test returned figures of seven for 54 in an England victory. A strong, bloody-minded batsman, he was a match-saver rather than a match-winner and he will always be remembered for making 71 in 257 minutes against Australia at Lord's in 1953 and with Willie Watson putting on 163 for the fifth wicket to deny the Aussies. In the same series he took 262 minutes over 38 in the second innings at Headingley when Australia were on top and the importance of these two backs-to-the-wall actions was emphasized when England won the last match at The Oval to regain the Ashes, Bailey making a crucial 64 in 228 minutes in the first innings. With 2,082 wickets in a first class career which stretched from 1945 to 1967 he was obviously top class and for me these are the only two guys to rival Botham.

Ian Terence Botham had the great gift of talent allied to luck. Maybe it's true that you make your own luck but there was no doubt it was on his side when he made his debut at Trent Bridge against Australia in 1977. It was the match which marked my return to Test cricket and when he came on to bowl he was obviously nervous. His first ball to Greg Chappell could kindly be described as a medium pace loosener but to be frank it was nothing more than a long hop which Chappell shaped to bang through the off side off the back foot but instead he got an inside edge on to his stumps. The gods were smiling on Botham and he finished with five for 74. Then, when he came back after a period of suspension to play against New Zealand at The Oval in 1986, Bruce Edgar edged the second ball he bowled straight to Graham Gooch at second slip. Gooch said, 'Who writes your scripts?' And he was right, you couldn't plan it.

If that was good fortune it was earned because he was an imposing figure with big shoulders, broad in the beam but with a slim waist which allowed him to gain that vital swivel which is crucial in producing outswing to the right hander, the most dangerous ball there is. He got close in to the stumps and his movement away from the bat dismissed some of the best in the world. He was also, along with Fred Trueman, the best I ever played with at getting rid of tailenders. As an opener when I'm getting mentally prepared to bat there's nothing worse than nine, ten and jack hanging around making runs. You want rid of them quickly and there was none better than 'Guy the Gorilla' as he was known in his early days (after the great ape in the London Zoo), long before the later nickname of 'Beefy'.

I'd be down at fine leg when seven wickets were down, shouting 'Get the gorilla on', because I knew he would see off the tail. He was not afraid to 'stick it up 'em', as the phrase goes, letting them have nasty, short, quick deliveries into the ribs. Tailenders don't like it so they move away to leg, are not in line and become a sitting target. They're backing off and the fear factor takes over. I wasn't worried at the tailenders taking offence at my shouting because as an opener I knew I was going to get some short stuff, so what the hell.

In his pomp Botham was much sharper than people

thought and the best I ever played with. Sadly, as age caught up he was a shadow of that great bowler when he played with Worcestershire and Durham, living off his well-deserved reputation. But let's not dwell on that; it happens to all players, none of us end as we were in our purple patches.

His superb bowling allowed his batting to flourish, letting him play shots and take risks. It's a great help when you're batting to know that if you fail you can succeed with the ball. In some cases when he had already bowled well he had the licence to do as he wanted and I believe that being a wicket-taking bowler gave him the freedom to bat expansively. We'd all like to bat the way he did but if you're purely a batsman and you fail, there's nothing to fall back on.

I've always disagreed with people who said that once his bowling talents faded he would be good enough to play for England just as a batsman. I never believed it. When you *have* to make runs with nothing else in your armoury you can't be free because if you get out to a loose shot you'll be criticized. Trying to construct a long innings just wasn't in Ian's nature and to ask him to play like that would have put him in a straitjacket, stifled his personality and dulled his natural talent. So it was that as his bowling waned so did his batting.

A substantial part of Ian's character was his supreme confidence and self-belief, an arrogance that he could do the impossible. Many great players have this, some in a quiet way, others shout it out. Mark my words, without it you don't get to the top.

He was also a great catcher in the outfield or at slip where he held them whether they were flying high or wide. He didn't miss many but when he did they were dollies and he always said he 'lost it in the crowd' and 'didn't see it', much to our amusement! At times he got closer and closer at second slip and I wondered if there was too much bravado. We were sure someone would flash, edge one and he was going to get a flyer which hit him in the chops but he never did.

The only blemish on his startling figures was against the West Indian sides of 1980 and 1981. They were at their peak with four brilliant fast bowlers and the best side I ever played against. But in nine Tests he made only one half century and never took five wickets in an innings. I'm not casting a slur – his record will stand the test of time – but it would be wrong of me not to say that, try like hell, as he always did, there was no match-winning performance.

He was too young when the selectors made a stupid miscalculation and appointed him captain at the age of 24. He was still one of the lads, larking around and enjoying himself and it wasn't his fault that he was given the job at the wrong time. He had a good cricket brain and if the selectors had waited until he matured a bit he could have been the right man for the job. When I played with him I always stood up for him because he never shirked responsibility. He was a big man always ready for the big stage and England's finest all-rounder.

The Wicketkeeper

For me this is a no contest with Alan Knott far and away the best.

People talk about **Thomas Godfrey Evans** being excellent standing up to Alec Bedser's medium pace cutters and he was something of a legend. He was ebullient, always positive, full of laughter, a generous sort and as the hub of the fielding side the wicketkeeper is the one to lift everyone when spirits flag. He was the man to do that but he didn't make runs under pressure like Knotty. Catches and stumpings are obviously important but in the modern game you must always be aware that the keeper has to make runs.

Now, **Leslie Ethelbert George Ames** of Kent averaged around 40 with the bat but people I have talked to who saw him play say that his glove work was never more than adequate, nothing special. An outstanding batsman, then, but just an average keeper. He managed the England side I toured the West Indies with in 1968 and I found him quiet, easygoing and a man no one could fall out with.

But the quality of the keeping is paramount for me and **Alan Philip Eric Knott** was simply fantastic. I roomed with him in St Lucia in 1968 and I told him then, 'You're going to be a legend in your own lifetime.' Even in those early days I thought he had quality and anyone who saw him keep to Derek Underwood on a wet pitch would have agreed. It was worth the entrance money alone just to watch Knotty.

On the 1970–71 tour of Australia under Ray Illingworth

when we regained the Ashes Knotty went four months of Tests, state games and up-country matches and never missed a chance. We got to the last Test and Illy lured Greg Chappell up the pitch, the ball went between bat and pad and Knotty missed it completely. There was a stunned silence in the field. No one in the side could believe what had happened – that's how good he was.

I've always judged keepers not so much by how many catches they take but how many they miss. The truth is that the bowler creates the chance and if it goes begging it can lead to a loss of confidence and keepers who get a lot of victims are usually profiting from quality bowling.

Bob Taylor was wonderful, with great hands and I played with him in the Golden Jubilee Test in Bombay in 1980 when he equalled the world record for catches in an innings, seven, on a bouncy seaming pitch. But Bob was not much as a batsman.

Knotty made runs under pressure. It wasn't so much the amount of runs but when he got them and I remember Ian Chappell, a real tough cookie, saying he was never through us until Knotty was out.

He was full of little idiosyncrasies: the handkerchief sticking out of his trouser pocket at just the right length; he used to cut the buttons off his shirt cuffs and do them up with Elastoplast; he had honey in his tea and was up at the crack of dawn lifting dumb-bells. When I roomed with him the alarm went off at six o'clock in the morning and when I asked what the hell was going on he said he was off to do his exercises with Bernard Thomas, the physio. I told him to get back to bed and get some sleep but he took no notice.

In addition to his great concentration he went about his job quietly but with ruthless efficiency. There were no histrionics, no excessive appealing, he didn't try to get up a batsman's nose, there was no gamesmanship. He just let his performances speak for him. He also had a wonderful cricket brain and it was Knotty who helped me work out John Gleeson, the Aussie 'mystery' spinner in 1970–71. Gleeson bowled his offspinner with the index finger, the usual way, but his leggie came off the middle finger, not the ring finger which is normal. He didn't turn his wrist but flicked the ball with strong fingers and big hands and he was very difficult to pick. Knotty and I sat for hours in our room flicking a tennis ball to and fro trying to work out how he did it and eventually we sorted it out.

In 1974–75 when Dennis Lillee and Jeff Thomson burst on the scene it was Knotty who developed the 'upper cut' over the slips and gulley to combat their very quick, bouncy, short stuff. He was the first to play a shot which is now commonplace and he worked out a way to counter the very real threat those two posed.

In all I'd say Knotty was a genius of a cricketer and I don't think there is any argument that he is the best ever seen, a top professional.

Sydney Francis Barnes (1901–14)

S. F. Barnes has to be the number one pick among the bowlers. Over six feet tall with wide shoulders and a deep chest on top of strong legs, his high delivery gave him lift off the pitch added to the accuracy of a spin bowler and had a well-concealed faster and slower ball.

Barnes was accepted by all his peers in Australia and England as the best and reading about him only reinforces those opinions. Wilfred Rhodes said, 'He was a very fine medium pace bowler and the best I ever played with. He had a lovely run-up to the wicket, carrying the ball in his left hand until only two paces from the crease then transferring it to his right. He kept a perfect length and direction and if you wanted to field at short leg you could stand up close to the batsman without any fear.'

Herbert Strudwick, the Surrey and England wicketkeeper, said, 'He was the best I ever kept to. He sent down something different each ball and he could turn it either way in remarkable fashion.'

The great Australian batsman Clem Hill said, 'On a perfect pitch Barnes could swing the ball in and out late and spin it.'

Wow, where did you come from? This is the stuff of comic books, like Wilson of *The Wizard*, yet the tributes paid to him and his figures prove that this was no fairy tale. There's a temptation to think that the stories about him have been embellished, that no one could make the ball talk like that. But then go and look at his figures: 4,069 wickets at 6.03 in the leagues, 1,441 for Staffordshire at 8.15 runs apiece and a total of 6,229 wickets in a career which stretched from 1895 to 1940 – and he did it all with not more than three hours' coaching but practised assiduously to perfect the leg break after mastering offspin quite easily!

His career started inauspiciously at Warwickshire in 1894 with two for 95 against Surrey at The Oval and after three more games he disappeared into the Lancashire League, playing five seasons with Rishton and two with Burnley. Word of his prowess reached Archie MacLaren, the captain of Lancashire and England, who put him in the county side for the last match of the 1901 season at Leicester. He took six for 70 and, amazingly, after taking just 13 first class wickets spread over seven seasons, MacLaren selected Barnes for the MCC tour to Australia that winter. In the first two Tests he took 19 wickets at 15.89 each before injuring his leg but he had made the leap from obscurity to international success.

He played in only 50 championship matches because there was more money in the leagues and he was a man who knew his own worth. He was a cantankerous character who was difficult to handle and when Johnny Douglas didn't give him the new ball in the first Test of the 1911–12 tour of Australia he got the huff; whether or not he wasn't trying we shall never know but he had figures of four for 179 in the match and England lost. To make his point he had five for 44 in Melbourne in the following Test when he got the new ball and England won the next four games, Barnes, opening the bowling, taking 30 wickets in the series at 19.96. His pride had been hurt, not least because you only got one ball to an innings in those days and he wanted it.

In South Africa, on matting pitches in 1913–14, he had

49 wickets in the first four Tests at 10.93 each but refused to play in the fifth because the management had promised to pay his wife's expenses and didn't come up with the brass.

Before anyone pooh-poohs South Africa it should be remembered that they had beaten England in the previous series and were no mugs with the bat. Herbie Taylor, one of their finest, averaged 50.8 in the series, a considerable feat given the threat Barnes posed.

Only Don Bradman dissented from those who thought Barnes the best in the world and said, 'Bill O'Reilly is better than Barnes because he could bowl every ball that Barnes bowled plus the googly.' The England man replied, 'That's quite true, I never bowled the googly. I never needed it.'

When asked which batsmen he found most difficult Barnes replied, 'Victor Trumper, no one else ever troubled me.' It was Barnes who was the originator of the modern phrase 'not good enough to get a touch' when, bowling at tailenders who played and missed and nicked it through slips, he remarked: 'They're not playing well enough to get out.'

Aloof, contrary, awkward, he disliked committees and hated batsmen and one contemporary commentator described him as 'a relentless, unsmiling destroyer of all batsmen that came his way'. No one can recall him having an off day or bowling badly (except when he was miffed at Johnny Douglas) and, whatever rosy glow is put on stories about him, his figures are amazing.

Against Australia he had 106 wickets at 21.58 and 77 of those were taken on their pitches Down Under which were flawless and the scourge of many a good bowler. In first class cricket in all he had 719 wickets at 17.09 to add to his staggering total of 6,510 wickets in league and minor counties cricket. He took a wicket every seven overs in

Test cricket against top batsmen on perfect pitches in Australia, while on the matting strips in South Africa he was unplayable.

I'd have loved to bat against him. I'd probably have got out just like the other poor so-and-sos but if you're a real pro you want to have a go. If, like Herbie Taylor, you come through it you've achieved the impossible, like walking up Everest.

Try as you might you can't ignore him as the best bowler the world has ever seen.

Frederick Sewards Trueman (1952–65)

Fred was my favourite bowler, one of the best I've ever seen or played against and blessed with the most perfect action you could ever wish to see. Poetry in motion. Exactly what you would want to teach any youngster: smooth, accelerating run-up, sideways-on delivery looking through the left arm with perfect poise and balance.

He bowled the most gorgeous outswinger at a real nasty pace and if you think of Waqar Younis producing those toe crushing inswinging yorkers, well Fred could do exactly the same with his outswinger and, like Waqar, do it at will.

He was one of the few bowlers I have seen who could genuinely bowl to a 7–2 split field (seven fielders on the off side and only two on the leg). When some captains try it most bowlers deliver the ball too wide of off stump for fear of being hit though the on side where there are only two fielders. But Fred was always difficult to work through the leg side because of the outswing and his tremendous control. Such control, in fact, that in seven seasons playing with him I can't remember him ever delivering anything like Steve Harmison's first ball of the 2006 Brisbane Test which ended up in second slip's hands.

When he first arrived at the Yorkshire indoor winter nets he was raw, fast and sprayed it about a bit but in those conditions, with poor lighting, the nets close together and the rest of the players on top of you, there was a feeling of claustrophobia and a young quick bowler was the last thing you wanted coming at you. When batters were asked by Arthur 'Ticker' Mitchell, the coach, what they thought about the young Trueman they all admitted how quick he was but stressed how wild he was too. The shrewd Mitchell laughed and said, 'Just think how good he'll be when we've taught him to bowl straight.'

The Indians found out how fast he was in 1952 when Fred made his Test debut at Headingley and they were reduced to nought for 4. They were terrified of him because they'd never seen pace like that and he had 28 wickets in the four-match series while still doing his National Service in the RAF but played in only seven home Tests in the next five years.

Len Hutton didn't do him any favours, make no mistake about that, and Fred got a reputation as being difficult. Fred became a larger than life figure. There were tales about his conduct on tour and he suffered from that; although half the stories told about him were true, the other half were about other people but sounded better if you used his name. One story still going the rounds had him saying, 'Pass the salt, Gunga Din,' to a West Indian official. Fred emphatically denied this until his dying day and I believe him. Privately he told me who did say it.

Fred missed 29 out of 36 Tests after that India series so just think what he might have achieved on top of his magnificent record of 307 wickets at 21.57, one every 49 balls. He held the world record for most Test wickets for nearly 12 years.

To listen to Fred after his retirement you'd think he was some kind of angel. He was not a drinker, just the odd pint, which most people find hard to believe. But he used to swear profusely on the field – not at the batsmen or umpires but at the nicks or the balls that beat the bat. One of his favourites was to stare down the pitch at some hapless lad, that black mane falling over his eyes, rolling up the sleeve which always unfurled in his delivery, and snarl, 'Tha's got more edges than a broken chamber pot.' I used to love to be at mid off or mid on to hear the banter.

He was already a legend when I got into the Yorkshire side and in my first championship match at Northampton Fred scored one of his three first class centuries. I struggled to make six before I was caught Allen bowled Lightfoot and I thought, If this is how good the bowlers can bat I've got no chance. Fred had a simple method: he played forward to everything and waited for the ball to hit the middle of the bat. If it was short and hit the top of his pad or thigh he'd look up the pitch and growl at the bowler, 'Pitch it up sunshine, two can play at that game and I'm a bit quicker than you.'

In that era, the early sixties, there were fewer net sessions than now but Fred got through twice as many overs as current bowlers manage in competitive matches. Like Brian Statham and Alec Bedser, Fred was a well-oiled machine – two or three balls to loosen up in the first over and then they were off full pelt. Current players are certainly 'gym fitter' than those of the past but they are not 'match fit'. Those old bowlers used to get through 1,000 overs a season and were well grooved. Nowadays there's too much resting and never in the history of the game has there been a player who got better by playing less.

It was hard work to get Fred to nets, unless he was trying to impress the selectors before an England match. His usual routine was to go into the opposition dressing room, tell the older players how well he was bowling and how many wickets he had, then seek out a young player, ask his name and what he did. If he was a batsman Fred would confidently assert, 'That's two more for FS then.' He'd get into our room 15 minutes before the start, get changed, whirl his arms a couple of times and that was his preparation. He always had 10 or 15 minutes' kip in the lunch interval, without fail. He'd have a ham sandwich, take a couple of bites and lie down with his sweater over his boots. Woe betide anyone who made a noise and woke him up. They would get a volley of abuse in the earthiest terms!

He was never short of repartee and when Richard Hutton interrupted one of his many tales of how he produced balls which swung and nipped back to ask if he ever bowled a straight one, Fred replied, 'Aye, it were a full bunger and it knocked out Garry Sobers' middle stump.'

But he was no paper tiger and Peter May once told me that his greatest attribute was to come back at the end of a long tiring day in the field and do the business. Brian Close, his captain at Yorkshire, knew that too and would call up Fred when the pitch was flat and the batsmen on top. He'd then set an attacking field so there were gaps which cost Fred precious runs but Closey remained deaf to the pleas for a more defensive field and just looked down at the grass. As Fred got more and more furious he got faster and faster and the end result was usually the wicket we wanted.

Between 1959 and 1963 he was without doubt the greatest fast bowler in the world with 776 wickets, 180 of them for England. In back-to-back Tests against the 1963 West Indians with Conrad Hunte, Rohan Kanhai, Basil Butcher, Garry Sobers and Frank Worrell in the side he took 11 for 152 at Lord's and 12 for 119 at Edgbaston. Two years earlier he had 11 for 88 against Australia at Headingley, taking five for 16 in one spell of fast stuff in the first innings and in the second bowling offcutters to have five wickets in 24 deliveries without cost. I doubt we shall ever see his like again.

Harold Larwood (1926–33)

The Nottinghamshire fast bowler only played in 21 Tests and his record of 78 wickets at 28.25 is not quite as good as some of the bowlers I have considered and discarded. But I think he was much better than those figures suggest. You have to realize that in that golden age of batsmanship fast bowlers were expected to aim at off stump, pitch it up and always had attacking fields. Short stuff or anything aimed at the leg stump was frowned upon and considered not the done thing and that's why you see most sides of that era obsessed with medium pacers and spin. Larwood made his debut in the second Test of the 1926 series against Australia but he was in and out of the side after that, missed out on 27 further caps and was not picked for the tours to New Zealand and the West Indies.

The amazing thing for me is how, given his record and the unwritten restrictions on the quick men, he was ever picked for the Bodyline tour of 1932–33 and how he did so well. I can tell you as a former opener that the biggest problem facing a fast bowler is not swing or movement off the pitch but the fear of being hit and put in hospital. In those days there were no helmets, chest protectors or arm guards and the batting gloves were flimsy. The biggest factor in a fast bowler's armoury is that threat of injury and frankly if you make him pitch it up outside off stump on a good pitch with gaps all over the field you've pulled his teeth and it all becomes so predictable. Take away that fear of being hit and it's all a hell of a lot easier. I know, I've been there.

But in those days of the amateur captain it was 'play up and play the game' and woe betide any fast man who let someone have it round their ears, it just wasn't done.

Then suddenly Douglas Jardine plucks him out of relative obscurity for the 1932—33 tour of Australia. The plan was to cut down the great Bradman. Somehow the shrewd Jardine assessed that, despite his previous pretty average figures in Test cricket, Larwood would have the pace and accuracy to bowl the 'leg theory', fast deliveries aimed at the batsman's ribs with a packed onside field. Remember there were no restrictions on the number of men you could have on the leg side. Not everyone could do it; too full and you'd get worked off the hip, too short and you'd be pulled in front of mid wicket, easy runs, too wide and it would be wasted energy. Larwood, however, proved brilliant at it and bowled like a demon with tremendous stamina and accuracy throughout the series. Nobody had bowled like this before and the Australians were shell shocked.

That's the reason I'd pick him for my side: if Larwood had been able to bowl like the quicks of the last 50 years just think of the havoc he would have wreaked. Think of the West Indians of the 1970s, Lillee and Thomson, John Snow in 1970—71, all masters of the short ball. For 16 of his Test matches Larwood had to bowl under the code of the age he lived in but when he was let off the leash he showed he had the capacity to frighten batsmen and the accuracy to destroy them. Like it or not Bradman was cut down to size.

Larwood finished the tour with figures of 33 wickets in the series at 19.51 and came home suffering from a sore heel. What happened afterwards really gets me and was the shabbiest episode in the history of Ashes cricket.

The Aussies got themselves into a state partly because they didn't have the bowlers to return the fire and partly because they were not good enough to cope with the short stuff. They threatened not to tour England in 1934 and to appease them MCC demanded that Harold apologize to the Australians. Quite rightly he refused and he never played for England again. What had Larwood to be sorry about? He hadn't done anything wrong, he'd just followed his captain's instructions, yet Jardine wasn't asked to apologize and led England in six Tests in 1933 and on the tour to India the following winter.

To have not done as Jardine ordered would have been tantamount to committing cricket suicide. You have to do as you're told. You might disagree and say so in the dressing room and tell the skipper he's wrong; I've done it. But you still have to do as the captain wants and in those days the amateur captains were gods on and off the field. They believed they were infallible and the stewards of the game. Lord Hawke, captain and president of Yorkshire, once wrote that if ever a time came when a professional captained Yorkshire it would signal the end for cricket. Well it happened in 1962 when Vic Wilson became the first pro captain and led them to the championship title and we're still going strong. But that's how the landed gentry thought. They felt that without their leadership, standards would drop and eventually the whole foundation of the game would collapse.

The pressure from the Australians got rid of Larwood while Jardine judiciously retired before the 1934 tour, jumping before he was pushed. The Aussies must have been laughing. They even sought to put pressure on Bill Voce, another member of the Bodyline tour and Larwood's partner at Trent Bridge, twisting MCC's arm to such effect that they told Voce not to play in the county match against the tourists so as not to upset them. Although he did turn out for his county against the tourists, he was not picked again for England against Australia until 1946–47.

The Aussies got exactly what they wanted and Bradman made 304 at Leeds and 244 at The Oval as they won the series 2–1 and regained the Ashes. To me it was pathetic that the Australian Cricket Board should be sending telegrams to MCC complaining that the English bowlers were hurting their players. You'd think cricket was a game for cissies.

Australia has always prided itself on being a sporting nation which plays to the rules. They're always hard, tough guys, coming at you hard but fair, which I admire. But to read some of the stuff that they wrote about Bodyline and how they squealed appals me. In later years as soon as they had the fire power through first Lindwall, Miller and big Bill Johnston and later with Meckiff, O'Rourke, Lillee and Thomson they had no mercy for any opponent. There was plenty of short stuff, bouncers and intimidation, believe me, and they won plenty of matches with it. So long as the umpires allowed it and they played to the rules that is fine by me. But if it's OK for them, then it was OK for Larwood and it was scandalous that Harold was made the scapegoat to pacify the cry babies.

Larwood played until 1938 for Nottinghamshire but the way he was treated was disgraceful and a blot on MCC's distinguished history.

I haven't picked Larwood out of sympathy but because of his ability to intimidate. If he'd been allowed to stick it up 'em like the quicks of the last half century what a record he would have had.

George Alfred Lohmann (1886–96)

Although he only played Test cricket for 10 years between 1886 and 1896, George Lohmann has a strong claim to be the greatest bowler ever. In 18 Tests he took 112 wickets at 10.75 each with a strike rate of one wicket every 34 balls – they are phenomenal figures. A lot of people look at the statistics from the last 10 years or so of the 19th century and dismiss them as not worth much. They say the pitches were bad, the overall standard of play not very good, but that's not fair. You can only judge a man's performance against his contemporaries but by any standards Lohmann's achievements with the ball were outstanding. Because they played so little Test cricket in those days the figures look insignificant. But look at it this way: England had 13 Tests in the 12 months from April 2007; over a 10-year period that's 130 matches, so if Lohmann kept up his strike rate of 6.2 wickets a game he would have 808 wickets and we would be sitting up and taking notice. The guys of that era had so little opportunity to play big games but it's wrong to discount them simply because of that.

Batsmen tend to be remembered more than bowlers because they are more aesthetically pleasing and that tends to colour the imagination, but I am trying to look at things objectively.

Lohmann played in the inaugural South African series of 1895–96 and while I accept that they were new to Test cricket and not very strong, he took 35 wickets in 103.4

overs at 5.8 each, taking one wicket every three overs. At Port Elizabeth in the first Test he had eight for 7 as they were dismissed for 30 in 94 balls and he finished the match with a hat-trick. Against Australia, a different cup of tea, he had 77 wickets at 13 each, one every 48 balls, and they were good. Altogether he took eight or more wickets in an innings 20 times, four of them in Tests, and 13 or more in a match 14 times.

Born in Middlesex, the son of a well-to-do stockbroker, he was 5ft 11in and 12 stone and by all accounts a handsome man who played a major role in Surrey winning seven championships during his 11 years with them. He bowled brisk medium pace cutters, what they used to call break backs, with swerve or swing, very similar to Sydney Barnes who followed him. Economical yet penetrative, Lohmann bagged 1,221 wickets at 13.19 for his county, including 200 wickets in a summer in three consecutive seasons, 1888 to 1890. He took wickets cheaply and regularly, one every 37 balls.

We tend to look at all sports with a modern perspective and think that these old codgers wouldn't live with today's generation, but you have to judge them in their own times. Would Fred Perry, a legend at tennis, live with the current crop with their carbon-fibre racquets and 130mph serves? Probably not, but do you erase the achievements of a previous generation because of that? The same applies to golf, football, you name it.

Five wickets in an innings 176 times, 10 in a match on 57 occasions; those figures will do for me and make him a must in my side. You have to assess players on how they performed in their own era and he was exceptional. If you're picking the best team it's not fair to rule out Lohmann simply because he played so few Tests. None of his contemporaries came close to his figures. You can make any excuse you want, bad pitches, quality of opposition, but his performances were mind boggling. It didn't matter whether it was on the matting pitches of South Africa, in the heat of Australia with four- and six-ball overs or on the pitches in England, he did the job.

I don't care if he is similar to Barnes. If he can take wickets so quickly and cheaply, who the hell cares if you have two of the same type? Bowlers hunt in pairs and Australia used to play two legspinners in Grimmett and O'Reilly, didn't they?

Unfortunately, Lohmann didn't enjoy good health and at only 35 years of age had to give up the game because of tuberculosis for which there was then no cure. He moved to South Africa to benefit from the drier climate of the Cape, near Worcester, and recovered sufficiently to manage the South African team which toured England in 1901. But a couple of months after his return he died of the disease at the age of 36, one of the most underrated bowlers in the history of the game.

John Brian Statham (1951–65)

We need to inject some pace into the side and to do that I've had to review at least five quality bowlers before settling on one of them.

The first to consider is **Frank Holmes Tyson**. He'll forever be remembered for that fantastic performance Down Under when he blew away the Aussies in the winter of 1954–55. After a poor start up in Brisbane where he had one for 160, in Sydney and Melbourne he put in incredible performances from a shortened run-up and finished the series with 27 further wickets at 15.8. I once asked Richie Benaud what Tyson did with the ball, swing it, move it off the seam or what, and he replied in his laconic way: 'Didn't have to do anything with it, Geoffrey.' That quick? 'That quick,' he said.

The problem with Tyson is that he missed so many matches with injury: three against South Africa in 1955, four out of five the next year against Australia and three out of five in South Africa in 1956–57. After that wonderful effort in Australia he was absent for 23 Tests over the next four years. I'm sorry but missing that many games through injury is not good enough for my side. He was called the Typhoon after that Ashes-winning series and just like a storm he blew himself out.

Alec Victor Bedser is another great bowler I would like to get in the side but can't. He was the modern day equivalent of Lohmann and Barnes with a great record.

Uncomplaining, dependable, hard working, a total pro and a captain's dream because you could set a field to him. Unfortunately for a man I respect and admire, Barnes and Lohmann had superior strike rates to his 67.44 balls per wicket and I'm sad to leave him out because he put in so many top class performances for Surrey and England.

John Augustine Snow is another with a great record, 202 wickets at 26.66. I remember him making his debut in the same team as me against New Zealand in the second Test of 1965. It was a bit of a surprise when he didn't get picked for the tour of Australia the following winter; instead he spent it in South Africa where he was encouraged to get closer to the stumps at the point of delivery and make the ball go out. When he started in county cricket he bowled mainly inswing and that spell abroad made him a much more dangerous bowler. His great strength was pitching it just short of a length and getting it up into the batsman's ribs and he did just that in the successful 1970–71 Ashes tour for which he will always be remembered.

Some people called him lazy because he was not always up for it in the county game but I wouldn't agree with that and prefer to say he was a bit laid back and sometimes needed geeing up. Raymond Illingworth used to send me to mid off when Snow was bowling with instructions to wind him up and I did it by taking the mickey out of his bowling. I'd say to him at the end of an over, 'I'd have scored 10 off that,' or, 'You'd never get me out with stuff like that.' He used to threaten me back, 'Wait until I get you on a quick pitch at Hove,' to which I'd reply, 'You're not quick enough or good enough.' A bit cheeky but it worked as I did stir him up. He'd broken my hand on the eve of the 1969 Gillette Cup final but, as I reminded him, he might have bust my hand but he didn't get me out!

There's no doubt about it, he was a very fine bowler as was **Robert George Dylan Willis**, another I considered for my side. Bob made his debut in the 1970–71 series after just half a season with Surrey, coming out as a replacement for Derbyshire's Alan Ward who went home with a stress fracture of the shin. It was mainly on the strength of a recommendation from John Edrich because half the team had never seen him bowl. He had a very long run and an ungainly action but those who only saw him at the end of his career when he was stiff-jointed and not too mobile would not have recognized the genuine athlete he was in his younger days.

He was unlucky that he played in Botham's era when people always focused on the derring-do of the all-rounder as at Headingley in that famous 1981 Test which they insist on calling 'Botham's Game'. There's no doubt Ian turned the match with his superb 149 not out, but it was Bob who won it with a magnificent spell of eight for 41 from just 15.1 overs. It was sensational stuff as he flew down the hill from the Kirkstall Lane end like a man possessed, really in the zone and unstoppable as England got home by 18 runs. I don't think he was ever given the proper recognition for his genuine quick bowling.

But the man I'm going for had 252 wickets at 24.84, Brian Statham, forever known as 'George'. Some have it that the nickname came about because of superstition. The Lancashire players believed that every time they had previously won the championship title there was a 'George' in the side – before Statham came along Winston Place, the opening batsman, was dubbed 'George'. When Place retired the new boy carried on the tradition. Others thought he got the name because his bowling looked as though it was on autopilot, but in my early days he was called the Greyhound because of his sinewy, loose-limbed run-up, an easy, repetitive action.

He may have been thought of as a quiet man but all his former team-mates I have spoken to have stressed that he had a steely determination and was a real competitor who loved winning. He was the complete opposite to Trueman, his England partner, both in personality and as a bowler and they entirely complemented each other. While Fred never stopped talking, George was quiet; while Fred always let you know about his feats, George was unassuming; while Fred was always at the batsman, George wore them down; while Fred was mostly abstemious, George liked a few gin and tonics. They made a formidable pair although, strangely, they did not figure together that often in the England team.

Statham was rarely injured and had great stamina but it was his pinpoint accuracy at no mean pace that made him such an outstanding performer over 18 years. He set great store by his ability to bowl on a line just outside the off stump. When asked by his Lancashire team-mate David Green one evening why he had such a long face he said, 'I like to be an inch or two outside the off stump and now it's getting to four inches wide and that won't do.' Modern day bowlers don't believe such accuracy is possible yet it was Statham's forte. If he had a winter off he would turn up to the spring nets, pick up any old ball and land it right on the spot. Any captain with a bowler like that is a happy man. He also had a mean bouncer which he didn't use often but when he did it was a nasty delivery from not much shorter than his normal length which skidded at you.

He was in and out of the Test side after his debut on the 1950–51 tour of Australia and didn't get established until the 1954 series against Pakistan and in Australia the following winter when he had 18 wickets at 28.3, proving an admirable foil for Tyson.

He was double-jointed, extremely supple and even now in my mind's eye I can see him reaching over his right shoulder and way down his back to pull off his sweater.

He got me out early on in my career at Bramall Lane with a ball which swung in, pitched about middle and leg, straightened, hit me on the back leg and pinned me leg before for nought second ball. At the end of the day's play both sides were invited to the committee room and I was standing on my own none too happy with life when he came over to me and said, 'If I bowl thee another like that in the second innings tha'll have bagged 'em.' He was trying to help but it didn't do my confidence much good although I knew what he meant; there's little or nothing you can do about deliveries like that.

With 1,816 wickets for the Red Rose county at 15.12 and 2,260 at 16.37 in his first class career at a formidable strike rate of a wicket every 44.67 deliveries, Statham eventually had one end of Old Trafford named after him but I think Lancashire got it wrong. Although the local council named a road at the City end Brian Statham Way he bowled the vast majority of his overs from the Stretford end. Surely it would have been more appropriate to dedicate that end to one of the county's and England's finest bowlers.

Wilfred Rhodes (1899–1930)

The left arm spinner was the most difficult to select because so many very great ones have played for England down the ages. The immensely talented **John Henry Wardle**, an orthodox left armer, also had the ability to bowl chinamen and googlies, the left armer's wrist spin. What's more he could drop it straight on the spot and on the South African tour in 1957 had 12 for 89 in the second Test at Cape Town. Yorkshire, however, wanted him to bowl traditional spin and he was absolutely brilliant at that with 1,846 wickets in his first class career at an average of 18.97.

You can win a bob or two asking which Test match bowler since the war with more than 100 wickets took them at the lowest average. The answer is Johnny Wardle with 102 at 20.39 and no one has ever got that right when I've asked the question of fellow broadcasters.

Wardle's great rival for a place in the England team was Surrey's **Graham Anthony Richard Lock**, a superb competitor and wonderful catcher at short leg. He had an excellent record in his 49 Tests but he blatantly threw it and Wardle should have had his Test caps if truth were told. There was huge rivalry between them and the merits of Lock, fast and flat, and Wardle, flight and guile, were hotly debated. With Peter May his Surrey captain in charge of England, Tony Lock often got the vote because the skipper was comfortable with what he knew and on the dry, turning pitches prepared for England's home series he was very effective. Lock came out to the West Indies in 1968 after Fred Titmus lost his toes in a boating accident and played in the last two Tests in Port of Spain, Trinidad, and Georgetown, Guyana. By then he had been forced to remodel his action and he wouldn't have given anyone a sleepless night. Two instantly forgettable bowling performances but with the bat he made 89 runs in the last Test to help save the match.

Another who merits the highest consideration is **Derek Leslie Underwood**. 'Deadly's' 297 wickets at 25.83 are formidable figures and I am full of admiration for him. Anyone who saw him bowl on a wet pitch knew he was unplayable. If Yorkshire were playing Kent and it was raining I'd joke with him, 'Is this a six for 40 pitch then, Deadly?' He'd reply, 'If it rains another hour or so, Fiery, it could be eight for 20.' I was proud to play with him and against him. Who can forget that day at The Oval when a freak thunderstorm hit and it looked as though play would be washed out? The groundstaff and spectators managed to get the ground fit for a start at 4.45 p.m. with Australia 86 for five. On that strip they didn't have a prayer against Underwood and he finished with seven for 50 from 31.3 overs.

Then there's **Hedley Verity** who Bradman said was the best England spinner he ever faced which is no surprise since he got him out twice in a day at Lord's in 1934 when Hedley finished the Test with match figures of 15 for 104. He only played for nine seasons before he was killed in the Second World War but in 40 Tests he took 144 wickets at 24.37 and had 1,956 first class victims at 14.9, with 10 wickets in a match on 54 occasions in his all too short career. When I read Verity's book he had the best advice I've ever heard for a spin bowler: 'Bowl as short as you can while making the batsman play forward.' Very wise words.

I could pick any of those and be quite happy and I know there will be people making a case not only for the ones I have mentioned but others, too. I wouldn't disagree with any of the arguments put forward, they're all valid. And you could make a case for Johnny Briggs of Lancashire, who suffered dreadfully from epilepsy and died in Cheadle Hulme asylum at just 40 years of age. In his 33 Tests he had 118 wickets at 17.74. Colin Blythe of Kent, another afflicted by the disease for which there was then no cure, had 100 wickets in 19 Tests at 18.63 before he was killed in the First World War. There is also Yorkshire's Bobby Peel, 20 Tests, 102 wickets at 16.81 and another 101 wickets for the county at 16.98 before his career was ended by Lord Hawke who took exception to him appearing on the field clearly inebriated.

But I'm going for Wilfred Rhodes because his wicket-taking ability was as good as the others', 127 in 58 Tests at 26.96, but also in those matches he made 2,325 runs at an average of 30.19. The thing is, before anyone starts quoting other batting averages, this was a tailender who started his England career at number 10 and ended up opening with Jack Hobbs 19 times. In other words he made many of his runs at the sharp end, where it matters. In the second Test at Melbourne on the 1911–12 tour Hobbs and Rhodes made 323 together in just 268 minutes, Hobbs 178, Rhodes 179. That's going some and it's still an England record first wicket stand against Australia.

The war cut his career by four summers, as it did to a number of great players, but this fellow was unique. It's been told and re-told down the years that if Wilfred got you out once, he'd know how to get you out again. It may be folklore but what it really says is that his colleagues and the public recognized a great cricket brain, held him in high esteem and revered that cricket knowledge.

As a young player in the early 1960s I was introduced to him at Scarborough. Now blind, he used to sit in the players' enclosure in front of the dressing room listening to the sound of bat on ball, the players' chat and taking in the nuances of the crowd. His first question to me was, 'Do you cut?' Well, I was a bit flummoxed because it was one of my favourite shots and I didn't know what to say to the great man. So I ummed and ahhed a bit before he broke in and said, 'Never cut till May is out.' I sometimes wish I'd remembered that and taken more heed.

Because these greats of a bygone era only played against Australia and South Africa it's important to take into account their domestic record. Here Wilf was supreme with more wickets, 4,204, than anyone in the history of the game, a figure that will never be reached given the curtailed programme of first class cricket. They cost only 16.72 each. He had five wickets in an innings 287 times and ten in a match on 68 occasions with a strike rate of a wicket every 44.18 balls. Incredible.

You need batsmen to make runs and put your side in a position for victory and bowlers to win games. No bowlers, however good they are, can do that if there aren't enough runs on the board. That's why I want five batsmen, an all-rounder, a wicketkeeper, a spinner who can bat and quality quick men. I think I've got them and choices for all situations.

James Charles Laker (1948–59)

Every side needs balance and when it comes to offspinners most people would go for Surrey's Jim Laker. There is no doubt he was a great bowler and I don't use that word lightly but in its truest sense. I had tremendous affection for him because he helped me enormously when I first started broadcasting and his knowledge and laconic style made working with him really enjoyable. I remember him telling me when I was in the BBC commentary box that whenever a new batsman came to the crease he always tried to give his first ball a real rip, turn it as much as he possibly could to make the batsman think every ball would do the same and sow doubt in his mind.

A heavy-set six footer who had 193 wickets at 21.24 in 46 Tests, he is the only truly great bowler that Yorkshire let slip through their fingers. He sauntered back to his mark with a nonchalance that hid an intelligence which was always working on the next delivery. With a high, classic delivery, he didn't have the modern day 'doosra' but relied on genuine finger spin with an arm ball which drifted away from the right hander allied to great control and accuracy. He was at his best in English conditions and first claimed attention when he had eight wickets for 2 runs in the England versus The Rest Test trial at Park Avenue, Bradford. He did the hat-trick four times, the first for Plum Warner's XI against The South of England in 1947, the next three for Surrey, against Gloucestershire in 1951 and twice in 1953 against

Warwickshire and Cambridge University. Then came the memorable summer of 1956 when in May he had all 10 for 88 in 46 overs against the Australians at The Oval and proved that was no fluke by taking 19 wickets in the fourth Test at Old Trafford, an astonishing feat which is unlikely to be repeated. On turning pitches against him the Aussies were pathetic. They played with the bat so far in front of the pad that there was a gap big enough to drive a bus through. They just hadn't a clue and some of them were reduced to slogging. Those figures will live in history as testimony to an absolutely sensational performance. With his Surrey spin twin, Tony Lock, on the dusty Oval pitches he helped win the county championship title seven times into the bargain.

I played against him once at Clacton in 1963 when he'd finished his career at Surrey and played a few games with Essex as an amateur. I can honestly say that of all the bowlers I've faced all over the world he was the only one who made the ball hum in the air. I could actually hear it coming towards me. He has to be very high on anyone's list when it comes to picking a side of greats and the only other offspinner to come near him is Bob Appleyard who only played in nine Tests and had 31 wickets at 17.87 each. The Yorkshireman is the only bowler to have taken 200 wickets in his first full season, 1951, but he played only one match the following year and missed the whole of 1953 with tuberculosis. But he fought back to have 154 victims in 1954 and played an important part in England's successful tour of Australia that winter with 11 wickets at 20.36.

On rain-affected or dry, dusty pitches Jim Laker was nigh on unplayable and to underline the fact had 135 wickets in 29 Tests on home soil at an average of 18.08 and 58 at 28.60 in the 17 Tests played on the flatter strips overseas, not bad figures. I don't dismiss his claims lightly but he might struggle to get into my final XI on good pitches although he would be invaluable on the subcontinent. I think I have choices for every type of pitch and all situations.

England

SQUAD

W. G. Grace

Jack Hobbs

Len Hutton

Wally Hammond

Denis Compton

Ian Botham

Alan Knott

Sydney Barnes

Fred Trueman

Harold Larwood

George Lohmann

Brian Statham

Wilfred Rhodes

Jim Laker

Australia

Sir Donald George Bradman (1928–48)

The first time I met the man with the most unbelievable figures in world cricket I was lying in a daze in a hospital bed and so mesmerized by his presence that I failed to ask the millions of questions that later occurred to me. I was only a young kid of 24 or so and taken ill in Ceylon on our way to tour Australia in 1965–66. I was so poorly I had to spend eight days in Singapore where a doctor injected me with something or other and I was in no fit state to take any part in the games in Perth. Feeling better when we got to Adelaide, I made 94 against South Australia but could hardly run in the field and so it was back to hospital where the medics discovered that the doctor in Singapore had narrowly missed the sciatic nerve with his needle. I was in a bad way but one afternoon I woke and there, sitting on my bed, was 'The Don', the greatest cricketer the world has ever known. He was chairman of the Australian selectors at the time and he'd brought me a book by his friend Johnny Moyes, but instead of talking to him my mind went blank and I could only lie there with my mouth open. The one thing we did manage to have some sort of conversation about was the cricket ground in Vancouver which he thought one of the loveliest in the world. I'd played there with Yorkshire on a tour so I didn't appear a right pudding, but what a chance missed. Bradman wasn't just the king, he was a cricketing god and if I'd had the chance in later years I'd have talked to him until the cows came home.

When you look at his performances this man is twice as good as anyone else. He averages just under 100 in Test cricket while other top players are around the 50 mark. Given that 99.94 figure, if he gets in he's going to make 200 a match on average while the best of the others will get half that. To catch up, the Len Huttons and Wally Hammonds of this world will need four innings, not two. For Australia it's like having two extra batsmen in the side so you're not going to beat them unless you get him out. To me, Douglas Jardine got it dead right. You had to focus on getting Bradman out to stand a hope in hell of winning and while you might not approve of the tactics you can't fault his thinking. The other great benefit he brought to the side was the way he made his runs. If he's scoring quickly and heavily at one end it makes it a lot easier for the guy at the other end to get some runs because the opposition are paying so much attention to Bradman.

The widely held image of the boy Bradman hitting a golf ball against a water tank with a stump at his home in Bowral is, I believe, the basis for his exceptional coordination of brain, eye and muscle. While the kid is amusing himself playing his own boyhood Tests in the eight-foot space behind the house he is unwittingly fine-tuning the dexterity, wrist work and speed of foot which would lead to his versatility and range of strokes.

In his book *The Art of Cricket* the Don wrote, 'I doubt if one could truthfully say there is a single key to the art of batsmanship but footwork is certainly one of the keys to unlock the innermost secrets. It is to batting what a foundation is to a house. Without it there can be no structure.'

What's interesting to me is that his self-taught methods went contrary to the coaching manual. We're told that in your stance you should have the toe of the bat behind the right foot (for a right hander, of course); he had it between his feet. We're told to pick the bat up as an extension of the arms, with it pointing towards first or maybe second slip; he picked it up pointing more towards gully, using the rotation of his shoulders rather than his arms, while remaining absolutely still with no premeditated movement until the ball was delivered. They still teach the orthodoxy and it's fundamental to all training films, while the methods used by the world's greatest batsman are never given a moment's thought. Here's a guy who's twice as good as anybody else and nobody teaches it – to me, that's amazing.

The great man himself said, 'Orthodoxy has greater limitations on versatile stroke play.' That says to me, and anyone else who cares to listen, that he couldn't have achieved the results he did batting the way everyone else was, and is, taught. 'My entire cricketing experience has been a practical one,' he added; that tells me a lot without rubbishing the technical way most of us have grown up with. It's interesting that we have taken not the slightest notice of what he says.

I have talked about him to Sir Alec Bedser and Bill Bowes and Sir Alec said it was a hard enough job to keep him quiet. 'He always got to the pitch of the ball and I never saw him stretch for it, he was always on top of the ball with his head over it.' Bill Bowes remarked that if you bowled him bouncers he would either sway out of the way or get his right foot across outside the off stump to get inside the line and play it down. With three men in the covers he would either find the gap or, if it was a bit short, pull it through mid wicket. Setting traps for him, Bill said, was a waste of time.

Despite his huge scores, two triple centuries, 10 doubles, he rarely batted for more than a day and although there may have been 120 overs bowled it's still a pretty formidable scoring rate. Headingley in Leeds was his favourite ground in England with the then world record 334 made in 1930 when he was 21 years of age, 309 of them on the first day, 304 in 1934, 102 in 1938 and 173 not out in 1948. No wonder Yorkshire made him their first overseas life member, and there aren't many of them.

It's astonishing to think he was dropped after his first Test against England in Brisbane in 1928–29 but in the third, in Melbourne, he made 79 and 112 and from then on it was just a procession. On his first tour in 1930 he made 974 runs at an average of 139.14 and the legend was built on just 80 innings in 52 Tests. He was so famous even in England that during the summer of 1930 newspaper sellers carried placards which just read, 'He's Out.'

After he retired, scientific tests on his eyes showed they were not abnormal in any way, he had the same vision as anyone else with good eyesight, and I'm convinced it was his upbringing which trained them so well. He felt very little physical or mental strain from all his deeds and wrote, 'If I made a mistake I felt that nine times out of ten it was a physical mistake. I had tried to do something and didn't get there in time, I was too slow or something like that. I am sure with a lot of players their mental attitude is terribly important, they imagine that there are difficulties that are not really there.'

See? It's as easy as that!

Keith Ross Miller (1946–56)

A big factor in the strength of any side is the quality of the all-rounder and anyone who saw Keith Miller play would remark on his great natural talent; even someone like Richie Benaud, who doesn't get carried away, thinks that Miller was a fantastic performer.

Built like a Greek god, he was a debonair six footer with a mane of black hair which was in sharp contrast to the short back and sides of the period. He was a warm and generous individual off the field and a fearsome competitor on it. He'd have nights out on the town with his great pal Denis Compton and then spend the next day trying to knock his block off. He lived life to the full and lit up the grey postwar days with his dashing performances in the Victory Tests mainly at Lord's where he scored three hundreds in 1945, 105 in May and 118 in August for the Australian Services, and followed that with 185 in 165 minutes for the Dominions against England the same month.

A distinguished fighter pilot with the Royal Australian Air Force, he had seen friends and colleagues die in battle and, not surprisingly, his attitude was to live life for the day and to the full. His flair and instinct caught the public's imagination and huge crowds flocked to see him play. He was once asked about the pressure, that much overused word, of performing in front of such huge audiences and he said, 'Pressure? Pressure is having a Messerschmitt 109 up your arse, not playing cricket.' That put the world in context for him and others who lived through the war.

His sportsmanship was legendary. When the 1948 Australians were murdering a poor Essex side at Southend in May, making 721 runs in a day, he thought it was overkill and when he went out to bat, told the umpire to tell the bowler to let him have a straight one and stood aside to let the ball hit the stumps. He didn't think much to kicking a man when he was down and Essex were one of the poorer sides in county cricket. When Yorkshire played them we only used to book in for two nights because they could be beaten in two days.

In the 1953 Test at Lord's he hit Johnny Wardle for six into the Grandstand scoreboard but was beaten in flight by the next delivery and Wardle said that before the ball reached him he said 'well bowled' and was on his way virtually before the ball hit the wicket.

As a bowler he shared the new ball with Ray Lindwall and was a real handful. Batsmen never knew what was coming next, a rip-roaring bouncer or a fast leg break, a yorker or a late-moving outswinger. When I asked Len Hutton about these two he acknowledged that Lindy was a fine, fine bowler but as for Miller he just rolled his eyes and shook his head.

Miller's contemporaries were convinced that how he bowled depended on what sort of a night out he'd had: a fun party with the champagne flowing and he'd bowl like the wind, a dull night in and a flat performance. It was that surprise element, his nonconformist attitude which made him so appealing to the public; if he had been playing in this time of instant heroes and nonentity celebrities I can only imagine what a sensation he would have been. There was a story that when Bradman imposed a curfew on the

Australian team he presented himself at the captain's door dressed in his evening clothes and said he'd been in by the appointed time and now he was going out. Bradman was not amused by Miller's antics and they rebounded on him when Australia brought Ian Johnson out of retirement to captain them when the job should have gone to Miller who Richie Benaud said was the best skipper he ever played under when he led New South Wales.

He made his Test debut against New Zealand at Wellington in March 1946 and in his next match, against England in Brisbane in the first Test of the 1946—47 tour, made 79 and took seven for 60 when England were caught on a 'Gabba sticky dog' after a thunderstorm. In the same series he registered his first Test hundred in the fourth game in Adelaide, an unbeaten 141.

Miller had a lot of back trouble which later hindered his bowling but three centuries on the 1954—55 tour of the Caribbean proved none of his old magic at the crease had gone: 147 at Kingston in the first Test, 137 in Barbados in the fourth and 109 back in Jamaica in the fifth. He left an indelible mark at Lord's, his favourite stage, with five for 72 and five for 80 in the second Test of the 1956 Ashes series, the only match the Aussies won in that Jim Laker-dominated summer, and, following his 109 in 1953, is the only tourist to appear on both batting and bowling honour boards at the ground.

Although he had charisma and a playboy image, make no mistake about it, at heart this fellow was a superb cricketer.

Alan Keith Davidson (1953–63)

A lot of people might think, Why pick Alan Davidson? Well, just look at his record and you'll be staggered by it. He took 186 Test wickets at 20.53 and of all those who have had more than 100 victims since the Second World War, only one man, Yorkshire's Johnny Wardle, got them at a cheaper rate. Although his strike rate of a wicket every 62 balls is not as good as some, if you look at his economy of under two runs an over it's clear that no one smacked him around the park. If he wasn't getting wickets you could set a field to him and be sure you weren't going to give any runs away. As a quality left arm over the wicket bowler who had a pretty fair pace he had the asset of allowing the captain to use prevailing conditions to the best advantage. It's rare to play a Test when there isn't some kind of breeze and with the left armer you can exploit the conditions from both ends.

A big, barrel-chested lad, he was a lot quicker than people think and he could swing it in and out, very rare, and move it both ways off the seam. Kenny Barrington thought he was 'absolutely outstanding' and he should know.

Davidson made his debut in the first Test against England at Trent Bridge in 1953 but he was very much a reserve bowler in a powerful Australian side which had Lindwall, Miller and Johnston, who was also a left armer, as its frontline attack. He struggled to get a bowl and although he played in all five Tests he bowled only 136 overs. If you're fourth in line behind those three you're not going to get much of a chance.

In the next four years he played in only 11 Tests with Ron Archer often preferred to him and didn't come into his own until the big three retired or were over the hill, finally becoming the number one bowler on the tour of South Africa in 1957–58. After being the understudy for so long he seized the opportunity and took 25 wickets at 17 as Australia won 3–0. He had six for 34 in the first Test at Johannesburg, six in the match in the innings win in Cape Town and nine for 82 from 46 overs in the eight wicket win in Port Elizabeth. He never had a poor series after that and when England toured Australia in 1958–59 claimed 24 wickets in the rubber at 19 runs each with six for 64 and three for 41 in the eight wicket win in Melbourne.

He had 12 wickets in three Tests in Pakistan and then in the five-match series in India which followed he took 29 wickets at 14.86 each and that's some record out there, believe me. In the second Test of the Indian series he had match figures of 12 for 124 at Kanpur on a newly laid turf pitch but that was not enough to stop India winning by 119 runs.

Perhaps the greatest game he played in was the famous tied Test, the first of the series with the West Indies in Brisbane in December 1960, and what a part he played in that. He had five for 135 as the West Indies batted first and made 44 in Australia's reply, then took six for 87 and followed that with 80 before he was seventh man to go, run out, with only seven wanted for victory. The rest is history but what an all-round performance from Davidson who became the first player to take 10 wickets and score 100 runs in a Test match. In the four Tests he played in that series he had 33 wickets at 18.54 including six for 53 in the second

Test at Melbourne, five for 80 in the third at Sydney and five for 84 in the fifth, again at the MCG.

He could make useful runs down the order and averaged 22 with the bat but, more importantly, in a tight situation he could take the initiative away from the bowler. A fine example was at Old Trafford when Australia were struggling and, with Graham Mackenzie, he put on 98 for the last wicket. Davidson remained unbeaten on 77 and the Aussies won by 54 runs. He bagged 23 wickets in that series at 24.86 and when England toured Down Under the following winter of 1962–63 he finished his last series with 24 wickets at 20 runs apiece.

For all his talents he needed careful handling because he was a bit of a hypochondriac and there was always something wrong with him. He constantly complained of aches and pains and wanted to take his sweater, but Richie Benaud, his captain for both Australia and New South Wales, always coaxed another over out of him and then was studiously looking the other way or doing something else so Davidson's complaints went unheeded.

His ability to swing the ball out set him apart; most left armers can swing it in to the right hander but rarely the other way and he could do it in the toughest conditions, like Pakistan and India, and, allied to his economy, he's a must after Miller. He provides options by being able to bowl 'em out or bottle 'em up, that rarest of breeds, an attacking bowler who doesn't give runs away, and that's a captain's dream. He's in my team any time.

Dennis Keith Lillee (1971–84)
Jeffrey Robert Thomson (1972–85)

Although they played in 121 Tests between them they were only partners in crime on 26 occasions but my word what a fearsome combination they were. Just the names – Lillee and Thomson – were enough to have most batsmen quaking in their boots. Two completely different types, Lillee with his high classic action, Thomson generating tremendous speed with his slingshot delivery, they wreaked havoc among the best in the world.

I first came across Dennis Lillee on the 1970–71 tour of Australia in the state game in Perth in November. Western Australia had batted first on what was then a tinpot little ground and our team was still in a state of undress when I went out to open the batting with Brian Luckhurst. In the first over he let me have a short one and as I jerked my head backwards my cap flew off. As I turned to pick it up I saw out of the corner of my eye players down at fine leg in their jock straps or with towels wrapped round them rushing out on to the balcony to see what had happened. Dennis stood a few yards from me snarling aggression but I avoided eye contact and let him get on with it. Although it was a sign of what was to come there was no recurrence and 'Lucky' and I both got hundreds and put on 215 for the first wicket.

He made his Test debut at Adelaide for the sixth game of that seven-match series, in which one match was completely abandoned. He took five for 84 in our first innings and although I wasn't one of them he had his moments later on!

He went to play a season in the Lancashire League at Haslingden in 1971 and I think it did him a power of good. It's no use just bowling like the wind on those pitches and in that league. If the batsman nicks it nobody's going to catch it and if he misses it's likely to be four byes, so he learned new tricks about varying his pace, using the crease and how to cut the ball while never losing his wonderful late out-swing. He became a craftsman.

Back home that winter Lillee played against the Rest of the World in a series of matches to replace the cancelled South African tour and had 23 wickets in four games including eight for 29 on his home ground at Perth. In England in 1972 he looked a real quality act with that lovely run-up and leap into the delivery stride and showed great control while generating genuine pace. He had everything expected of a great fast bowler with 31 wickets in five Tests at 17.67, the highlights being six for 66 at Old Trafford in the first, five for 58 and five for 123 at The Oval. The only time the Aussies came unstuck on that tour was at Leeds where a growth of fusarium affected the pitch. Derek Underwood came back for that game to bowl England to victory and to this day the Aussies think it was a plot and won't be told it was all an accident of nature. I say it couldn't happen to nicer people!

On the Caribbean tour of 1972–73 Lillee broke down in February with a stress fracture of the back – the first of the sort of injuries we hear about all the time now – was in a plaster cast for six weeks and there were grave doubts about whether he would ever play again. But 20 months later when England toured in 1974–75 he was back, teamed up with 'Tommo' for the first Test in Brisbane. The Lord Mayor of the city was Alderman Clem Jones who sacked the groundsman eight days before the match and decided to prepare the pitch himself. This must have been music to Lillee's ears and he and 'Tommo' duly destroyed England with 13 of the 20 wickets to fall. Dennis had 25 at 23.84 in the series and with his awesomely quick partner at the other end he was even better.

Jeff Thomson made his debut in 1972 against Pakistan in Melbourne and returned none for 110 in the match. What wasn't known at the time (because 'Tommo' didn't tell anyone!) was that he played with a broken bone in his foot but it looked like a huge gamble to bring him back nearly two years later. Nobody could have anticipated what followed as the duo blew England away, winning four of the first five Tests. Thomson finished with 33 wickets at 17.93 each and so began one of the most feared new ball attacks cricket has seen. 'Tommo' had a superb physique and just sort of jogged up to the wicket before unfurling his huge chest and shoulders and hurling the ball down at not much short of 100mph. From wide of the crease his bouncer followed the batsman and even fuller length balls would lift awkwardly. He was made for the hard, bouncy pitches out there and as England were decimated the Aussies, never slow to crow, had a little rhyme which went, 'Ashes to Ashes, dust to dust, if Tommo don't get you, Lillee must.'

'Tommo' was built up as the archetypical Aussie, a real Okker, a larrikin, a bloodthirsty bastard who wanted to hurt batsmen and didn't give a monkey's cuss for anyone. But most of these newpaper articles were written by other people and, in truth, he wasn't and isn't anything like the image portrayed and I think he's a great guy. One thing he did do was swear non-stop. He used the F word just about every ball but, as with Fred Trueman, I never heard him swear at a batsman or an umpire. There was no subtlety about him, it was all raw pace and bounce, but he caught the public's imagination and crowds all over the world flocked to see him.

On the softer pitches in England in 1975 he had less success, 16 wickets at 28.56 but at home against the West Indies the following winter he had 29 wickets in six Tests against a team which included Gordon Greenidge, Roy Fredericks, Lawrence Rowe, Viv Richards, Alvin Kallicharran and Clive Lloyd. No mugs there. They had Andy Roberts, Michael Holding, Keith Boyce and Vanburn Holder, but it was a case of who has the best fast bowlers holds the aces and Australia won 5–1. By now they were very much the top dogs in world cricket, but on Christmas Eve 1976 the Aussies suffered a major setback when 'Tommo' collided with Alan Turner in going for a return catch in his ninth over in the first Test against Pakistan in Adelaide and dislocated his collarbone. I don't think he was ever quite the same again and what looked like a golden period with these two didn't happen.

Lillee took 11 wickets in the Centenary Test in Melbourne but then signed for World Series Cricket and Thomson was on his own for the Ashes series in England in 1977. 'Tommo' had 23 wickets at 25.34 in the five Tests and followed up with 22 against India in five home Tests and 23 in the Caribbean in a five-game series. The deadly duo were reunited for the one Test against the West Indies at Brisbane in December 1979 and against England the same month. By now Dennis had become a clever bowler and the last thing you needed to do was stir him up. But in the first Test at Perth on the 1979–80 tour he came in at number nine with an aluminium bat. After a couple of strokes Mike Brearley, the captain, complained to the umpires that it was marking the ball and they ordered him to change it. Lillee lost his rag, chucked the bat away and had a real temper in front of his home crowd who lapped it up. I ask you, here's a man with a batting average of 13, a mug with the bat but deadly with the ball, so why fire him up? That's real Cambridge University thinking for you and Lillee nipped out me and Derek Randall for ducks in a furious opening burst.

In the Centenary Test at Lord's in 1980 in the first innings he bowled me a beauty from the Pavilion end which nipped back up the slope and did for me when I was 62; he finished with four for 43. When the Aussies were going on the field for England's second innings Dennis said to Dickie Bird, the umpire, who he knew was a friend of mine, 'If we get your mate out early we'll be up the road before tea, Dickie, I'll bowl the rest of 'em out.' Well, Ian Botham had told me, 'Forget going for the runs, Fiery, stay there.' With those instructions I batted for five and a quarter hours and made 128 not out. It was one of my best innings because there was the motivation of playing against the world's best on the biggest stage of all, Lord's, in front of a full house who were gripped throughout the day. It's what every top sportsman wants to do, to test himself against the finest of his peers, the challenge to your character and ability. Dennis set me a real examination and it was with great satisfaction that I passed it.

He paid me a nice tribute sometime later when he went to the same Sydney hotel where I had stayed during my season playing with Waverley in grade cricket and had become good friends with the manager. In all innocence he asked Dennis what he thought of my batting and the great bowler replied, 'He's like a good red wine, he gets better with age.' Well, all I can say is, so did he.

Lillee and Thomson were together for one last series in New Zealand in March 1982 when they shared 15 wickets, the third and final Test in Christchurch being their last together.

'Tommo' carried on and just as it looked as though his career was petering out he came back for four Tests against England in 1982–83 and took 22 wickets at 18.68. It was his last hurrah because although he played in the first and last Tests in England on the 1985 tour he managed only two wickets at a cost of 174 runs at Leeds and one for 101 at Edgbaston.

They were a formidable pairing, as good as any in the world. Dennis was the more skilled, 'Tommo' more reliant on the brute force of that burly body. Lillee is a must in my team but Thomson's virtues have to be weighed against some pretty formidable competition.

Gregory Stephen Chappell (1970–84)

Greg Chappell has been one of my favourite batsmen since he made his debut against England at Perth in the second Test of our 1970–71 tour and made a hundred batting at number seven. They were in trouble at the time but with Ian Redpath, who also made a ton, they put on 216 for the sixth wicket in the first ever Test in Western Australia.

Tall and upright, he looked as though he meant business when he walked to the wicket. I'm a great believer in body language; it's part of the equation of batting and lets the opposition know you're keen for the fray, up for the challenge. I hate to see a batsman trailing out to the middle with rounded shoulders and head bowed as though he's going to a funeral, it sends the wrong message. I liked Greg's attitude; he was composed, controlled, there wasn't a lot of emotion and in that first match I remember him hitting Ken Shuttleworth wide of mid on from balls pitched on and outside the off stump. 'Shuts' wasn't used to anyone doing that on the uncovered pitches in England and it took a bit of time for the penny to drop. By that time Chappell was away and never looked like getting out. That was one of the things that characterized his batting. Once he was in he took some shifting because he played straight, didn't take risks and, while pretty orthodox, put the loose delivery away with a bang.

The next season Australia played the Rest of the World in the home series arranged to replace the South African tour and he made 115 in Sydney and 197 in Melbourne against some pretty good bowlers. Two more hundreds followed on the tour of England in 1972, 131 at Lord's and 113 at The Oval, and he averaged 48.55 in the Tests. In March 1973 he and his elder brother, Ian, set up a unique Test record when they both got hundreds in each innings against New Zealand in Wellington: Greg 247 not out and 133, Ian 145 and 121. It was only the fourth time a batsman had made a double and a single hundred in a Test match, the others being Lawrence Rowe, Sunil Gavaskar and Doug Walters. The only other recorded instance of brothers making hundreds in both innings of any match was Reginald (134 and 101 not out) and Wilfrid (140 and 172) Foster for Worcestershire against Hampshire at New Road, Worcester, in July 1899. So that was a bit special for the Chappell brothers and the Kiwis must have been sick of the sight of them by the end of the game.

In 1974–75, when Lillee and Thomson were dominating the English batsmen, Greg accumulated 608 in 11 innings at an average of 55.27. His only poor run came after the first World Cup in England in 1975 in a non-Ashes series of four Tests in which he managed only 106 runs in six innings. He soon put that behind him with a superb series as captain against the West Indies at home, making 702 runs and being dismissed only six times for an average of 117. He made a hundred in each innings again, 123 and 109 not out in Brisbane, the only instance of a captain making a ton in his first game as skipper. Phenomenal batting against Roberts, Holding and company.

As captain he lost the Ashes in 1977 when I felt that the Australian batting wasn't anything special. They had good quick bowlers in Lenny Pascoe and Jeff Thomson, good swing bowlers in Max Walker and Mick Malone, but Ray

Bright versus Derek Underwood was no contest. It was also the prelude to World Series Cricket and a number of them, including Chappell, had signed up but were sworn to secrecy and this must have had an effect. I'm not making excuses because England were the better side; I made my comeback and got hundreds at Trent Bridge and Headingley, Ian Botham was in his first series, Bob Willis was pretty quick and, in English conditions, there were few better seamers than Chris Old and Mike Hendrick. Greg did OK but was not the dominant force he had been. He was back in form with 235 in Faisalabad in March 1980 and 204 against India in January 1981 in Sydney and in his final Test at the SCG made 182 against Pakistan, his eighth innings of 150 or more, and became the only batsman to start and finish a Test career with a hundred. There were no frills to his batting, he rarely hooked and you'd never see him play a reverse sweep; he kept it simple and was dominant in a classic way.

If there was one blot on his copybook it was when he instructed his younger brother Trevor to bowl an underarm grubber when New Zealand wanted six to tie from the last ball of the third game of the Benson & Hedges World Series finals at Melbourne in February 1981. It caused a hell of a row and the New Zealand prime minister called it 'cowardly'. I wouldn't go that far but it was against the spirit of the game and, although I've never talked to him about it, I bet it's something he regrets. To me he always played fairly and competitively, was as gracious in defeat as he was in success, a bit different from his elder brother, and I admire his demeanour as a cricketer and a man. He's a must for me at number four.

Arthur Robert Morris (1946–55)

Arthur Morris was the first player to score a century in each innings on his first class debut when he made 148 and 111 for New South Wales against Queensland in December 1940 at the age of 18. Who knows what he might have achieved but for the Second World War.

A medium-build, compact left hander, he used his feet to spin, drove elegantly and averaged 46.48 over his 46 Tests with 12 centuries. That's one every four matches, not bad going in anyone's book. England's Alec Bedser caused him problems when he swung the ball around leg stump and a myth grew up that he was Alec's 'bunny'. It's true Alec got him out 18 times in Tests but, for me, it's not who gets you out but how many runs you've made before they get you out and Arthur Morris made plenty. In 24 Tests against England between 1946 and 1955 he ran up 2,080 at an average of 50.73, including six centuries in 10 Tests and if that's being someone's 'bunny' then I'll take those figures every time because they look pretty good to me.

If a great opening bowler is taking the new ball against a top opening batsman it's his job to get him out and he's not doing his job if he doesn't. Similarly, if a quality batsman doesn't come out on top from time to time he's failing in his. To be called a great bowler or batsman you have to be able to produce the goods against other great players or, by definition, you're not great.

In his first Test series, against England in 1946–47,

Arthur Morris scored three consecutive centuries after starting at Brisbane with just two. In the second innings of the third Test in Melbourne he made 155 and in the next match at Adelaide he had one in each innings, 122 and 124 not out, to finish the series with 503 runs at 71.85. In six of the seven innings he was out to Bedser; some 'bunny' eh?

On the 1948 tour of England he amassed 696 runs at an average of 87, outscoring even Bradman, with hundreds at Lord's in the second Test, and a match-winning 182 at Leeds where the Australians were set to make 404 in 344 minutes and won by seven wickets. Morris and Bradman put on 301 in 217 minutes for the third wicket and Arthur improved on that at The Oval where he was run out for 196.

On the tour of South Africa in 1949–50 he had 111 in the fourth Test at the old Ellis Park ground and 157 in the fifth at Port Elizabeth, terrifically consistent run making. When England went to Australia in 1950–51 it could be said that Alec had the better of the argument, getting Arthur five times quite cheaply. But the little left hander still managed a double century at Adelaide where he made 206 out of a total of 371 and held the innings together as Australia won. He had a couple of poor series, at home against the West Indies in November and December 1951 with 186 in six innings, while in England in 1953 he got starts but didn't go on to make the big scores associated with him. However, when Len Hutton won the toss and put the Aussies in at Brisbane in the first Test of the 1954–55 tour, the first in Australia with complete covering of the pitch, he ran up 153 in the total of 601 for eight declared.

Although he tended to tail off a bit at the end of his career he was the sort of opener a side needs. You've got to have someone to stick at it because pretty twenties, thirties and forties don't win Test matches. You need openers who can build a platform for a substantial score and in my book Arthur Morris was just the job.

Clarence Victor Grimmett (1925–36)
William Joseph O'Reilly (1932–46)
Shane Keith Warne (1992–2007)

Of Grimmett, O'Reilly and Warne, to my mind the three greatest legspinners Australia has produced, Clarrie Grimmett came first. Curiously he was born in Dunedin, New Zealand, went to Australia on a working holiday and stayed 66 years.

He was 33 years old when he made his debut against England in Sydney in the fifth Test of 1925 with the Aussies already 3–1 up in the series and was the fifth bowler used. That didn't stop him taking five for 45 in the first innings and six for 37 in the second; match figures of 11 for 82 in your first game can't be bad. He quickly established a huge reputation in his new homeland where he was variously known as 'The Gnome' or 'Scarlet' after the Pimpernel's 'they seek him here, they seek him there'. Batsmen of the day found him hard to fathom and he was the first bowler to develop the 'flipper' (the one that goes straight on and keeps low) and the topspinner (similar to the flipper with tennis ball bounce) into deadly deliveries on the hard Australian pitches. He first toured England in 1926. While there wasn't quite the magic on the slower, softer English pitches he still finished with 13 wickets from the three Tests he played in, although they cost 31.84 each. When England toured the following winter he bowled a lot of eight-ball overs, 398, and took 23 wickets at 42.6 each, but by the 1930 trip to England he was now bowling at some of the greatest batsmen England, or cricket for that matter, has ever produced in Jack Hobbs, Herbert Sutcliffe, Wally Hammond, Patsy Hendren and Frank Woolley. In the first Test at Trent Bridge he had 10 for 201 in the match England won by 93 runs, eight for 272 at Lord's where Australia won by seven wickets, six at Leeds and five at The Oval to finish with 29 wickets at 31.89 in the series.

He mesmerized the raw West Indies on their first visit to Australia, taking 33 at 17.96, but on the next tour, to South Africa in 1931–32, had 33 wickets in four Tests at 16.87 apiece against a side which should have known how to play wrist-spin given they virtually invented it in the 1920s.

Back home against the Springboks, Grimmett was joined for the first time in the Australian side by Bill O'Reilly and completely overshadowed his partner with 14 in the match, seven in each innings, for 198 runs in the fourth Test in Adelaide. In the Bodyline series of 1932–33 England had Larwood and Voce, Australia Grimmett and O'Reilly. Well, I know which I'd rather face, but the spinners did bowl their side to victory in the only match Australia won in that infamous series, by 111 in the second Test at Melbourne, where O'Reilly had five in each innings and Grimmett just the one wicket.

The two were very different in style, Grimmett more the old-fashioned type relying on flight and guile to deceive and O'Reilly a big six footer who was not called 'Tiger' for nothing, always in your face, aggressive, fast, off a longish run with a whirl of arms, always wanting to dominate the batsman. Bradman said he was the greatest bowler of his time and by all accounts he was so quick it was difficult to adjust to his googly and topspinner and batsmen couldn't get down the pitch to him. With his Irish background O'Reilly had the hostile temperament of a fast bowler, in stark contrast to the gnome-like approach of Grimmett, the patient enticer of batsmen into his web. The pair's best joint performance came at Trent Bridge in the first Test of Australia's 1934 tour of England when they shared 19 wickets in a 238-run win. Grimmett had five for 81 and three for 29, O'Reilly four for 75 and seven for 54 and they got through 184 overs in the match!

There was a good-natured rivalry between them but 'Tiger' had great respect for the man he first saw bowl when, as a boy, he went to watch an upstate match and saw a player whose name appeared on the scorecard as Grummitt. He called him 'Grum' ever after. The pair routed the South Africans on the tour of 1935–36, Grimmett taking a series record 44 wickets and his partner 27. In his affectionate obituary in *Wisden* O'Reilly wrote:

On that 1935–36 South African tour, Grum set an Australian record for a Test series with 44 wickets, yet he came home to be dropped forever from the Australian side. He was shoved aside like a worn-out boot for each of the five Tests against Gubby Allen's English team in Australia in 1936–37 and he failed to gain a place in the 1938 team to England, led by Bradman. It was illogical to assume that age was the reason for his discard. He was 47, it is true, when the touring side was chosen, yet two years later, at the age of 49, he established an Australian record of 73 wickets for a domestic first-class season. Which raises, rather pointedly, the question of why the hell was he dropped? By now Don Bradman was Grimmett's captain for South Australia, and also Australia's captain. As such he was an Australian selector, and Bradman, it seemed, had become inordinately impressed with the spin ability of Frank Ward, a former clubmate of his in Sydney. It was Ward who was chosen for the first three Tests against Allen's side in 1936–37 and who caught the boat for England in 1938. Bradman, it seemed, had lost faith in the best spin bowler the world has seen. Grum's departure was a punishing blow to me and to my plans of attack. His diagnostic type of probing spin buttressed my own methods to such a degree that my reaction to his dismissal was one of infinite loss and loneliness.

Chuck Fleetwood Smith, a left arm back of the hand bowler, got the vote in front of Grimmett and had ten for 239 in the 148-run win in Adelaide in the fourth Test. On the 1938 tour of England, O'Reilly had five for 66 and five for 56 in Australia's five-wicket win at Leeds in the fourth Test. Even in the fifth where England made 903 for seven at The Oval he finished with three for 178, including Len Hutton, caught Hassett bowled O'Reilly 364. Fleetwood Smith will always be remembered for his one for 298 in the same match!

O'Reilly didn't play Test cricket again until after the war when in his final appearance in March 1946 at the age of 40 he signed off in great style with five for 14 as New Zealand were bowled out for 42 and three for 19 when they made 54 in the second innings. What a way to go. A schoolteacher, he went on to become a cricket writer noted for his fiery columns and he was 86 when he died in the same year Shane Warne made his debut for Australia against India at Sydney in January 1992. That was the start of a career in which, for me, he became the greatest spinner of all time. He was voted one of the five greatest ever cricketers by *Wisden* and it's hard to dispute that, given his 708 wickets, but he also captured the public's imagination as very few others have done.

It all started with that delivery in the first Test of the 1993 Ashes series at Old Trafford when he bowled Mike Gatting with a ball which pitched miles outside the leg stump and hit the top of the off. They called it the Ball of the Century and a legend was born. The reason he was so good is that he bowled so very few bad balls. Every batsman knows that leg-spinners can deliver wicket-taking balls but if you wait and be patient, they'll let you have a long hop or a half volley you can put away. He didn't do that. Accurate with huge spin – and I mean huge, enough to pitch well outside leg and miss off – he hemmed you in with fielders in front on both sides of the pitch and drifted the ball into your pads. In effect he closed off the off side and made you want to drive against the spin through mid on, which is hellish difficult against someone who spins the ball so much. He could bowl around the wicket into the rough and nobody can drive with any confidence in the second innings of a Test when he's dropping the ball on the worn patches – that's a serious problem.

Warne was strong enough to bowl long spells and he loved it. You couldn't get the ball off him once he got going and until that shoulder trouble he had an unbelievably good 'flipper' and an equally lethal topspinner. They were a large part of his armoury; with him and McGrath bowling together there was nothing to hit and both were capable of producing wicket-taking balls out of nowhere. Just any captain's dream, because you can control the whole game. Warney followed Richie Benaud's credo that to be successful a wrist-spinner has to be able to bowl a stock legspinner and drop it on a sixpence. He could do that within his first two years and added all the variations afterwards.

Most people around the world have seen him bowl on television or during a Test and they don't need telling how good he was. He has a heart of gold and whatever he may or may not have got up to off the field I couldn't give a damn. If I'm going to pick 11 saints I'm not going to have a very good team, and none of them would be Australian. I've only room for two leggers and with Grimmett being slightly similar in style to Warne I'm going for the 'Tiger' as partner to the best of them all.

Robert Neil Harvey (1948–63)

A short, stocky left hander, Neil Harvey was a boy wonder in Australia when he became the youngest Aussie to make a century in a Test, 153 at Melbourne in the fifth Test against India in 1948 at the age of 19 years 122 days. It was only his second innings after a debut at Adelaide in the fourth Test where he went in at number six with the total at 503 for four and it was a case of after the Lord Mayor's Show following 112 from Sid Barnes, 201 from Bradman and 198 not out for Lindsay Hassett. He contributed only 13 to a total of 674 in an innings win but at Melbourne his talent was obvious. A fluent, attacking player, he liked to get on top of the bowling, and at times his footwork to the spinners was quite brilliant, appearing to me that he was very much like Compton. That's why I want him at number five in my side.

In 1948 he toured England with 'The Invincibles' and made 112 in the fourth Test at Leeds after not being selected for the first three, incidentally the first century in England by an Australian left hander. In South Africa in 1950–51 he had hundreds in four successive Tests, 178 at Cape Town in the second, 151 not out in Durban in the third, 56 not out and 100 at Ellis Park, Johannesburg in the fourth and 116 at Port Elizabeth in the last. Half a dozen hundreds in your first 13 Tests is pretty good going and perhaps not surprisingly he couldn't keep up that rate of scoring. He had an average series against England in

1950–51, getting in and then not going on to make the big ones, and a poor series against the West Indies in 1951–52 with only one half century. But at the end of 1952 he was back with a bang against South Africa in the home series with 109 in the first Test at Brisbane, 190 in the third at Sydney, 116 in the fourth at Adelaide and his career best 205 in the fifth at Melbourne. By golly he loved those Springboks, eight hundreds in 10 Tests against them; in fact he loved them so much he married a South African girl.

On the 1953 tour of England he had to work hard for his runs because the bowling had improved and had depth; Trueman, Statham, Bedser, Bailey, Laker, Lock and Wardle were some attack on uncovered pitches, a real handful that no one would fancy. But he made a fine 122 in the Manchester Test. It was the same again when England went to Australia in 1954–55 but now there were Tyson and Appleyard into the bargain, yet Harvey played two of the great innings in that series. In the first Test when Len Hutton put them in at Brisbane he made 162 and at Sydney he made an unbeaten 92 out of 184 all out, the next highest innings being 16 from Arthur Morris in the 38-run defeat, by all accounts an exceptional knock.

When I met him I was struck by his vitality and confidence, as you might expect from a man who got a hundred in 21 of 79 Tests, a strike rate of better than one in four. He got big hundreds, too, and as I've said before, pretty little thirties and forties don't win matches. When a batsman gets in he's got to finish the job and Harvey certainly did that.

In the Caribbean in 1955 he had 133 in the first Test in Jamaica, the same score in Trinidad in the second and when they went back to Jamaica for the last match in the series he ran up 204 in which, incidentally, he hit the only six of his Test career. It proves that quality players can attack the bowling without hitting the ball in the air. It's nonsense to think you have to hit it into the stands and he proved it. Bowlers love batsmen like him – so long as they're on the same side – men who make big scores and give them something to bowl at. On the specially prepared pitches in England for the 1956 tour he struggled like everyone else against the sharply turning ball and Tony Lock got him six times, four of them cheaply. But possibly the worst day of his life (and for that matter most of the Australians') came at Old Trafford when Jim Laker got him out twice in one day for nought.

It was a different world in India and 140 in Bombay in October 1956 must have come as some relief after the earlier part of the year. In the New Year's Test against England at Melbourne in 1958 he made 167 and back in India in December 1959 had 114 in Delhi and the following January 102 in Bombay in the first and third Tests. His last century came in his penultimate Test against England in Adelaide in January 1963, his 154 being another example of the man going on to make the *big* hundred. Of course he had one or two poor series – we all do, if we didn't there wouldn't be any point in being a bowler – but 80 of his 137 innings were at number three where it's a lot more difficult; for me he'd make a top-notch number five behind Bradman and Chappell.

Allan Border and Steve Waugh were other candidates for this spot in my batting order and both were terrific players. Border was always prepared to battle it out and his 11,174 aggregate will take some beating, while Steve became a mentally strong player, cut out the hook and showed great determination, characteristics I admire. But I want something more than that and Neil Harvey gives me the attacking flair I need down the order.

Raymond Russell Lindwall (1946–60)
Glenn Donald McGrath (1993–2007)
Frederick Robert Spofforth (1877–87)

Ray Lindwall could have taken up rugby league before the Second World War but in peacetime he concentrated on cricket and there were a lot of batsmen, particularly English ones, who wished he'd stuck with the oval ball. As a kid he used to play in the streets of Sydney and hoped to catch the eye of the great 'Tiger' O'Reilly as he walked home from the SCG and later, at the city's St George's club, became his protégé.

Not tall at 5ft 10in, he had a deep chest and broad shoulders and developed his lovely, flowing approach to the crease while serving in the South Pacific during the war. He could swing it both ways while maintaining extraordinary control for someone of genuine pace. He could bowl an awkward skiddy bouncer but he didn't overdo it, using it mainly to keep a batsman in order, and his main weapon was the full, very fast delivery which swung late. If you can bowl those you're going to get wickets all right and he did.

Lindwall made his debut against New Zealand in Wellington in March 1946 and his first two victims were both bowled. That's significant because he hit the stumps for more than 40 per cent of his 228 Test match wickets, which underlines how accurate he was.

When England toured in 1946–47 he played little part in Australia's win by an innings and 332 runs in Brisbane and missed the second Test with a recurrence of the tropical disease he caught in the Pacific and which afflicted him for the rest of his life. It was his batting that caught the eye in the third Test in Melbourne, scoring a century in 113 minutes and 88 balls, then the second fastest hundred by an Aussie, and putting on 154 for the eighth wicket with Don Tallon which effectively won the game. In the last match, in Sydney in February 1947, there was a sign of things to come when he had seven for 63 from 22 eight-ball overs and Australia won by five wickets. Against India at Adelaide the following November he had seven for 38 as India followed on in the fourth Test and then took England by storm when Bradman's all-conquering Australians toured in 1948 with 27 wickets at 19.62.

In those days there was a new ball every 65 overs and given the Aussie bowling line-up on uncovered pitches it was crazy. They were queuing up to get their hands on it. I ask you, what sort of administrators make a rule like that? They must have been wrong in the head, it was brainless and Lindwall and company extracted full measure. In the fifth Test of the series at The Oval, after England won the toss and batted first he took six for 20 as they were bowled out for 52, Len Hutton the last man out for 30 of them. The Aussies won the series 4–0 and Lindwall was one of *Wisden*'s five players of the year.

Bradman used Lindwall sparingly in the early days and that extended the fast bowler's career to 14 years at the top. When I met him much later on in Australia I was struck by his bull neck and shoulders and it was easy to see how he generated so much real pace.

He toured South Africa in 1949–50 and had 12 wickets at 20.66 from slightly more than 100 overs in five Tests and was similarly lightly used on England's tour of 1950–51 with 15 at 22.93. When the West Indies toured Australia in 1951–52 he was in his pomp and claimed 21 wickets at

23.04 and he was back on the rampage against England on the Australian tour of 1953 with 26 at 18.84. He took five for 57 in the rain-affected draw at Nottingham in the first match, five for 56 in the second at Lord's, a couple at Old Trafford in another match badly affected by the weather and then at Leeds in the fourth Test stunned the huge Yorkshire crowd by bowling their hero Len Hutton with the second ball of the game, finishing with five for 54 and eight for 158 in the match. He even had four for 70 when England finally won back the Ashes at The Oval, but the following winter was outbowled by Frank Tyson and Brian Statham when England retained the urn. But he was far from finished and in his thirties on flat pitches in the Caribbean against the three Ws he had 20 wickets at 31 each, including six for 95 in Trinidad.

After the spin-dominated tour of England in 1956 he undertook a trip to Pakistan and India at the age of 35 and in three matches against India had 12 wickets at 16.58 including seven for 43 at Madras in October 1956. His last four Tests were on the subcontinent, finishing at Eden Gardens, Calcutta, in January 1960. He took half his 228 wickets in 29 Tests against England, 114 wickets at 22.44, and that marks him out as one of the finest genuine speed merchants of all time as well as being a fast, athletic fielder with a flat, accurate throw.

Glenn McGrath never looked much like an athlete; a tall beanpole with long legs, he always appeared a bit stiff, a bit mechanical. But it was that automaton-like repetitive action that made him the fine bowler he was, a real destroyer. Not especially quick, but sharp enough, his secret was that he got the ball into the most difficult areas for batsmen more often than any other modern day bowler since Richard Hadlee. McGrath bowled very few bad balls and the batsman was always under pressure against him. If you get the ball into that corridor of uncertainty, four to five inches wide of middle and off stumps, and you can land it on a good length, not short or a half volley, at over 80mph the batsman has a third of a second to decide six things: play or leave it, go forward or back, block it or hit it! You can get five things right but one wrong and you're gone – that's how difficult it is facing someone like McGrath. Every youngster should practise bowling in that area; don't try to be clever, just aim for a good repeatable action and control.

McGrath had a useful bouncer and a yorker but swing was not his forte and he relied on seam movement. From that great height if there was a bit of bounce in the pitch it brought added difficulty because it was hard to get forward to him. His figures don't flatter him: 563 wickets in 124 Tests at 21.64 were well earned by a craftsman but he let himself down with his sledging and abuse of batsmen. It was uncalled for, unnecessary and against the spirit of the game. Steve Waugh called it 'mental disintegration' of the opposition. I call it crude. I've always maintained that if McGrath said the same things he did to batsmen out in the middle to anyone in a pub he'd have been decked. If behaviour is not acceptable in society, then it's not acceptable on the cricket field and it shouldn't be tolerated. The umpires who let him get away with it have a lot to answer for because they are the custodians of the game and it always saddened me that Waugh, who I respect and admire as a cricketer, allowed it to go on when he was captain. In the West Indies in May 2003 in Antigua he had an exchange with Sarwan which became serious and at long last the Australian Cricket Board stepped in and told their team to cut it out. For me it was long overdue and it is an ongoing problem which should be tackled by the ICC and the authorities.

Fred Spofforth was one of those rare creatures, a man whose first names were hardly known. He was simply referred to as 'the Demon Spofforth' and his figures in only 18 Test matches are remarkable: 94 wickets at 18.41 and he got someone out every 44.5 balls, the best strike rate of any Australian bowler with more than 50 wickets. He was the greatest figure in the early years of Australian cricket but it is difficult to make a judgement of his true value since I've never met anyone who saw him play. He must have been a bit of a character because he refused to play in the first ever Test when the selectors decided not to pick his pal in the New South Wales team, Billy Murdoch, as wicketkeeper. He got his way in the second match, also in Melbourne, in March 1877 against England, but really earned his reputation in January 1879 when he had six for 48 and seven for 62, 13 for 110 in the match and did Test cricket's first hat-trick.

Tall and slim, he was fast medium with a leap before his delivery stride and he could do the hundred yards in under 11 seconds, which was pretty fast for those days. Esentially a seamer who varied his pace a lot, he was on the trip to England for one Test in 1882 when the Ashes were born after England's seven-run defeat at The Oval in August and the Demon Spofforth took seven for 46 and seven for 44, record match figures for Australia which lasted until Bob Massie took 16 in a Test at Lord's 90 years later. A newspaper published an obituary to the death of English cricket, and according to legend a set of bails were burned and the so-called Ashes created.

Spofforth did much to increase the popularity of cricket in his native country. He was the first genuinely quick bowler and as his fame spread he became a revered figure. Had he not finished with Test cricket in 1886 at the height of his powers and moved to England to pursue his business interests, heaven knows what figures he might have ended up with. Looking at the records of that period, there were a lot of low-scoring games and it was much harder to make runs on some iffy pitches. Judging Spofforth is tricky. There is that great strike rate but the rules were different and if you were simply picking a team on figures anyone could just go through *Wisden* and do it. I'm picking my team for all conditions but on decent pitches. In the last 20 years or so things have become a lot better for batting and since 1969 pitches have been covered, which makes it harder work for the bowlers. McGrath played all his career in more difficult conditions for bowlers and I've got to have him in front of Spofforth. Ray Lindwall produced tremendous performances against the top sides as well as England so I'm having him instead of Jeff Thomson.

The Wicketkeeper

My view is that with such high quality batting and bowling I want the best man for the job and there are some legendary characters like Wally Grout, Bertie Oldfield, Don Tallon, Rod Marsh, Ian Healy and Adam Gilchrist to be considered. I have great affection for **Arthur Theodore Wallace Grout** because he kept for Australia in my first Test match at Trent Bridge in 1964 and was responsible for one of the finest pieces of sportsmanship I have ever seen. I opened with Fred Titmus because John Edrich had stood on a ball at practice the previous day and was unable to walk when the match started. Early in the innings I pushed a ball into the on side and called for a single but as Fred set off Neil Hawke, a big lad who played Aussie rules football, flattened him as he went to field the ball and when it arrived in Wally's hands Fred was still trying to get up. He could have run him out by miles but instead threw the ball away and let Fred recover his ground. That's the sort of Australian I remember with fondness, hard and fair and good sports, what I regard as the *real* Aussie.

Few chances escaped the agile Grout behind the stumps. In Test cricket he dismissed 187 batsmen, 163 of them caught and 24 stumped. Of these, 23 fell to him in the series with the West Indies in Australia in 1960–61; 21 in England in 1961 and 20 against England in Australia in 1958–59. Only Godfrey Evans, who played in 40 more Test matches for England, possesses a better record. On two occasions

Grout claimed eight victims in a Test match and his six catches in one innings against South Africa at Johannesburg in 1957–58 set up a world record which has since been equalled by Denis Lindsay for South Africa and John Murray for England. On five other occasions Grout disposed of five batsmen in an innings. Outside Test cricket he created a world record with eight catches in an innings for Queensland in a Sheffield Shield match at Brisbane in 1960 against Western Australia. He also had a nice line in Aussie wit and, when asked by an Englishman if he'd attended a public school, he replied, 'Eton. And drinkin'.' He ignored doctors' warnings about his weak heart and kept on playing until he was 39 and died from a heart attack less than three years later.

Donald Tallon, another Queenslander, had great hands but not much of a batting average in Tests although he made hundreds against all the state sides in domestic first class cricket and **Rodney William Marsh** turned himself from a bit of a joke into a legend. When he first started out he kept dropping the ball and we called him 'iron gloves' but he was a tough nut and 'c Marsh b Lillee' appeared 95 times in Test scorecards. He made his debut against England at Brisbane on our 1970–71 tour, went on to play in 96 Tests and when he retired had what was then a world record 355 dismissals. **Ian Andrew Healy** continued the dynasty of acrobatic wicketkeepers and in 119 Tests overtook the Marsh record and finished with 395 victims.

In an earlier era when there were more spinners about **William Albert Stanley Oldfield** was considered to be the best, with lightning fast hands and nimble footwork. In his 54 Test matches his bag was 130 dismissals, 78 catches and 52 stumpings, the latter still a record for Test match cricket. In the Melbourne Test of the 1924–25 series he stumped

Hobbs, Woolley, Chapman and Whysall in the same innings and Bradman called him the best.

But batsmen don't use their feet to get to the pitch of the ball as they did then and now it's all sweep and reverse sweep based on length, and modern day batsmen all tend to play spinners from the crease. Bertie will forever be remembered for the third Test of the Bodyline series when he was hit on the head by Harold Larwood at Adelaide and was carried off unconscious. When he came round he said, 'It was my fault, I ducked into it.' He and Larwood later became firm friends. There is no doubt he was a very fine keeper and a proper sportsman into the bargain.

But can I keep out someone like **Adam Craig Gilchrist**? At one stage he was averaging in the mid fifties with the bat and that put him up there with some of the greatest batsmen of all time like Len Hutton and Greg Chappell. The 2005 Ashes series cut him back a bit when he struggled against lively swing bowling from around the wicket which exposed his lack of footwork. He didn't get his front foot forward and far enough across and because he hadn't seen much bowling of this quality, his judgement of what to play and what to leave wasn't great. Since then he's not been in such devastating form in Tests.

Three Gilchrist innings rank among the most amazing by Australians: his unbeaten 149 from 163 balls against Pakistan at Hobart in only his second Test when all seemed lost; his savage 204 not out against South Africa in the first Test at Johannesburg in 2002 made from 213 balls with 19 fours and eight sixes, then the fastest double ton on record; and his 57-delivery Ashes century at Perth in the third Test of the Ashes series in December 2006 when he missed equalling Viv Richards' fastest hundred by a ball and finished with 102 from 59 balls with 12 fours and four sixes.

A natural hitter, there's little wonder he's smacked more sixes in Test cricket than anyone else and he plays like that from the off. If he comes in when you're in trouble with men round the bat he counter-attacks and seizes the initiative; if you're already on top he just blows the opposition away.

He's been exceptional for Australia and what a bonus it is to have not just an ordinary batsman but one who rates with the greats coming in at number seven. His keeping may not be that clever and he misses low and wide catches but the point about batsmen-wicketkeepers is that someone who averages around the high twenties and lets chances go begging can't make up the ground but someone like Gilchrist, averaging around 50, can be forgiven the odd mistake. Another thing I like about him is that he's a true sportsman who is honest enough to walk when he's on nought or a hundred. I know a lot of people who'll walk when they've got a ton but aren't quite so keen when they've got nowt and you've got to admire him for that. Gilchrist showed that he meant to get to the top when he left his native New South Wales and moved across the country to Perth because he couldn't get into the state side. It's tough if you're a wicketkeeper in Oz because there's only six places up for grabs and that's what keeps Australian cricket so strong, that constant competing for places. You can't afford ever to be complacent because there's always someone ready to jump into your boots. When he packs up Gillie's will take some filling.

Victor Thomas Trumper (1899–1912)

It's very difficult to assess the great names of an era when there was no television, film or radio because you're left with contemporary accounts which sometimes appear to have been written by people wearing pretty heavily tinted rose-coloured glasses. But there's no doubting Vic Trumper's place in Australian cricket, universally acknowledged to be the best until Bradman came along.

In his obituary *Wisden* said:

Trumper at the zenith of his fame challenged comparison with Ranjitsinhji. He was great under all conditions of weather and ground. He could play quite an orthodox game when he wished to, but it was his ability to make big scores when orthodox methods were unavailing that lifted him above his fellows.

To average 39.04 in 48 Tests on what we know were not the greatest of pitches at the start of the 20th century took some doing and by all accounts Trumper was at his best when the going was toughest. On good strips he had fluency and timing and there was no limit to his range of strokes. Unusually for the times, he was a young man when he made his debut at Nottingham in 1899, making nought and 11, but in the second Test, at the age of 21, made 135 not out at Lord's, batting at number six.

He moved up to open without a great deal of success in the 1901–02 series in Australia but flourished when the

Aussies toured England in 1902, making 103 before lunch on the first day of the fourth Test at Old Trafford and averaging 32 for the series. In South Africa on unfamiliar matting pitches in 1902–03 he averaged 47.8, while against England in the first Test of the 1903–04 series in Sydney made 185 not out in 230 minutes batting at number five in the second innings, the first hundred coming in 94 minutes. Back at the top of the order he made 113 and 59 at Adelaide in the third Test and ended with 574 runs at an average of 63.77, stupendous figures for those days.

I look at *Wisden* again for an assessment and find:

Under all conditions Trumper was a fascinating batsman to watch. His extreme suppleness lent a peculiar grace to everything he did. When he was hitting up a big score batting seemed quite an easy matter. He took so many liberties, however, and scored from so many good balls, that in order to do himself justice he had to be in the best possible health and condition. The strokes with which he drove even the best bowlers to despair demanded a marvellous union of hand and eye. His game at its highest point of excellence could only be played by a young man.

I don't think he could have been in the best of health all the time in those pre-penicillin days and there were fluctuations in form. In 1905 in England he had a poor series with 125 runs at 17.85 and a top score of 31 and in the next series in 1907–08 he bagged a pair in the fourth Test in Melbourne. But his powers returned with 166 in 241 minutes batting at number three in the second innings of the fifth Test at Sydney, a match-winning knock. Back at the top of the order for the second Test against South Africa in 1910–11 he made hundreds in consecutive innings: 159 in Melbourne and, at number five in Adelaide in the next

game, 214 not out in 242 minutes; at the time the record
Test score by an Australian. In the series he made 661 runs
at 94.42 while batting just about everywhere in the order.
Maybe it was a case of the Australians thinking he was so
good he could make runs whatever the situation, but his
popularity was huge and a benefit game for him in Sydney
between New South Wales and the Rest of Australia in
February 1913 raised £3,000; just think what that would be
worth in today's money. But Victor didn't have long to
enjoy it and succumbed to kidney disease at the age of 37.
When he died in June 1915, even with the First World War
killing millions his passing was announced on newspaper
placards throughout Australia.

I think he's got to open with Arthur Morris because he
had obvious quality. If you just pick people on averages then
the current side would walk it but a cricket team is more
than a set of figures and Trumper, a modest man even at the
height of his fame, seems to me to be the right sort for
my team.

Two I had to consider were Bill Lawry and Bob Simpson,
tremendous opening partners who hold the Australian
record for the first wicket, 382 against the West Indies in
Barbados in 1965 when they both made double hundreds.
They had an almost telepathic understanding when it came
to running between the wickets and I had plenty of time to
observe them when they put on 201 for the first wicket at
Manchester in July 1964. We were in the field for two and a
half days as Bob compiled 311 – I thought I was never going
to get a bat. Bill was always hard to get out; Bob was a very
clever player and the best slip fielder I have ever seen. He
caught me in my first Test at Trent Bridge in that same
series and what a catch it was. It went to second slip's left
hand but Ian Redpath missed it and Bob came behind him

to take it. *The Cricketer* magazine featured a picture of it on the front cover and I got sick to death of being asked to autograph it.

Bob caught me in both innings at Headingley and the second time when I said 'well held' he replied, 'You keep nicking 'em and I'll keep catching 'em.' I thought, In that case I'd better learn very quickly to stop nicking them. If that wasn't enough he got me out at The Oval when I made 113 in the second innings of the fifth Test and this time I edged one of his legspinners to Ian Redpath at slip. I'm very well aware of their capabilities, a pair of very fine players who come very close to the two I've picked.

Australia

SQUAD	RESERVES
Arthur Morris	Jeff Thomson
Victor Trumper	Clarrie Grimmett
Donald Bradman	Fred Spofforth
Greg Chappell	Wally Grout
Neil Harvey	Don Tallon
Keith Miller	Rod Marsh
Adam Gilchrist	Ian Healy
Alan Davidson	Bertie Oldfield
Dennis Lillee	
Glenn McGrath	
Ray Lindwall	
Shane Warne	
Bill O'Reilly	

South Africa

The Openers

For many South African players a proper assessment is difficult because they didn't have the chance to show what they could do on the world stage and it must have been terribly frustrating. With no aspirations above provincial games or English county cricket for the 22 years South Africa was banned from Test cricket, a whole generation of players had nowhere to go.

Every sportsman has to have ambition; you want to test yourself against the best. That's what keeps you going forward; you want to climb Everest, get to the top, be the number one. That's what stimulated me throughout my career, to measure myself against my peers and the great names of the past. For those not that good, that's OK, they can find a comfort zone, but for the players with that extra special quality it must have been soul destroying to know there was no higher hill to climb than first class cricket.

Then there are those who were given a flavour of life at the top just before South Africa's exclusion only to have it taken away. I'm not sure what was worse, never knowing, or getting a taste and having the cup snatched away. A bit like giving a child a toffee apple, letting it have a bite and then grabbing it back. The kiddie would scream its head off and those players inwardly must have felt much the same as they watched and listened to the cricket world passing them by.

With no focus or heart it was little wonder that the South Africans snatched Kerry Packer's hand off when he came up with the World Series format; it was a lifeline, a ticket into the big picture.

Among this body of players for whom I have so much sympathy is **Barry Anderson Richards** who played in only four Tests before the curtain came down. Wherever he went he made runs be it in the provinces, county cricket, Sheffield Shield, for Packer or for the Rest of the World. Tall, fair-haired and good looking, Richards made batting look so easy, so effortless. With a high backlift and an economy of movement he never appeared rushed and that's always a sign of quality.

At 18 years of age he captained the South African schools side to England in 1963 and a lot of people don't realize he had a month with Gloucestershire two years later before joining Hampshire in 1968. I first recognized his exceptional talents when he made 224 for South Australia against Ray Illingworth's England team at Adelaide on the 1970–71 tour. I well remember the match because I got 179 but Barry was out of this world. In that season he made 356 against Western Australia in Perth, 325 of them coming in one day, and finished their season with 1,538 runs at 109.86! He wasn't a big hitter but a clean, classical striker of the ball with the skill to put it where he wanted. Nine times he made hundreds before lunch in county cricket, and he had a century in each innings twice, at Northampton in 1968 and at Southampton against Kent in 1976.

For Natal in the 1972–73 season he was sponsored by Clover Dairies, an ice cream firm, for two Rand a run (when the Rand was worth something). He scored 1,247 at an average of 69.27. Then when World Series started in 1977–78 he made 207 for the Rest of the World against Australia in Perth and in his first innings in such a lamentably short Test career, he completed his hundred against Australia in the first over after lunch. He did it all over the world and averaged 72.57 from just seven Test innings. Later in life he gave the impression he was bored with county cricket and while I don't know whether that was true I could understand it if he was. Of all the 'lost generation' perhaps he was the most frustrated.

One of my favourite cricketers is **Edgar John Barlow**. He was very talented and had a wonderful self-confidence, an intelligent cricketer with an irrepressible spirit. He also had that rare gift, and it is a rare one, of being able to lift a dressing room. He was never down for more than a few seconds and immediately thinking positively about how to win the match. Graeme Pollock told me that he was 'the key guy in the resurgence of South African cricket' in the 1960s. 'On the 1963–64 tour to Australia we were all young players – for many of us it was our first trip abroad. Eddie was so uplifting all the time,' Graeme said. Problems? Feeling down? Loss of confidence? Send for Eddie who went out of his way to motivate everyone. What a fantastic guy to have in the side.

He played the game hard and his obduracy caused a major upset on England's tour of 1964–65. At Newlands in the third Test he was clearly caught behind off Ian Thomson in the first innings early on the first morning but stood there and was given not out by the umpire. The crowd, the press, everybody noticed because when he reached his hundred nobody in the England side applauded. What made it worse and caused an even bigger furore was that when Ken Barrington was given not out on 49 to an appeal for a catch behind, Kenny put his bat under his arm and walked off and all hell was let loose in the media. It was a difference in philosophies; English players of that era walked, others didn't and Eddie was certainly a non-walker.

He hit three centuries in that series in Australia, 114 at Brisbane in the first, 109 at Melbourne in the second and 201 at Adelaide in the fourth. For the Rest of the World in England in 1970 he took four wickets in five balls at Leeds, including the hat-trick. In that match he got me out twice which gave him great pleasure because he was one of my seven victims in Tests, caught by Peter Parfitt at slip for 69 in the fifth Test at Port Elizabeth on the 1964–65 tour.

As I passed him he was grinning all over his face and said, 'I've waited a long time to get my own back, Fiery.' But I had the last laugh. When I got a parking ticket in Scarborough I told the authorities I'd loaned the car to Eddie and I got off the hook. Then I told him what had happened and added that when he came back to England the bobbies would be waiting for him! That wiped the grin off his face, I can tell you.

For all our friendship down the years and my admiration for him I have to leave him out in favour of **Bruce Mitchell**. He played his first Test in 1929 and his last 20 years later, making a record 42 consecutive appearances for his country. Studious, careful and very determined to occupy the crease for as long as possible, he was a man after my own heart. He had a steely determination, good footwork against the spinners and they said that once he got in, you couldn't get him out. He didn't play much for Transvaal, making only 56 appearances in 25 years because he had a well-paid job, couldn't get leave and there was no money in Currie Cup cricket.

In his first Test of the 1929 series Mitchell made 88 and 61 at Edgbaston and at the age of 20 finished the tour with more runs than anybody else. Not a big man at 5ft 10in, he relished batting and if he didn't make that many big scores, he played many a gem on some very poor pitches, particularly at home.

He played a major role in South Africa's first win over England, by 157 runs, making an unbeaten 164 out of 278 for seven declared in the second innings at Lord's in 1935, then his and his country's highest individual innings.

The war years deprived him of five summers but on the 1947 tour of England he made 597 runs at 66.33 including a century in each innings of the final Test at the Oval, 120 in the first and a career best 189 not out in the second. Then the following winter against England he made 475 at 52.77, including 120 at Cape Town in the third Test, four days before his 40th birthday. In the last match of the series and of his career at Port Elizabeth, Alec Bedser had him caught behind on 99 but it didn't get him down and he showed the determination which marked his cricketing life with 56 in the second dig to round off a remarkable career.

The Number Three Spot

I want a man at first wicket down who can handle the new ball and, as in my England squad, someone who is also an opener is ideal. **Herbert Wilfred Taylor** who played before and after the First World War has a very strong claim, averaging 40.77 from 42 Test matches. You may look at those figures and think they're not that impressive, but Victor Trumper, considered to be the doyen of batsmen of that period, averaged only 39.04 from his 48 Tests. You have to remember that there were a lot of low-scoring games and matches were played on some poor grass pitches or on matting, a far cry from today with covered pitches, heavy bats and small boundaries.

Herbie Taylor was the ideal batsman to emulate with a great defence and complete mastery of the matting pitches played on in South Africa until the 1930s.

On his first tour of England in 1912 for the triangular tournament which included Australia he made nought on his debut against the Aussies at Old Trafford and in the second Test at Lord's against England, Sydney Barnes got him out in both innings for one and five. People must have thought this was the end of him. Just over a year later, in 1913–14, Barnes took 49 wickets in four Tests in South Africa and, although Barnes had Herbie on five out of eight occasions, Taylor made 109 in the first Test at Durban and ended the series with 379 runs at 47.37 and was the only guy with any idea of how to play Barnes. An oft-repeated story is that SF threw a wobbly and hurled the ball down, cursing, 'Bloody Taylor, Taylor, Taylor all the time.' A good friend of mine tried to flesh out the story and, having struck up correspondence with SF, finally asked him if the story was true. Barnes replied with one word: 'Rot'. But he also wrote to Herbie asking the same question and he confirmed the story without any further explanation.

Taylor was the undisputed master of the mat, staying back with great concentration and, by all accounts, was a very cultured player. With Barnes bowling out his com-patriots at two a penny he stood alone. The problem is that if a matting pitch is not stretched out to be taut the ball goes all over the place. Richie Benaud told me that when he first went to India he detailed a man to go to the ground early each morning to make sure that the strip hadn't been loosened up overnight when Australia were batting!

Herbie's figures under those conditions are compelling. On England's 1922–23 tour he had 176 in the first Test and 102 in the fourth, both played at the old Wanderers ground in Johannesburg, and 102 in the fifth at Durban, a total of 582 runs at 64.66. In 1927–28, again against England, he finished with 414 runs at 41.4. To prove he could do it on grass pitches he amassed 121 at The Oval in 1929, with an average of 55.25 for the three Tests he appeared in, and the first time South Africa played a home Test on grass, at Cape Town in 1931, he made 117. He was no dumpling, he could play and among his contemporaries he has to be judged as one of the best.

So is it Herbie or Eddie at number three? Taylor has a record as good as Trumper's, judged the best of his age, but Barlow brings that indefinable quality to the dressing room, the ability to give it a lift. A captain looks after the tactics, the policy and the on-the-field stuff, but every top side has someone who gees up the lads, provides that extra spur, goes the extra mile. It's a special quality. I have to judge by figures and reputation against a guy I knew well, played with and admired. I think in the end Eddie Barlow may just shade it.

Robert Graeme Pollock (1963–70)

When it comes to picking any South African side Graeme Pollock has to be the first name you write down. He was voted the country's Cricketer of the Century by the public in 2000 and he won it by a mile, as well he might.

He was one of the best four batsmen I've ever seen; a big, tall lad, left handed and with that heavy bat of his driving off the front foot was something else. Length didn't matter to him: he hit on the up with power and placement and it was fantastic to see him in action. He was such a commanding player, like a left handed Viv Richards, with that same economy of movement in his shots and the ability to score at will, effortlessly leaning into his strokes. He has the distinction of being one of only four batsmen who have played in more than 20 Test matches to average over 60 along with Sir Don Bradman, Herbert Sutcliffe and George Headley, with 2,256 runs in 23 Tests at 60.97.

Right from the off it was plain he was more than useful, scoring his first century in the third Test of the 1963–64 series in Australia as a 19-year-old, 122 at Sydney, and followed that up with 175 in the fourth game at Adelaide. He became only the second man after George Headley to make three Test hundreds before his 21st birthday when he took 137 off England at Port Elizabeth in the 1964–65 season. Strangely for such a fluent player, he struggled against the flight and turn of Fred Titmus and David Allen, our offspinners, in the first two Tests of that series but finally got it together.

One of the finest moments of my career as a bowler came when I got him out in Cape Town, the biggest and best of my seven Test scalps. He was cruising along in a match heading for a draw on a flat pitch with a very nice quiet little hundred beckoning when I bowled him for 73. I always remind him of it when we meet up and, like Fred Trueman would have done, I tell him that it swung late and nipped back off the seam while he just shakes his head in disbelief.

Perhaps one of his most outstanding innings came on the 1965 tour of England when he made a quite magnificent 125 out of 160 scored while he was at the wicket on a seaming pitch at Trent Bridge where South Africa were reduced to 80 for five through some wonderful seam bowling from Tom Cartwright. Where everyone else struggled he middled the ball with fluent strokes and looked a different class. Tom broke his thumb in that match and in the second innings I was pressed into service and bowled 26 overs. I didn't get him out that time!

When Australia went to South Africa in 1966–67 he had 209 in the second Test in Cape Town, the first hundred coming from only 139 balls, and 105 in the fifth Test at Port Elizabeth, his sixth in all on his 23rd birthday. This feller could play all right.

He had an odd superstition that when a wicket fell he would leave the dressing room and then come back in to get his gloves; he did it without fail. When he was playing with Transvaal under Clive Rice he used to get very wound up when the captain regularly told him, 'Don't give it away, Graeme.' As if he would.

His Test career ended and South Africa's participation

was suspended at Port Elizabeth, where Graeme grew up, 81 years after the Springboks, as they were known then, played their first Test in 1889.

When World Series Cricket started in 1977 he was signed up to be one of the star attractions but two West Indian politicians, Michael Manley of Jamaica and Forbes Burnham of Guyana, kicked up a stink about West Indians playing in the same team with the now ostracized South Africans. Kerry Packer, apparently, spoke to the Australian Prime Minister, Malcolm Fraser, who struck a deal at the Commonwealth Heads of State conference in Singapore which, in effect, said it was acceptable for the West Indians to play alongside South Africans who had turned out in English county cricket but not others. It was a load of codswallop and while it mollified the West Indian politicians, it meant that both Graeme Pollock and Denys Hobson were sacrificial lambs and never played in World Series, despite receiving full pay.

Arthur Dudley Nourse (1935–51)

A powerful man, Dudley Nourse hit the ball very hard and was particularly effective off the back foot. By all accounts his cutting and hooking were something else, the product of strong forearms and a burly frame, his style a little like the West Indian Clyde Walcott. In 34 Tests he averaged 58.61, not bad going at all, and although he never toured Australia he made three trips to England in 1935, 1947 and 1951.

The son of Arthur Nourse, universally known as 'Dave', he got little help from his illustrious father who himself played 45 times for South Africa. Dave told young Dudley, 'I learned to bat with a paling from the fence – you go and do the same.'

In his first three Tests in England in 1935 Dudley made four, three and two but he was starting to find his feet with a couple of thirties at The Oval in the last game of the series. The following winter he made 231 against Australia at the old Wanderers ground in the second Test and ended the series with 518 at 57.55, so he must have played a few shots and proved he was capable of big scores.

When England toured South Africa in 1938–39 he amassed 422 in the series at an average of 60.28 and in the 'timeless Test' at Durban in March 1939 he made 103 in 364 minutes to add durability to his shot-making prowess.

A bout of pneumonia while serving in the Western Desert during the Second World War almost cost him his life but in the first Test of 1947 at Trent Bridge he made 149 and took part in the then record stand of 319 for the third wicket with Alan Melville, following that up with 115 at Old Trafford and half centuries in each innings of the Tests at Leeds and Lord's. He finished the series with 621 runs at an average of 69, pretty phenomenal figures.

In the winter of 1948–49, with England touring, he made 120 at Cape Town in the third Test and 129 not out at the notorious Ellis Park in the fourth to finish with 536 runs at 76.57, while in 1949–50 against an Australian side containing Ray Lindwall, Keith Miller and Bill Johnston, he averaged 45 with 114 at Cape Town.

But the best was saved for last. On his final tour of England in 1951 he made 208 in the first Test at Trent Bridge, an innings which was all the more remarkable because he broke his thumb three weeks earlier and must have been in excruciating pain for every one of the 555 minutes he was out there. When he was finally run out he took no further part in the match even though he was captain. Importantly, South Africa's first double hundred against England also brought their first victory over them for 16 years, 28 Tests dating back to 1935. By golly it must have taken some courage.

So we have a man with bags of shots, stickability and guts. What more could you want? Arthur Dudley Nourse was clearly the outstanding South African batsman of his generation and it fascinates me that he, with his fence paling, Don Bradman with his stump and golf ball against the garage and Jack Hobbs in the fives courts with a stump and a tennis ball, were virtually self-taught.

These are three of the biggest names in the batting game yet what bit of technical stuff they might have learned was grafted on well after their teenage years. I was brought up to play the game strictly according to the MCC coaching bible and was a technical or textbook cricketer. There's nothing wrong with the coaching manual but these three guys showed there is another way to learn the game, training eyes and hands and having a wonderful ball sense. Doing things their way makes your feet work quickly and properly, develops your hand–eye coordination – there's nothing in their book about keeping your left elbow up or how you hold the bat. Let's face it, if they didn't master the way they were learning they'd have been forever fetching the ball back when they missed it or have it coming back at them from impossible angles. They just had that incredible, almost uncanny instinct for the game.

I also considered two other middle order players, Alan Melville and Colin Bland. **Alan Melville**, public school and Oxford University, could bat anywhere in the top three and averaged 52.58 in his 11 Tests, captain in 10 of them. He skippered the Varsity and Sussex to great effect and in his 86 games on England's south coast the county finished runners-up three times. He made 103 in the 'timeless Test' of 1939 and followed with 189 and 104 not out in the Trent Bridge Test of 1947 and 117 at Lord's in the next, to register four Test hundreds on the trot although they were eight years apart. So there is little doubt about his credentials.

Kenneth Colin Bland, tall, long-legged and very athletic, will always be remembered for his astonishing ability in the field and while there is no doubting how terrific he was it rather overshadowed his batting – indeed, he averaged 49.08 in 21 Tests, not to be sneezed at, and made 127 at The Oval in the final Test of the 1965 series which proved to be the last between the two sides for a long time.

I remember when he came on the 1961 tour with the Fezelas (the young South Africans) under Roy MacLean they played their first game at Scarborough and he managed

W. G. Grace as a young man.

The doctor in his later years
gives little indication of the fine
athlete he was in his youth.

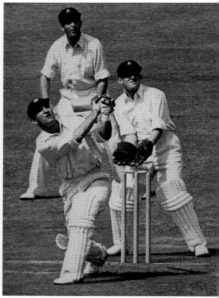

Sir Jack Hobbs, the first professional cricketer to be knighted. What a player he must have been!

Sir Len Hutton, better known for his fluent cover drives than hitting sixes over mid-wicket.

Wally Hammond: simply the best, top of the shop.

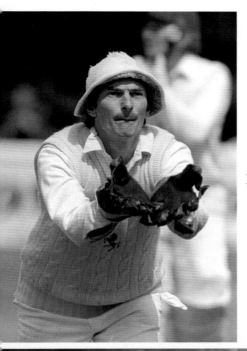

Alan Knott. For me, no contest, far and away the best ever.

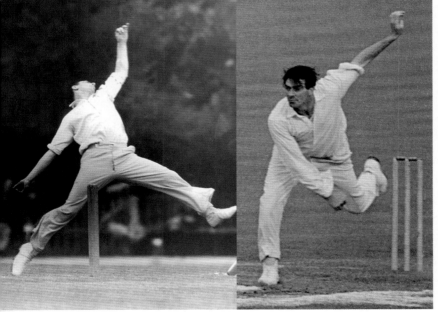

red Trueman at full stretch, the most perfect action you could wish to see.

George Lohmann: strong claims to be the greatest bowler ever.

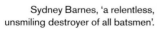

Sydney Barnes, 'a relentless, unsmiling destroyer of all batsmen'.

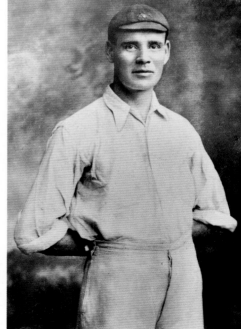

Left: Wilfred Rhodes pictured at Scarborough. Started at number 10, ended up opening and took 127 wickets.

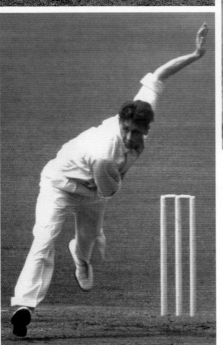

Above: Jim Laker. He could make the ball hum in the air as it came towards you.

Left: Brian Statham, steely determination and a real competitor.

Sir Donald Bradman. Setting traps for him was a waste of time.

Bill O'Reilly. One of the three best leg spinners Australia ever produced and 'The Don' thought he was the best.

Ray Lindwall. A lot of English batsmen wished he had stuck with rugby league.

Dennis Lillee. He said of me: 'Like a good red wine, he got better with age.' He did, too.

Shane Warne captured the public's imagination as very few have done.

Adam Gilchrist, one ball short of the fastest Test hundred of all time.

to throw the ball from one scoreboard to the other with one bounce. Let me tell you that's a mighty big throw on North Marine Road.

The moment when he ran out Ken Barrington at Lord's in 1965 sticks in most people's memories. With Kenny strolling along to a century he reached 91 before pushing a ball out on to the leg side and going for a single. Bland moved from mid wicket towards mid on and in a single moment so quick it almost beat the eye scooped the ball up, threw and hit the bowler's wicket all in one blurred movement. Sensational. He's the best outfielder I've ever seen, including the young Clive Lloyd, Viv Richards and Jonty Rhodes and anyone else you care to name.

Melville and Bland, both strong contenders, certainly, but in the end I have gone for Nourse's toughness and determination and plenty of runs for my middle order.

Michael John Procter (1967–70)

The strength of any side has a lot to do with the quality of the all-rounder because he gives the side balance but it has to be real top-drawer stuff not just any old bats-a-bit, bowls-a-bit jobber. Mike Procter was absolutely terrific, a real match-winner and wherever he played produced exceptional performances with bat and ball.

Some said he bowled off the 'wrong foot' but he didn't. Normally a bowler pivots on his front foot and delivers the ball over a braced front leg. What Procter did was let the ball go just before his front foot hit the ground and gave that impression of being wrong-footed by throwing himself forward. A burly six footer, broad in the shoulders and beam, he charged in with a windmill, chest-on action. But none of this affected his accuracy or pace and he was really, really quick; by throwing himself forward, as he did, he got the ball to overspin and skid at you with big inswing. He moved it so far in to you that he had you playing at wide deliveries and when he rolled his fingers over the top of the ball it would go straight on or be like a big leg cutter. He was very awkward because of that huge swing and it was very hard to drive him through the off side unless it was a very full delivery. He also had this amazing ability to bowl very fast inswingers from around the wicket at right handers. It's very difficult to maintain control of the swing at pace from this angle without running on the pitch, but he could do it.

He did the hat-trick four times: in 1972, 1977 and twice in 1979, the last two occasions all leg before. The first was against Leicestershire at Bristol and in the following match he did it against Yorkshire at Cheltenham. Richard Lumb, Bill Athey and John Hampshire were all given out by Ken Palmer, a Test match umpire and former fine bowler with Somerset, who said after the sixth ball, 'That's over and thank f*** for that.' They were all stone dead, absolutely plumb in front and I know because, in the words of Len Hutton, 'good player were at t'other end'.

His first hat-trick came at Westcliff on Sea against Essex in 1972 when he scored a ton in the second innings and he added another hundred, 122, to his third three-in-three against Leicester in 1979, the only man to score a century and do the hat-trick in a match twice. As a batsman he was a wonderful striker of the ball off front and back foot, very dangerous, and like all talented, wicket-taking bowlers his ability with the ball gave him licence to play shots and do serious damage very quickly.

He started his career with Natal but then went up to what was then Rhodesia, now Zimbabwe, in 1970–71 to play in the B section of the Currie Cup. They brought him in to stimulate the game and did he ever give it a shot in the arm.

In his first season he had hundreds in six consecutive first class innings, equalling a world record jointly held by Sir Don Bradman and C. B. Fry. They came against Natal B in Bulawayo 119, Transvaal B in Salisbury 129, Orange Free State in Bloemfontein 107, North-eastern Transvaal in Pretoria 174, Griqualand West at Kimberley 106 and his career best 254 against Western Province in Salisbury.

In 1972–73 he had a hundred in each innings for Rhodesia against the International Cavaliers and in 1979 for Gloucestershire hit the fastest ton of the season in 57 minutes to win the Walter Lawrence Trophy. So he could bat a bit, couldn't he?

When he went back to Natal in 1976–77 he produced the best bowling the Currie Cup had seen by taking 59 wickets at 15.86 each and again showed that amazing ability to transform matches.

I believe that if he'd had a proper Test career rather than just the seven Tests he played he would have been up there with legends of the game like Ian Botham, Richard Hadlee, Imran Khan and Kapil Dev and numbered among the top five bowling all-rounders the world has ever seen. He had 41 wickets at around 15 apiece in Tests so I can really only judge him on his performances in provincial and county cricket. They were phenomenal and we can only wonder about what might have been.

Jacques Henry Kallis (1995–)

In addition to picking a bowling all-rounder in Mike Procter I want a batsman who can bowl. **Clive Edward Butler Rice** was an outstanding player of his time although he never had the chance to play Test cricket because of his country's exclusion from international competition. His record in first class cricket, mainly for Transvaal and Nottinghamshire, was brilliant with 26,331 runs at 40.95 including 48 centuries and 930 wickets at 22.49. A fierce competitior, he was the strong silent type, a man of deeds not words, and what he did say was usually short and to the point. He was a likeable guy and although there may have been more aesthetically pleasing players, those who were easier on the eye, when you are in trouble you want someone like Ricey at the other end – a no-nonsense effective battler and very much my sort of cricketer. As a bowler, when he bent his back he was quite sharp with an unfurling action which made the ball skid on to you and he could run through sides.

When he joined the Packer circus he was not out of his depth against some of the quickest bowlers who were a big test of his courage and character, qualities Ricey had aplenty that were as much a part of his cricket as his ability. Anybody who saw what he did at Nottinghamshire, leading them to trophies and forging a powerful partnership with Sir Richard Hadlee, couldn't fail to be impressed by the way he got the most out of his players, never settling for second best.

Unfortunately I can't pick him because Jacques Kallis has emerged as one of the finest all-rounders of all time with a record to set alongside the incomparable Garry Sobers. I first saw Kallis as a young unknown playing for Western Province and I recommended him to Yorkshire but they had already signed Michael Bevan. A big lad, tall and broad shouldered, he is technically correct with a big stride forward and when he goes back he gets right on top of the ball; whatever the length it's no problem. In well over 100 Tests for South Africa he's been like a machine, bringing quality to the side with his simple, effective method.

There's nothing flashy about what he does and in this modern era of bashing the ball all over the place and unorthodox shots he shows that the outstanding players don't need to be cute or clever. His full range of strokes, judgement of length and quality of placement are enough. He made half centuries in eight consecutive Tests, had hundreds in five matches on the trot against the West Indies and New Zealand in 2003–04 and is the only South African to have twice scored a century and taken five wickets in an innings.

For a burly man he is surprisingly light on his feet; something that all great players have in common is good footwork. If I'd known in my playing days what I know now I would have taken dancing lessons to become more nimble. Get the feet in the right place and the rest will follow and, well balanced, you can use your hands to great effect. Kallis does all this and in many respects is a batsman of the old school.

Averaging in the mid fifties with the bat, his bowling was pretty smart as well. Before his knees started giving him trouble he bowled beautiful outswing with a lovely action and that strength in the upper body produced dangerous bounce into the bargain. He's still lively at fast medium but in his early days he was quite sharp.

Kallis has been South Africa's go-to player for the last 10 years and is arguably the best all-round cricketer the country has produced.

The Fast Men

Any side needs some real pace and there are some pretty strong contenders for a place in my side. The first to consider is **Neil Amwin Treharne Adcock**. Tall, fair-haired, very quick and very nasty, he was a real tough nut. From a high action he got bounce and sharp inswing and those who played against him describe him as 'a real awkward b****** who got up your nose'. Certainly he had lots of aggression combined with stamina and, by all accounts, he liked hitting batsmen. When New Zealand toured South Africa in 1953–54 they played the second Test at Ellis Park. The pitch there wasn't too clever and Adcock was lethal. In the Kiwis' first innings he put Bert Sutcliffe and Lawrie Miller in hospital and two others were bowled off their chests!

Neil Adcock never got into the top sides as a schoolboy and was never selected for the Nuffield weeks where all the top youngsters from the country got a chance to show what they could do. It was former Test opener Eric Rowan who spotted his potential and encouraged the lad to bowl fast. He shared the new ball with another contender, **Peter Samuel Heine**, who was 6ft 5in tall and equally aggressive. While Adcock swung it in Heine made it go the other way and they made a pretty fearsome, nasty pair, a real handful.

Peter Richardson, the England opener, told me that in the first Test of the 1956–57 series at the new Wanderers ground in Johannesburg Heine hit him on the side of the head and sat him on his backside. As he lay there dazed (no helmets in those days) he looked up to see the bowler glowering down at him. 'Get up, and I'll hit you again,' he said.

Well, he did get up and went on to make what was then the slowest century in Test cricket. At the end of the first day England were 157 for three, with Richardson 69 not out; he eventually reached three figures after eight hours and eight minutes in the middle. But it turned out to be a match-winning effort as South Africa collapsed in the second innings. There's no doubt about it, Heine was out for blood and often drew some!

Just as these two devils were coming to the end of their careers another nasty piece of work stepped on to the stage in 1961. **Peter Maclean Pollock**, Graeme's elder brother, had 116 wickets in 28 Tests at an average of 24.1 but that's only half the story. Nicknamed 'Pooch' because he used to squeal his appeals like a toy poodle, we had other less friendly names for him. He was part of the 'new kids on the block' along with his brother, Colin Bland, Eddie Barlow and Denis Lindsay who went to Australia in 1963–64 and drew the series 1–1. Against a strong Aussie line-up of Bob Simpson, Bill Lawry, Peter Burge and Brian Booth, Pollock had 25 wickets at 28 apiece, so he could bowl a bit. But there was always a mean streak and I came face to face with it on the MCC tour of South Africa in 1964–65. I'd been having a lean time on the tour but at Port Elizabeth against Eastern Province things came together and I was heading for a double hundred, my first. Mike Smith, the captain, sent out a message that the declaration was coming at the interval and I should bear that in my mind if I wanted to reach 200. As I recalled in my autobiography:

Pollock probably guessed the situation. In any event he took absolutely ages to bowl the last over before lunch, whipped in a couple of bouncers that I couldn't have reached with a step ladder and included two beamers which didn't miss me by much. [Bob] Barber was not playing in that match but was in the bar later that evening when Pollock remarked that Boycott hadn't liked his beamers. Bob stopped him short. 'Do you actually mean to say you bowled those on purpose? If you bowl any of those at me you'd better not miss because I'm coming straight for you with the bat. And you'd better not bowl any more at Geoff while I'm at the other end,' he said.

From then on Bob took the mickey out of him which used to enrage Pollock. If he let him have a bouncer Bob would sway out of the way and then go down on one knee and play a 'pretend' sweep shot grinning all over his face while Pollock stood glaring and fuming a few paces away. It was all great theatre.

Mean side apart, Peter was one hell of a competitor and on the 1965 tour of England had 20 wickets in a three-match series. In the second Test at Trent Bridge he produced match figures of 10 for 87 with five for 34 in the second innings from 24 overs.

I was at the other end in the first Test of that series at Lord's when he hit John Edrich on the head in the second innings. He went down like a sack of spuds, retired hurt and didn't come back – he was in no fit state. There were no helmets and no sightscreens at the Pavilion end in those days and an inch or two either way might well have been fatal.

Given his nature on the field, when he finished playing he went from one extreme to the other and turned to religion, becoming a passionate preacher from the pulpit. Some say it was to atone for his sins on the field; I say he needed to!

Two other bowlers who have to be worthy of consideration are Vince van der Bijl and Garth Le Roux. Neither of them had the opportunity to play Test cricket and so my judgement has to be on what they achieved in the Currie Cup and in English county cricket.

Vintcent Adriaan Pieter Van der Bijl was a tremendous bowler, a lot like Joel Garner, fastish medium with a high action and pitched the ball up just that fraction short of a length so that it was never really up to the batsmen and never really short, very awkward. This guy was quality and it was a pity he never got to play any Tests because I think he would have got wickets at the highest level. For Middlesex in 1980 he had 85 wickets at 14.72 and in his time in county cricket he won a lot of friends on and off the field with his amiable attitude. You couldn't ask for a nicer bloke.

Garth Stirling Le Roux was in the same mould though with a better physique. What a build for a quick bowler. I played against him when he was at Sussex, always found him a handful and when he went off to play for Packer in the SuperTests of 1978–79 he was voted man of the series with 17 wickets at 15 each and in the one-day games 17 wickets at 13 apiece. They're fantastic figures for limited overs cricket and show just how good he was. He had pace and bounce from that huge frame and, like Vintcent, he was a super guy off the field. These two were tops and if they'd had Test careers I think we'd be talking about them as two of the great bowlers. As it is they have to be assessed against those who did.

The most outstanding of all the South African quick bowlers has got to be **Allan Anthony Donald** who played in 72 Tests and took 330 wickets at 22.25. He was there right from the start after his country's readmission to the international arena, playing in the first ever official game against the West Indies in Barbados and although they lost that there were better days ahead.

He had an easy run-up, a silky approach, never seeming to strive, and then exploded into the delivery stride. A class act with accuracy and the ability to bowl fast yorkers. He had good control from around the wicket, something not many pace bowlers can do well. When India became the first coloured side to officially play in South Africa he had his best match figures in the third Test of the series in Port Elizabeth, 12 for 139, and on two other occasions had 11 wickets in a game: against Zimbabwe, when they had a decent side, in Harare in 1995 and against England in 1999 in Johannesburg.

Donald could also be pretty hostile when he was stirred up, as Michael Atherton found out when he gloved a catch behind at Trent Bridge in 1998 and was given not out. Michael wasn't one for walking and paid the price as Donald really let him have it.

He played a major role in South Africa's rise after their years of exile because with one truly great fast bowler operating at one end it was much easier for Shaun Pollock and others to perform at the other. Towards the end of his career he had a few injuries and I wonder if a lot of that wasn't down to the amount of one-day cricket he played. In addition to 72 Tests over 10 years he also bowled in 164 limited overs internationals and that's roughly the equivalent of another 33 Tests. Add in all the extra travelling involved and it's bound to take its toll. Added to that he had a fine career with Warwickshire with 536 wickets at 20.82 but it all made for a huge workload. That he managed it with such distinction is a great tribute to him.

Donald's got to be in my side with Neil Adcock and the

third place goes to Vintcent van der Bijl. The others all have strong claims but the main strike bowler usually favours one end over the other; it's slightly downhill, or he wants the wind behind him or maybe there's more bounce at one end. But someone has to perform at the other where it will be a bit harder with all those factors working against him. I think Vintcent would be ideal. He's not busting a gut every ball for extra pace, you're not going to get anything to hit and he has the strength, character and skill to do it magnificently.

The Wicketkeepers

It comes down to three really, John Waite, Denis Lindsay and Mark Boucher.

The remarkable thing about **John Henry Bickford Waite** is that he opened the innings as well as keeping and in his first seven Tests had to face new ball bowlers like Alec Bedser, Brian Statham and Trevor Bailey in England in 1951 and the following winter in Australia Ray Lindwall, Keith Miller and Bill Johnston. How hard is that? Little wonder he averaged just over 30 with the bat from his 50 Tests. There's never been a successful wicketkeeper-opener in Test cricket for obvious reasons. It's mentally draining and physically tiring. Take 90 six-ball overs in a day, and that's 540 times you have to squat on your haunches, never mind the no balls, wides and wild throw-ins you have to cope with. Just try it. There's professional athletes who can't manage that. Then just imagine having to go out and face the new ball straight afterwards. I don't think so. Yet he did it with a degree of success, making four centuries, although he now admits it was a bit naïve to try and do both.

When I asked him about it he said nobody wanted to do the opener's job and he volunteered because it would help him to get in the side. 'I was young, keen, just out of school really and desperately wanted to play,' he said. Can you imagine starting out facing new ball bowling of that calibre? You wouldn't be queuing up to face them even if you were a specialist.

But Waite was a technically sound batsman and an excellent keeper particularly against 'Toey' Tayfield, that fine offspinner. In one of my many long conversations with him he told me an oddity: his first victim in Test cricket was Len Hutton, caught off Athol Rowan at Trent Bridge in 1951 and his last? Me. At Port Elizabeth in the last Test of the 1964–65 series caught behind off left arm seamer Mike Macaulay.

Another contender is **Denis Thomson Lindsay** who shared the job with John until taking over from him. A wonderful attacking batsman, he made 1,130 runs at an average of 37.66 in his 19 Tests. I knew him pretty well, playing against him in club cricket in South Africa when I had a winter there preparing for the English season and turning out for Pretoria High School Old Boys. Naturally as a Test player I got quite a few hundreds at that level and when we went to Benoni, Denis's club, it was a gorgeous day, with the sun high in the sky and I was looking forward to a good pitch and a few more runs. The sun may have been beating down but to our amazement the pitch was sopping wet. Denis said there had been overnight rain and I said it's a bloody funny thing it only rained on that 22 yards. The rest of the ground was bone dry. He laughed and said, 'You won't be getting another hundred here, Fiery.' I didn't but the 20 or so I did get on a pitch where the ball was leaping at my throat was worth a ton.

I'd first come across him when he played for the Fezelas side, a touring team of young South Africans who went to England in 1961. They included Colin Bland, the Pollock brothers, Graeme and Peter, and Eddie Barlow, the young turks who were to take the Test world by storm. They mainly played against county second XI sides and I was just making my way with Yorkshire, little knowing what lay ahead for all of us.

Denis had a fabulous season in the series against Australia in 1966–67 and I saw two of his Tests in Johannesburg where I was coaching the primary and secondary lads at King David's High School. In the first innings Denis made 69 out of 199 and with the Aussies totalling 325 in reply South Africa were rocking at 268 for five when Denis came in a second time. In one of the most astonishing knocks I've ever seen he savaged the Australian bowlers and murdered Dave Renneberg and Graham Mackenzie. They kept putting two men back for the hook but Denis just smacked the short deliveries out of the ground. He had 25 fours and five sixes in 182 as South Africa easily won the game and it was some spectacle to see him in full flow. I've seen some great knocks in my time but that was about as good as it gets, I can tell you. Also in that series he had 137 in the third Test at Durban when South Africa were 83 for four and that innings won that Test as well. Then, coming in at number six in the fourth Test in Johannesburg, with South Africa 120 for four, he cracked 131 from 139 balls, the first 50 coming in 47 minutes, and rain saved Australia on the last day. Amazing stuff. There was no intimation of this sort of destructive ability in the previous summer's tour of England where he amassed just 92 runs in six innings. His Test career finished, like so many others, at Port Elizabeth in 1970 and when he died of cancer in 2005 I lost a good friend.

Mark Verdon Boucher also has to come into contention, if only for his never-say-die attitude. In many respects he reminded me of David Bairstow, the late Yorkshire and England wicketkeeper. The game was never lost while 'Bluey', as he was known, had a breath in his body. Tough, pugnacious, always ready for a scrap, Boucher had the sort of bloody-minded attitude that means a game was never over until the last ball was bowled. Just the sort of lad you want alongside you when you're going into battle.

There's not that much to choose between the three on wicketkeeping ability or batting but I have to go for John Waite. While Denis Lindsay had that one cracking series, making 606 at an average of 86.5, it was only one series. Waite made a lot of his runs up the sharp end where they are harder to come by against the new ball and his glove work was a little more artistic than both his rivals. So John Waite just edges it. But he definitely won't be opening in my team.

Hugh Joseph Tayfield (1949–60)

Called 'Toey' because of his habit of stubbing his right toe into the ground behind him at the start of his run-up, Hugh Tayfield was a captain's dream. Every pitch suited him, he always wanted to bowl and although not a great spinner of the ball he could get it to drift away from the right hander with fantastic control, as his figures of conceding only 1.94 runs per over in 37 Tests underline.

John Waite who kept wicket to him for most of the offspinner's career told me he had a sixth sense of when the batsman was going to come down the pitch to him and even the great Australian hitters like Keith Miller never got after him. 'He was as good an offspinner as there has ever been,' John said. 'If you were waiting for a bad ball you'd be waiting for ever.'

He bowled to an unusual field with two men at shortish mid wicket and a man out behind them, and such was his control of flight and length that a batsman could play six lovely shots in an over driving with the spin but fail to pierce the field and not get a run. Hugh also got through a lot of overs and John told me that he would always give the captain an argument if he tried to take him off.

Part of Tayfield's philosophy was that he didn't have to spin the ball a lot to take wickets. 'Three inches is enough to get past the bat or find the edge,' he would say, and proved it with 170 wickets in 37 Tests. Remember, there were no easy pickings in his day because South Africa only played against Australia, England and New Zealand; no Bangladesh and Zimbabwe to feed on and no dusty turners on the subcontinent either. Most pitches, too, in South Africa at that time were prepared for seamers which made his feats all the more remarkable.

He got through an astonishing number of overs and together with Trevor Goddard acted as the perfect foil to the two pacemen Neil Adcock and Peter Heine. What captain wouldn't want someone who could shut one end up tight while his strike bowlers attacked at the other end? But he was far from being just a model of economy. When conditions suited him he could win you matches and when they didn't he'd play a crucial supporting role. A rare gem.

He made his debut in the first Test of the 1949–50 series **against** Australia and quickly made his mark, taking seven for 23 in the third Test in Durban when the Aussies were all out for 75. But despite 17 wickets in the series he was not picked for the tour of England in 1951; that's selectors for you!

On the tour of Australia in 1952–53 in the second Test at Melbourne he had match figures of 13 for 165 as South Africa beat the Aussies for the first time since 1910–11 and finished with 30 wickets in the series against a side which included Colin MacDonald, Neil Harvey, Keith Miller, Lindsay Hassett and Arthur Morris. No mugs.

Against New Zealand back in South Africa in 1953–54 he had nine for 97 in the first match and then took six for 13 in 14 eight-ball overs at Johannesburg in the fourth, at one stage taking five wickets without conceding a run. Incredible stuff.

In England in 1955 he produced some more stunning figures, taking nine for 164 in the win at Leeds in the fourth Test while getting through 88 overs in the match and in the series had 26 wickets at 21 against a side which at times included Peter May, Denis Compton, Trevor Bailey, Tom Graveney, Brian Close and Willie Watson.

The quality of either winning the match by his guile or tying up one end and helping others to win it was even more apparent in 1956–57 when England visited South Africa and Tayfield bowled 24 eight-ball overs, 17 of them maidens, at a cost of just 21 runs for only one wicket in the third Test at Durban. *Wisden* records that at one period 137 balls were bowled without a run being scored and in the second innings he turned destroyer and had eight for 69 from 37.7 overs. In the fourth match of the series in Johannesburg he had four for 79 in the first innings from 37 overs (eight balls, remember) and had a hand in all 10 dismissals in the second with nine for 113, catching the tenth man, Doug Insole, off Trevor Goddard as South Africa won a tight game by 17 runs. He played a big part in the victory at Port Elizabeth in the last game of the series, bowling 22 overs for 43 runs in the first innings while Heine and Adcock cleaned up with four apiece at a total cost of 42 runs, and followed up with six for 78 from 24.3 overs. In all he took 37 wickets for 639 runs at 17.27 each.

While statistics don't always tell the story, you look at his figures, look who he was bowling to, look at the match circumstances and come to only one conclusion: he was some bowler was this feller, a real crackerjack.

Major George Aubrey Faulkner
(1906–24)

Aubrey Faulkner was one of the earliest exponents of legspin and played a major role in South Africa's first ever Test match win on his debut at the old Wanderers ground in Johannesburg against England in January 1906 with six wickets for 61 in the match. His four for 26 in the second innings set the stage for a thrilling finish with South Africa's last pair putting on 48 to bring victory by one wicket.

In 25 Tests he made 1,754 runs at an average of 40.79 and took 82 wickets at 26.58 each, a tremendous record for the period when you think that Trumper, rated the best batsman of his age, averaged under 40. The pitches weren't all that good and there were a lot of low-scoring games so his batting assumes greater importance while his legspin and the 'new art' of googlies were mystifying when the game was in its infancy.

When English batsmen first got a look at him on the South African tour of 1907 they found it so deceptive they thought he was cheating! It was all so different from anything that had gone before and together with Bert Vogler and Reggie Schwarz, Faulkner developed the skills of the wrist-spinner which are taken for granted these days.

He had a phenomenal season with the bat in Australia in 1910–11, making 732 runs at an average of 73.2 and cracking a double ton, 204, at Melbourne in the second Test, the first hundred coming in 114 minutes. At Adelaide in the next match he made 56 and 115. He made 123 against

England at the old Wanderers in 1910 and in the triangular tournament in England in 1912 scored 122 not out against the Australians at Old Trafford.

In the final game of that series he produced his best bowling with seven for 84 against England at The Oval, his last real appearance on the Test match stage although he did play one further match 12 years later.

South Africa have had so few world class spinners and, 'Toey' Tayfield apart, Faulkner is outstanding not least because he pioneered a new type of bowling and did it on grass as well as matting. At Leeds in the second Test of the 1907 series he had six for 17 and three for 58 and in Durban against England in 1910 he took six for 87.

During the First World War he was awarded the Distinguished Service Order, settled in England and set up the famous London Cricket School which produced a number of good players under his highly rated coaching. He was turned 40 when Archie MacLaren, the England and Lancashire captain, asked him to turn out for an England XI against Warwick Armstrong's all-conquering Australians of 1921 at Eastbourne. Faulkner made 153 and bagged six wickets for 63 as the Aussies suffered their only defeat of the tour. Storybook stuff.

When South Africa toured England in 1924 he was pressed into service again for one more Test at Lord's but age and the privations of the war had caught up with him and he took his own life at the age of 49.

Denys Hobson is the only other wrist-spinner of any quality worthy of consideration. He played for Western Province in the 1970s and 1980s, was a big spinner of the ball and everybody who played against him said how good he was. At Newlands in Cape Town, where there is usually a breeze blowing down the ground, he was particularly effective bowling into it, getting the ball to hang in the air so that batsmen never quite got to the pitch. He was signed up by Kerry Packer but, like Graeme Pollock, never played a game because of the behind-the-scenes politics.

For all his ability I'm not sure he would get in ahead of Faulkner because the Major could really bat. Not many sides play two spinners these days unless they are handy with the bat and Faulkner brings variety, balance and runs.

South Africa

SQUAD	RESERVES
Barry Richards	Herbie Taylor
Bruce Mitchell	Clive Rice
Eddie Barlow	Denys Hobson
Graeme Pollock	Alan Melville
Dudley Nourse	Colin Bland
Mike Procter	Peter Heine
Jacques Kallis	Peter Pollock
John Waite	Garth Le Roux
Neil Adcock	Denis Lindsay
Allan Donald	Mark Boucher
Vintcent van der Bijl	
Hugh Tayfield	
Aubrey Faulkner	

West Indies

Sir Garfield St Auburn Sobers
(1954–74)

Most people would say that Garry Sobers is the greatest cricketer there has ever been. Blessed with so much natural talent, gifted beyond imagination, a natural genius, he allied all that to concentration, determination and great stamina which allowed him to play long innings and make big scores. If you're picking any side he's got to be number one because he can win you the game with his batting or bowling.

The image I shall always have of him in my mind is of his walk to the wicket, tall and lithe with that easy loping stride, like a panther stalking its prey. He gave the impression he was looking forward to the battle ahead, though a smile was never far away, and there was the expectation that something was going to happen.

Sobers was born with five fingers on each hand and had the extra one removed in boyhood. Maybe it was God's way of telling us that here was someone exceptional but you'd never have known it from his start in Test cricket at the age of 17 against England in Kingston, Jamaica, in the fifth Test of 1954. He was picked as a left arm orthodox spinner, bowled 30 overs and had four for 75. Batting at number nine he had 14 not out and 26. In 1954–55 when Australia were in the Caribbean he played in four Tests and had three wickets for 213 runs and made 231 in six innings with the bat, going in mainly at six or seven although he did open once. On the tour to New Zealand in 1955–56 he managed 81 runs in five innings and took two wickets for 53, while in

England in 1957 he batted up and down the order, averaged 32 in 10 innings and took five wickets for 355 runs. That's 672 runs in 22 innings spread over 14 Tests with an average of 30.54. By no stretch of the imagination would you think that this kid is anything more than ordinary even if you're his mum or his best friend. Batting like that wouldn't get you picked and as for the left arm spin, you'd think, yeah, I wouldn't mind having some of that.

But suddenly the whole thing changes. It's 1957–58, he's 21 and Pakistan are in the West Indies. He makes three half centuries in the first two Tests in Barbados and Trinidad and then, in the third at Kingston, Jamaica, he breaks the world record with 365 not out made in 10 hours 14 minutes. It's extraordinary, you just couldn't see it coming. Now he's on a roll with a century in each innings of the fourth Test in Guyana, 125 opening and 109 not out from number three, and on to India in 1958–59 with 142 not out in the first Test in Bombay, 198 not out at Kanpur in the second and 106 not out in Calcutta in the third: total 557 runs at 92.83. He might have got more but they stuck him down the order to give the others a chance!

When England went to the West Indies in 1959–60 Sobers had 226 in the first Test in Barbados, 147 in Jamaica in the third and 145 in Guyana in the fourth: 709 runs at 101.28. In three series he's gone from someone you'd struggle to call ordinary to a paragon.

If his left arm spin was nothing special his left arm swing bowling could be devastating and there was something freakish about the way he started in this mode. In 1961–62 he had the first of two seasons with South Australia and because there isn't much for run-of-the-mill spinners out there he picked up the ball and found he could swing it. Just like that! It came so easily to him that he took 50 wickets and scored 1,000 runs in an Australian season twice and that takes some doing in their Shield cricket.

It was also in Australia that he played a masterly innings, compiling 254 for the Rest of the World at Melbourne in the third game of a five-match series which was arranged to replace the cancelled South African tour in 1971–72. Sir Donald Bradman, a man not given to dishing out praise lightly, called it one of the best innings he had ever seen.

I came across Garry in 1966 when he had a blistering summer in England with the bat, making 722 runs at 103.14 with 161 at Old Trafford, 163 not out at Lord's when they were in trouble and 174 at Leeds. He nearly did me for a pair at Trent Bridge, getting me leg before with a real big, late swinger second ball in the first innings and in the second only the thinnest of inside edges to a similar delivery saved me from a queen pair. Starting as a left arm orthodox spinner he had no guile or flight and tended to be flat through the air. I'm not surprised at that because if you throw it up anywhere in the West Indies except Trinidad they're going to hit it miles. They think spinners are a free hit. He could also bowl chinamen and googlies which were OK if you didn't read him or he was bowling at tailenders. If you could separate his figures I'd love to know what proportion of his 235 wickets came from swing and seam as opposed to the spinners and at what cost. The quick stuff came to him relatively late in his cricket life, almost by chance, but I can say he's the greatest swing bowler I ever faced.

He'll always be remembered for his graceful batting with that high backlift and the flourish at the end of the shot, but like all truly great players he could cut it when the going was rough.

When England played the second Test in Jamaica on the 1967–68 tour there were huge cracks in the pitch, so big you could put your hand down them up to the wrist. We were well on top and had them following on 233 behind. When Basil Butcher was out caught down the leg side in mid after- noon on the fourth day we were in the driving seat. The locals didn't like it and suddenly all hell was let loose. There were hundreds of bottles and cans thrown, the riot police went into action and there was so much tear gas about we had to bathe our faces in the dressing-room sinks. Garry, out first ball in the first innings, had been dropped second ball by Basil D'Oliveira at slip off John Snow and went on to com- plete a tremendous hundred on the fifth day on this awful pitch (which by now had craters in it) and then declared with the West Indies 158 in front. We'd agreed to make up the 75 minutes lost because of the riot on the last day and didn't we live to regret that when we ended up 19 for four with yours truly and Colin Cowdrey both out to Sobers for nought. The one that did for me pitched outside the leg stump, hit a huge crack and struck the wicket about about six inches up. It was a pretty hairy hour and a quarter next morning and there was so much pressure out in the middle with every fielder round the bat as we struggled to survive that when Fred Titmus pushed one out on the off side, Doug Sang Hue, the umpire, who'd moved over to point, picked it up and threw it back to Lance Gibbs, he was so caught up in the drama. Fred was furious and said so!

Garry was the supreme batsman, remembered also for his contribution to English county cricket, most famously for hitting six sixes in an over off Malcolm Nash bowling slow left armers, not his usual medium pacers, for Nottingham- shire against Glamorgan at Swansea. But along with Viv Richards he's the best I've ever seen. That match in Jamaica proved that if you could get him out once cheaply, it was never enough, you had to do it twice.

Sir Isaac Vivian Alexander Richards
(1974–91)

On his debut for the West Indies on the 1974–75 tour of India there was no hint of the great player Viv Richards was to become with scores of four and three in the first Test at Bangalore. But he made up for it with an unbeaten 192 in the next match in Delhi, so he soon showed his class. The following winter in Australia against the mighty Lillee and Thomson he batted in the middle order and didn't do much in the first four Tests then, unbelievably, he was moved up to open. A youngster with an average of 21 against the old ball was suddenly asked to take on the best in the world with a new one. Again, however, the class came through with 30 and 101 in Adelaide and 50 and 98 at Melbourne and he was on his way to being one of the most formidable opponents you could wish to see on a cricket field.

The way he walked to the wicket with that swagger, chewing his gum and with a faint smile on his face – the whole presence was enough to give bowlers the jitters. With great shoulders, powerful arms, a slim waist, at 5ft 10in tall he had the physique of a boxer allied to a quick eye and fast reflexes and he hit the ball tremendously hard. His great hero was 'Smokin' Joe Frazier, the former heavyweight champion of the world, who was renowned for always going forward, taking the blows and never backing off. In his mind he thought, Whatever you've got, I've got more – that was the way Viv batted, determined right from the off to dominate the bowling, 'beat the ball' as they say in the West Indies, and let everyone know who was boss. To Viv it was always a test of physical and mental strength; he never wore a helmet, and hated ducking, somehow thinking it showed weakness. He was very much the macho man looking for the head-on confrontation and his body language said, Whatever you do to me, you can't hurt me, I won't back off. He attacked from the first ball and, of course, sometimes got out, but he felt that if he won the opening rounds, as it were, as he did most of the time, the bowlers and fielders would quickly become demoralized.

I watched him a lot and it was noticeable that once he had asserted himself, shown who was in charge and got the field spread out he would settle down to bat at a more normal tempo. A fine example of that came in the first Test ever played in Antigua, his home island, the fourth of the 1981 series in the Caribbean which started three days after his marriage. In the previous one-dayer at Berbice, Guyana, we'd got him out cheaply with a bouncer from Graham Dilley which he hit straight down long leg's throat. So in the Test he knew we'd bounce him and we knew he wouldn't duck. Graham dropped one in short, Viv hit it miles out of the park and then walked right up the pitch tapping an imaginary spot nowhere near where the ball had pitched, looked up at Graham and just grinned. In the same match when Yorkshire's Graham Stevenson came on to bowl he was very nervous but Viv calmly patted back the first five balls of his first over. As he came back to his mark Stevo looked at me at mid off and said, 'Is he taking the mickey out of me or what?' I said, 'No, he likes you,' and he patted back the last ball of the over as well. He made 114 but he was at the crease for five hours making sure he got a hundred in this historic match.

For people he didn't take to or who tried to show off in

front of him he could be as brutal as he was kind to Stevo. There is a story that Greg Thomas, the fast bowler, who played for Glamorgan and Northamptonshire and five times for England, beat him a couple of times outside the off stump during a Benson & Hedges match at Taunton. Thomas, who fancied himself a bit, sneered at Viv, 'What you're looking for is red and round.' A couple of deliveries later Viv hit him out of the ground and into the River Tone and while they were trying to find the ball he said to Thomas, 'Why don't you go and get it? You know what it looks like.'

A lot of the old-timers thought that Viv got away with too much because of the way he could hit balls from middle and off stump through the leg side at will. Famously when Viv and Andy Roberts, the West Indies fast bowler, first went to Alf Gover's cricket school in London the former England and Surrey paceman gave his verdict that Viv played across the line too much and Roberts had a better chance of becoming a top batsman.

A couple of years ago I had a few friends over for lunch before the Headingley Test and Fred Trueman was regaling a mesmerized audience with his tales when Jonathan Agnew, once of Leicestershire and England, and now the BBC's cricket correspondent, walked into the room. 'You're a lucky bugger, Aggers,' said Fred, 'you got to bowl at Viv Richards. I'd have let him have a late outswinger starting about leg, he'd have tried to hit it through the leg side, got a leading edge and been caught.' Aggers, who had suffered some rough treatment at the hands of the great West Indian was, needless to say, stunned.

I think Fred might have won one or two jousts with him but Viv would still have got hundreds. As Richie Benaud once remarked, 'If a great bowler is bowling to a great batsman, if either doesn't win some of the time, they're not great, are they?'

What people forget about Viv is that he had a big, big stride and was always looking to come forward so that when he played across the line his head was right over the ball, very close to its pitch, and he was so much in control because his balance and weight were forward. He didn't like to play back but if the ball was short he would rock back, transferring his weight so quickly. That air of arrogance upset some but it never bothered me. Great players have to have confidence in themselves and the conviction they are the best or they don't succeed. That desire and drive to win took the World Cup away from us in 1979 because the West Indies were under the cosh until Viv made an unbeaten 138; similarly, when he made a second ball duck in the first innings of the third Test of England's 1980–81 tour at Barbados he made 182 not out in the second. He also had the fastest Test century made from 56 balls against England in Antigua in 1986 with seven fours and seven sixes.

I think his purple patch came in the 1970s before he became captain and in 1976 he made 1,710 Test match runs in a calendar year. He murdered England that sweltering summer, making 232 at Trent Bridge, 135 at Old Trafford and 291 at The Oval, but he could make runs anywhere without any problem.

An astounding batsman, he was knighted and appropriately stands alongside Sir Garfield Sobers. The two best batsmen I ever saw.

Brian Charles Lara (1990–2006)

I first saw him in Sharjah playing in a one-day match against Pakistan in November 1993 when he made 153 from 143 balls to win the Pepsi Champions Trophy for the West Indies. Everybody raved about a double hundred he made against Australia, 277 at Sydney, in only his fifth Test the previous January, taking nearly eight hours against an attack boasting Craig McDermott and Shane Warne; but here, on a flat pitch, he was terrific. He was the kind of batsman who made it all look so easy and the hallmark of his innings was the way he sliced up the bowling, seemingly piercing the field at will. Beautiful timing and that ability to find the gaps allowed him to score so quickly with rapier-like shots. In all the many innings I've watched him play that uncanny skill set him apart and, for me, is the mark of greatness.

When he broke the world Test match batting record at Antigua for the first time he was 320 not out overnight against England and all the great and good, including Garry Sobers, the record holder, flew down to the island to see him do it. I remember thinking how it would spoil the party if he got out in the morning but there was a seeming inevitability about his batting and he never looked like failing to pass Garry's 365 against Pakistan.

Shortly after that he played for Warwickshire and made 501 from 427 balls with 62 fours and 10 sixes. It may have only been against Durham, the new boys in the county championship, and he may have been dropped early on, but

I recall talking to Sunil Gavaskar about it and we were both in awe. We both got double hundreds and know a thing or two about making big scores but to make 300, 400 then go on to 500 was beyond our comprehension, just mind boggling.

For the West Indies in England in 1995 he made three consecutive hundreds, 145 in the fourth Test at Old Trafford, 152 in the next at Trent Bridge and 179 in the last at The Oval. For most of his career he was playing in a very ordinary West Indies side which made his scoring feats all the more remarkable. He was a master of the spinners and even Muralitharan came to grief against him when the West Indies went to Sri Lanka in 2001. Lara had 178 in Galle, 221 and 130 in Colombo using the sweep to great effect. Murali was such a big spinner of the ball he had to pitch outside leg stump to the left hander when he was bowling over the wicket and he didn't much like going around the wicket, so Lara was able to sweep him or pad him off at will. If Murali pitched on the stumps the ball turned so much it was a free hit outside the off. Brian could pick his 'doosra' and was nimble enough to get down the pitch. In the series he made 688 runs at an average of 114.66 – phenomenal figures.

After Matthew Hayden took away his world record Test score he regained it in April 2004 by making 400 not out against England in the first innings of the fourth Test, again in Antigua. He was 313 not out at the end of the second day and there was that same inevitability that he would pass Hayden's 380.

Lara made his runs against the very best attacks of his day with excellent judgement of length and a huge range of shots. After Viv Richards and Sobers he was as good as it gets.

George Alphonso Headley (1930–54)

Born in Panama, George Headley was taken to Jamaica by
his parents at the age of 10 and first came to prominence
in 1927 before the West Indies became a Test playing nation.
The Hon. Lionel Tennyson took a side to the Caribbean
to nurture the game and on his home island George made
211 at the age of 18. He wasn't on the first official tour to
England when the West Indies lost all five of their inaugural
Tests but in 1929–30 he played in the first ever Test on
Caribbean soil in Barbados and made 21 in the first innings
and 176 in the second batting at number three, to force a
draw. In the second Test at Port of Spain, he made 8 and 39
and the West Indies lost; in the third at Guyana he made a
hundred in each innings, 114 in the first, adding 196 for the
second wicket with Clifford Roach who made a double hundred, and 112 in the second, and the West Indies won easily.
At Kingston in the fourth Test he made 10 and 223 in six
and a half hours to earn a draw and it seemed they could only
win or draw when George did well, a theme that was to
continue throughout his career. To have scored four Test
hundreds in an inexperienced side before his 21st birthday
was just astonishing and he had an excellent series against
Australia in 1930–31, making 1,066 runs on the tour at 44.41.

The West Indies were lambs to the slaughter in the first
four Tests against what was a really strong side but George
was head and shoulders above the others, making 102 out
of 193 at Brisbane in the third Test and 105 in the fifth at

Sydney. His mastery of Clarrie Grimmett led the Aussies to dub him 'the black Bradman' and it stuck, although at home he was better known as 'Atlas' because he carried the rest of the side on his shoulders.

Mainly a back foot player with a superb square cut, he didn't do anything very special in the Tests on the trip to England in 1933 with one hundred in six innings, an unbeaten 169 at Old Trafford in the second game of the three match series, but in 23 first class games on the tour he made 2,320 runs with seven hundreds and an average of 66.68. In 1934–35 it was the same old story with George making 25 and 93 in the win at Port of Spain, Trinidad, in the second Test and 270 in the fourth on his home ground of Sabina Park in an innings victory.

Sadly he played only 22 Test matches in 10 years and there was a four-year gap until the West Indies came to England in 1939. George made a century in each innings at Lord's, 106 and 107, 213 out of a total of 502 runs scored by the West Indies, 42.43 per cent. He was revered in the Caribbean and widely respected throughout the cricket world. I've never heard a bad word said about him. With his son Ron playing for the West Indies and grandson Dean winning England caps, he could justifiably be called the granddaddy of West Indies cricket.

The war took another five years out of his career and then in January 1948 he was given the distinction and honour of being appointed the first black captain of the West Indies, in the series against England. Before that the game had been run mostly by the white Bajans but after leading his country in the draw in Barbados he was laid low with back trouble and didn't play again in the series. In India in 1948–49 he played in the first Test in Delhi but injury kept him out of the other four Tests.

In all he played only 17 first class games in the postwar period, just two of them Tests when he was recalled to the side on his home ground in Kingston for the first Test of the 1954 series with England. It was a sentimental gesture really because he'd only played in four first class matches since November 1948 and he was 45 years of age going out to face Trueman, Statham and Alan Moss of Middlesex. Fred told the story of how, when Headley came out to bat to rapturous applause, he asked Len Hutton, the captain, 'Who's this old cock?' Len warned him not to bowl any short stuff because he was a legend in West Indian cricket and it might provoke the crowd. Fred went on, 'I pitched the ball up and he kept propping forward so I thought, You've got to have one, sunshine, and let him have a short one. It hit him under the heart and he went down like a sack of potatoes. The crowd went mad, climbed over the fence and we had to run for the pavilion.'

He didn't make any runs in a sad end to a remarkable career and his figures alone were fantastic. Just imagine if he'd had more Test matches what he might have achieved. But by now there were new young bucks coming up and George's day was gone.

The Three Ws

Nobody can ever have a discussion about West Indian cricket without talking about Clyde Walcott, Everton Weekes and Frank Worrell who collectively and affectionately became known as the three Ws.

The first two made their debuts in the first Test of the 1947–48 tour against England at Barbados and the third of the trio played his first game at Port of Spain, Trinidad in the second match of the series. Sir Alec Bedser told me that all were exceptional and he couldn't think of any better three anywhere which is pretty big praise coming from a man of Sir Alec's experience. I've talked to a lot of people about them and while they all find it hard to separate them Everton Weekes marginally gets the vote; I know Fred Trueman had him at the top of his list.

Everton de Courcey Weekes was short and stocky with quick feet, and when you think he batted at number three against the new ball his record is fantastic. At the start of his Test career he was facing Trueman, Statham and Moss for England and Lindwall, Miller and Johnston in Australia – that's not a bad half dozen for starters. Incredibly, he made five centuries in consecutive innings starting with 141 against England at Kingston in the fourth and final Test of his first series and followed that on the tour of India with 128 in Delhi, 194 in Bombay and one in each innings, 162 and 101 at Eden Gardens, Calcutta. He almost made it six centuries on the trot but he was run out for 90 in the first innings of the fourth game of the series in Madras. But five hundreds in his first seven Tests before his 24th birthday, massive performances; he was 'in the zone' for sure and finished with 779 runs at an average of 111.28. In England in 1950 he averaged 56.33 from six innings with one hundred, 129, in the draw at Trent Bridge.

By his own standards he had a poor tour of Australia and New Zealand in 1951–52, but was back in mint form when the Indians toured the Caribbean in 1953. The first Test was played on matting at Port of Spain and he hit 207 and when they went back there for the third Test, this time playing on grass, he made 161; it all came the same to him and with 109 in Jamaica in the fifth match he had racked up six centuries in eight Tests against the Indians.

In the four-match series against an England attack of Trueman, Statham, Bailey, Laker and Lock in 1954 he had 487 runs at an average of 69.57, and against Australia in the West Indies the following year scored 469 at 58.62 with 139 and 87 not out in Port of Spain, where he hit Bill Johnston for six which, amazingly for an attacking batsman, was the only one of his Test career. New Zealand were the next to suffer when he toured there in 1955–56 with centuries in the first three Tests, 123 at Dunedin, 103 at Christchurch and 156 at Wellington.

The only time he didn't do anything special was on the tour of England in 1957 when the pitches were specially prepared for Jim Laker and Tony Lock, and in the fifth Test at The Oval he bagged a pair. His last century came in the first match of his final series in Barbados where he made 197 against Pakistan.

Clyde Leopold Walcott, who made his debut in the same game as Everton, was an entirely different kettle of fish. Where Weekes was compact and stroked the ball about,

Clyde was a massive 6ft 2in, 15 stone and gave it a terrific thump.

He did the almost impossible job of keeping wicket and opening the batting in the first match but after making 8 and 16 he was soon moved down the order. It didn't take him long to find his feet with 152 against India in Delhi in the first Test of the series, his fifth, and he added another ton (108) in Calcutta. He had a poor series in England in 1950 and didn't bat very well at all, making only one substantial contribution, 168 not out in the massive 326-run win at Lord's. He was an adequate keeper for 14 Tests until his back started giving him trouble and it was after he gave up the gauntlets and played purely as a batsman that we really saw him prosper. In New Zealand he made 115 in the second Test at Auckland, two more hundreds followed in the Caribbean against India in 1952–53, 125 in Guyana and 118 in Jamaica, and when England toured in 1953–54 he really got stuck in and made 698 runs at an average of 87.25 with 220 in Barbados, 124 in Port of Spain and 116 in Jamaica. The Australians were the next to feel his raw power when they toured in 1954–55. This time Walcott pasted them for five hundreds, 108 in Jamaica in the first Test, one in each innings in the second at Trinidad, 126 and 110, and, incredibly, he had one in each innings again when they went back to Kingston for the fifth game, 155 and 110.

Frank Mortimore Maglinne Worrell made up the trio when they all played together for the first time in the second Test against England in Trinidad in February 1948. Frank first played for Barbados as a left arm spinner but was soon opening and at the age of 19 had a triple hundred, 308 not out, against Trinidad, then with his old schoolmate Clyde Walcott (314 not out) he made 255 and put on a record

574 for the fourth wicket in February 1946, again against Trinidad in Port of Spain.

A slim, elegant and orthodox right hander, he was a graceful timer of the ball, a beautifully unhurried batsman and he made 97 on his Test debut and 131 in Guyana. He missed a number of games, however, and didn't go on the tour to India but in England in 1950 he made a marvellous 261 at Trent Bridge in the third Test and 138 at The Oval in the fourth. In Australia in 1951–52 he averaged 42 with the bat but also picked up 19 wickets at 21.57, nice figures, including six for 38 at Adelaide where the West Indies came out on top. His left arm swing and seam was pretty handy and he regularly took the new ball, returning his best figures in the fourth Test of the 1957 series in England, seven for 70 from 38.4 overs at Headingley.

Worrell was absent for 14 Tests but then, famously, took part in a fourth wicket stand of 399 with Garry Sobers in Barbados, batting 11 hours 22 minutes for his unbeaten 197. England went two days in the field without taking a wicket; the end of the third day, West Indies 114 for three, end of fourth, 279 for three, end of fifth, 486 for three. Those scoring rates, 165 runs on the fourth day and 207 on the fifth, give the lie to the perception that the ball was bashed all over the place while sides kept attacking fields.

In 1960–61 he took over as captain of the West Indies, the first black man to be appointed for a whole series. Despite his wonderful achievements with bat and ball Frank is known as the unifying force in West Indies cricket, a man who brought together the islands. He led the West Indies in the famous tied Test at Brisbane in 1961, opening the bowling and scoring 65 in both innings, and in the dramatic finish at Lord's in 1963 when England withstood a battering from Wes Hall and Charlie Griffiths to hang on for a draw, with Colin Cowdrey coming out to bat at nine down with his arm in plaster.

He was knighted the year after his retirement in 1963 and, sadly, died of leukaemia in 1967. Forever linked with his two compatriots, Everton and Clyde, Sir Frank was a big player on the world stage.

The Openers

This is where it gets tricky. I still haven't got an opening pair and yet I've talked about six West Indians who are among the best batsmen the world has ever seen. Of the specialists at the top of the order Desmond Haynes and Gordon Greenidge had an absolutley outstanding record in the all-conquering team of the 1970s and '80s. You could say they would have been tested more severely if they'd had to face their own bowlers but that's pure speculation and I have to deal with the facts. Alongside these two there is **Conrad Cleophas Hunte** who never had a settled partner yet produced some telling performances; most people forget that when Garry Sobers made his then record 365 not out in Jamaica, Hunte was at the other end and made 260 before he was run out. A handsome strokemaker, particularly good on the hook, he made big scores in England, 182 at Old Trafford in the first Test of Sir Frank Worrell's tour of 1963, and 135 in the first Test of the 1966 series, again at Old Trafford, so I'm well aware of just how good he was.

Desmond Leo Haynes had a lovely attitude, a wonderful smile, never lost his love of the game and was generous and helpful to everyone. I regard him as the best hooker I've ever seen (that does not include ladies of the night!), always hitting the ball down safely unlike Viv Richards who wanted to smack it out of the park. I felt he was always waiting for the short ball to hit in front of, or just behind, square leg. At Lord's in 1980 he and Viv put on 223 for the second wicket (Desmond 184, Viv 145) and England never looked like getting them out for most of a very hot second day in front of a full house. In mid afternoon Ian Botham said to me, 'Come and have a bowl.' I won't tell you what I replied but it wasn't very polite. But 'Beefy' insisted and some people may remember it was when I bowled from the Pavilion end with my cap on back to front. Desmond patted every ball back down the pitch and at the end of the over, a maiden, the two batsmen had a chat. 'Beefy' said, 'Have another over, I heard what they were saying and Desmond's asked Viv to come down that end, he's terrified of getting out to you.' What? Two of the best batsmen in the world don't want to face my fiery bowling? Apparently sometime earlier I'd told Desmond that if I ever got him out I'd ring him up every year on the anniversary to remind him and he hadn't forgotten. Just for the record my figures were 7–2–11–0!

Desmond was a really good player with 468 runs at 93.6 in the home series against the Australians in 1983–84 with hundreds in Guyana and Barbados, while in 1986 in England he amassed 469 at 78.16.

His partner, **Cuthbert Gordon Greenidge**, was a very different sort of player and personality. Although he was born in the West Indies he went to England at the age of 12 and I think that created some kind of inner conflict. He wrote that he never really felt totally at home in the West Indian dressing room and he was certainly difficult to get to know. Some got the impression he was morose, others thought he just wanted to be quiet and left on his own; whatever, he was one heck of a player.

With a very good technique he wanted to take control as soon as he could to subdue the bowlers, and the lesser ones got some fearful stick. Against Glamorgan in 1975 he got

177 in a one-dayer, in a 55 overs Benson & Hedges Cup match against the Minor Counties in 1973 he hit a record 173 not out and in the 40 overs John Player League he made an unbeaten 163 in 1979 with 10 sixes. He was dismissive of bowlers who weren't out of the top drawer and he absolutely loved belting people out of the ground. He may have lacked finesse but in the third Test at Old Trafford in 1976 on a very poor up and down pitch he made 134 out of 211 in the first innings (only one other man, Collis King, made double figures) and 101 in the second, some going.

If those innings were proof of his technique then at Lord's in 1984 there was clear evidence of his destructive power. David Gower set West Indies 342 to win on the last day and, as he said, 'It seemed a good idea at the time.' They made the runs from 66 overs with Greenidge lashing an unbeaten 214 from 242 balls with 29 fours and two sixes. He had a damaged leg for a large part of that knock and found running difficult, so it gave rise to the legend 'beware a limping Greenidge'.

At Old Trafford in the fourth Test of that series he made 223 but it took him nearly 10 hours to again illustrate he could play in different modes, belting the living daylights out of it at Lord's and cleverly and steadily amassing runs at Old Trafford, both grounds, incidentally, celebrating 100 years of Test cricket that summer. This was real quality and showed his completeness. He had a terrific career with Hampshire and I believe that harnessing what he learned in county cricket to his natural ability made him a very rounded batsman, a man for all situations. That's why I'm picking him in front of Desmond and Conrad and I'm going to have Everton Weekes as his partner. Clyde Walcott's going to bat at number six and be my enforcer, so the top seven reads: Greenidge, Weekes, Richards, Headley, Lara, Walcott and Sobers.

No Frank Worrell, no Clive Lloyd, no Rohan Kanhai – all terrific players with solid claims for inclusion. Clive Lloyd with his railway sleeper of a bat and huge frame, beating the ball to death and thrilling the crowds, the gifted Kanhai who could sweep medium pacers off the front foot and out of the ground and who made runs all over the world including a century in each innings in Australia in 1960–61, and Frank who we have already discussed. I'm sorry, I just can't get them in.

The Fast Men

Malcolm Denzil Marshall was as good as, if not better than, any of the modern fast bowlers and certainly along with Fred Trueman and Dennis Lillee among the three best quick bowlers I ever faced. He had everything, real speed on a quick pitch and with the ability to cut his run down and bowl clever swing and seam if the conditions demanded. He had all the attributes of a fast bowler and could be a mean little so-and-so out in the middle but a genuinely nice man off the field. We would be getting our stuff out of the car in the morning at the ground and he'd look over and say to me, 'You hookin' today, Boycs?' and I'd say, 'Not if you're bowling I aint.' He nearly always gave me a really quick bouncer in the first over and, finishing his run-up a couple of paces from me, smile and say, 'Ok, man?' I don't think he ever got me out in a Test and if you had his respect you'd earned it.

    Michael Anthony Holding has to be my second choice. Nicknamed 'Whispering Death' because of his light-footed approach to the crease, he bowled the fastest over I ever faced at Kensington Oval, Barbados, in the first innings of the third Test of the 1981 series, got me with the last ball of the over and in the second innings had me caught off the fourth ball I faced. I was having dinner in the hotel none too chuffed at getting out for nought and one and noticed the waiter hovering. He was clearly dying to say something but no doubt the look on my face put him off but as he was leaving he plucked up courage and asked, 'Did you see any of 'em?' 'I saw them all,' I said. 'I just couldn't play any of them.'

The great thing about Michael was that in addition to great pace he had great control. It's no use being quick if you spray it all over the place. He didn't; he harnessed that speed to pinpoint accuracy. The real test of a pace bowler is how he performs on flat pitches and he passed that exam at The Oval in 1976 with flying colours when he took eight for 92 in 33 overs in England's first innings of 435 and six for 57 when they were bowled out for 203. A fantastic match-winning performance of 14 for 149 on a pitch where two men, Viv Richards and Dennis Amiss, made double hundreds.

Phil Carrick, the former Yorkshire captain, went in as nightwatchman in an MCC game against the West Indies, faced three balls and spent a sleepless night worrying about the quick bowlers lined up the next morning. After a couple of deliveries Michael made the sign of the cross and said to Phil, 'Next one, man,' and it did for him. That's what genuine quick men can do to tailenders, frighten them out, and they intimidate others with pace like fire. In the last Test he played, against New Zealand in Wellington, he went wicketless and after an appeal for a clear catch at the wicket was turned down he followed through and kicked the stumps out of the ground. No batsman could frustrate him but poor umpiring did!

Joel Garner might not have been as quick as some of the others but he could get really awkward bounce from just short of a length. Six feet eight inches tall, he delivered it from a great height and had a magnificent yorker that was always too much for tailenders as well as plenty of those further up the order. He was rarely given the new ball for the West Indies and usually came on as first change, not that he was any the worse for that. When I batted against him I wasn't too bothered about a helmet but I needed a chest protector because of his ability to make the ball nip back and cut you in half. Sometimes I let the ball hit me in the chest rather than try and fend it off with a man at short leg or just round the corner at leg gulley.

I remember an England team meeting when we were discussing how to score off him and Ian Botham said, 'You don't, nobody does.' I asked, 'What about when he bowls to Viv Richards in the nets at Somerset?' Ian said that even Viv couldn't hit Joel and I thought, On that note I'll go to bed before I get even more demoralized.

Those three are definite picks in my squad but I want two more and among those to be considered is **Colin Everton Hunte Croft**. Clive Lloyd told me that he had the most stamina of all his bowlers and could get through long spells. He was certainly a handful and I don't think I've ever known any bowler who loved to hit batsmen like he did. He really didn't care if he knocked you out or got you out and I had the impression he preferred hitting you.

He's the fiercest, nastiest fast bowler I faced. I remember before the Antigua Test in 1981 the two teams went to a reception at Government House and he told Graham Stevenson, 'You easy to hit, I hit you all right.' Stevo replied, 'You'll not hit me unless you're aiming at the square leg umpire because I'll be hiding behind him.' Most of the time his 'frighten 'em to death' psychology worked and John Emburey and Graham were both out ducking balls which yorked them.

Wesley Winfield Hall and **Charles Christopher Griffith** spearheaded the attack in the 1960s. Wes had a lovely rhythmic approach, that gold cross swinging on its chain an unforgettable sight. Charlie chucked his bouncer and yorker and that made him more of a menace because you never knew when they were coming. He did a fair bit of damage in his time, hitting John Hampshire on the head in a Yorkshire match and laying out Nariman Contractor of India.

Those two hunted as a pair as did **Courtney Andrew Walsh** and **Curtly Elconn Lynwall Ambrose** who shared 924 wickets between them with Courtney, who had terrific stamina, holding the world record for a spell. He took his 519 wickets at 24.44 each while his partner had 405 at 20.99, tremendous figures, and that's why I have to pick Curtly. He might not play in the same side as Joel Garner but the West Indies need four fast bowlers in their team. That's part of their strategy and it worked more often than not. The use of a battery of quicks depends on three things: the quality of the pace men – you don't want people who spray it about; the quality of the opposing batsmen – some can just be blown away; and lastly, the quality of the pitch – genuine pace can take wickets on good surfaces and skill can get men out when there is moisture about or grass on the pitch.

My fifth choice is **Anderson Montgomery Everton Roberts**, the original leader of the four-pronged attack, who made his debut in the third Test of England's Caribbean tour of 1973–74. He was the one the others all looked up to and they took note of what he said. He was very deceptive with a superb change of pace and he hit a lot of batsmen because they were lulled into a false sense of him not being very quick and they'd go to hook or pull, only to find out they were wrong when the ball thumped into them. He was a very smart bowler who could swing it and bowl an awkward skiddy bouncer and he, too, was a fearsome competitor.

I've gone for these five and haven't even got to Wayne Daniel and Sylvester Clarke who were lightning quick. In the fast bowling department the West Indies have an abundance of riches.

The Spinners

Lancelot Richard Gibbs broke Fred Trueman's world record with two wickets in the last Test match he played, the sixth of the series against Australia at Melbourne in 1975–76, finishing his 79th Test with 309 wickets at 29.09. Tall and gangly with long fingers, he had a bouncy action and got through his overs quickly. He was always trying to get you out, not interested in containing and pinning you down. He had a chest-on action, clever variations in flight, used the crease well and spun it a lot, rarely bowling around the wicket because he couldn't do it all that well and on the covered pitches and good batting strips of the West Indies there was never that much turn.

He was perfect for his side; they had guys who amassed big totals, fast men to use the new ball and Lance was the ideal foil to fiddle a few out. He was always willing to try something different and he had great fielders like Garry Sobers at short leg to snap up the half chances. In Pakistan in 1957–58 when he was only 23 he had 17 wickets at 23 each, in 1960–61 in Australia 19 wickets at 20.78 in three Tests, and in England in 1963 he had 26 wickets at 21.3. He had a wonderful attitude for a spinner and would still come at you even if you were taking a few runs off him.

Lance was an extremely nice chap on and off the field and particularly kind to me. In 1967 I was playing for the Rothman's Cavaliers in Wales (no Sunday League cricket then) when the Test team was announced. No one got any phone calls in those days and we had to listen to the one o'clock news to find out who was in the team. When it came out that I had been dropped for slow scoring after making 246 not out in the win over India at Headingley, I was devastated, absolutely devastated. I was still comparatively raw at 26 years of age and very near to tears. The press were gathering in large numbers and I was very, very down and must have shown it for suddenly Lance grabbed me by the arm and dragged me into one of the tents. 'Listen to me,' he said. 'Hold your head up high. You've nothing to be ashamed of, it's the selectors who should be feeling ashamed. If you were a West Indian you'd be a national hero, always remember that.' It was unbelievable kindness from an experienced Test player to a youngster and, as I discovered as I grew older, typical of the man.

The other spinner is, of course, **Sonny Ramadhin** who in 43 Tests had 155 wickets at 28.98. He was entirely different from Lance; where the offspinner was tall and slim, Sonny was short at 5ft 4in and chubby. Interestingly he bowled his legspinner not with the wrist but off his middle finger and he was extremely difficult to read, like John Gleeson, the Australian, some years later. He mesmerized England in 1950 taking 11 for 52 at Lord's in only his second Test, and along with Alf Valentine, who had seven for 127 in the match, their feats were commemorated in a calypso, 'Those two little pals of mine, Ramadhin and Valentine'. He bowled 115 overs in that match, 70 of them maidens, and it was clear that the batsmen couldn't pick the legspinner.

In 1953–54 against Len Hutton's tourists he had 23 wickets at 24.3, and he was still a mystery to English batsmen when he toured in 1957. He had seven for 49 in the first innings at Edgbaston, but in the second Peter May and

Colin Cowdrey made a record 411 together for the fourth wicket, Ramadhin's 98 overs in the innings earning two for 179. Most of the time they played him with the pad — they wouldn't have got away with it these days when umpires are prepared to give you out if you hide the bat behind the pad and don't play a real shot. Sonny often complained about 'bloody footballers', batsmen who spent their time kicking him away, and with some justification in my book.

Not that I owe him any favours because he stopped me from getting into the record books with four hundreds in consecutive Roses matches. In my first three championship games against Lancashire I made 146 at Bramall Lane, 113 at Old Trafford and 131, again at Old Trafford. Nobody had ever made four on the bounce and I was going along nicely with 60 at Headingley in 1964 when he got me out leg before. I think it was turning too much and would have missed leg stump! Some batsmen say you can see which way it is spinning in the air but I never could, I just played him off the pitch.

I have to have two spinners in my squad for games on the subcontinent where you can't ignore the fact spinners are necessary, and these two are the best available by a long chalk.

To complete the side we need a wicketkeeper and I think **Peter Jeffrey Leroy Dujon** is the best man for the job. He averaged 31.94 with the bat, kept to all the pace bowlers of his time and was comfortable. More importantly, the quick men will be most comfortable with him because the last thing a fast bowler wants when he finds the edge is to have the wicketkeeper punching it round the post — the bowler wants to be sure the guy with the gloves is going to catch it.

I did consider that Clyde Walcott could do the job but he made his best runs after he gave up the gloves; with that back trouble he might get away with it for one match but not much more than that. So Dujon it is.

West Indies

Gordon Greenidge

Everton Weekes

Viv Richards

George Headley

Brian Lara

Clyde Walcott

Garry Sobers

Jeff Dujon

Malcolm Marshall

Michael Holding

Joel Garner

Curtly Ambrose

Andy Roberts

Lance Gibbs

Sonny Ramadhin

RESERVES

Conrad Hunte

Frank Worrell

Clive Lloyd

Rohan Kanhai

Wes Hall

Colin Croft

Courtney Walsh

New Zealand

Sir Richard John Hadlee (1973–90)

He was a truly great fast bowler, the best 'in the corridor' bowler I ever faced. Off his short run he was very sharp but with fantastic control around off stump and always got the ball in that awkward 'no man's land' when, as a batsman, you have a split second to decide whether to go forward or back. He kept you under pressure all the time; hardly anything to hit and swinging it in a little and cutting it both ways off the seam with the odd very quick bouncer to keep you on your toes and stop you getting forward. In his first eight overs you were lucky if you got one half volley and if you did you'd better put it away because there wouldn't be another for a while.

He is by some distance the best cricketer New Zealand have ever had and remains the jewel in the crown of Kiwi cricket. They've never had a match-winner like him and for my money he'd have got into any side in the world, even the great West Indies team.

When he started his Test career in February 1973 as a 21-year-old he was very raw and in three Tests against Pakistan made 47 runs in four innings (with two ducks) and had five wickets for 347 runs. The first real sign that he was a match-winner came against India at Wellington in 1975–76 when he took seven for 23 in the second innings of the third Test to finish with 11 for 58 in a victory by an innings and 33 runs.

The next time he produced something special I had a

close-up view because I was captain when he bowled New Zealand to their first win over England in 48 attempts dating back to 1929. I put the Kiwis in on a poor pitch at the Basin Reserve in Wellington in February 1977 and John Wright batted all day for 55 not out having gloved the first ball of the match to Bob Taylor and been given not out. When I see him now I always ask if his hand has healed and he smiles and says, 'I couldn't walk, it was my debut.' I don't blame him for that but it was a shocking pitch and they didn't play another game there for three years. In the last innings we wanted 137 to win and Hadlee, with the gale force wind that blew throughout the game at his back, bowled like lightning, as quick as Michael Holding at his best, and took six for 26 in 13.3 eight-ball overs. He had 10 for 100 in the match as they got home by 72 runs, a win that set the country alight.

After that season he went to Nottinghamshire and when I spoke to him in New Zealand during England's tour in 2008 he said it was the best thing that happened to him. At home the Kiwis only played five three-day games a year in the Plunkett Shield over Christmas and the New Year and the rest of the time it was weekend club cricket. 'I just ran in hard and gave it everything,' he said. 'I didn't really know what I was doing apart from getting it to the other end as fast as I could. At Nottinghamshire it was a dramatic change and bowling every day I learned fitness, skill and it was a bit like fine tuning. The more you bowl the more you learn about your trade.'

In 1980 he had a few injuries and towards the end of the summer bowled off his Sunday League run-up which, in those days, was limited to 15 yards. He had a fair amount of success and the chairman asked him to come back even if he bowled off his short run.

'In point of fact I was three times more successful off my short run,' he told me. 'I got closer to the stumps and if I lost a little pace I made up for it in skill. But when I went back to New Zealand they didn't like it at all. Some players, commentators and the media gave me stick and even suggested I wasn't trying! They wanted the fast man they had seen before and it took a long time to convince people.'

If proof were needed it came in the second Test against Australia at Auckland in March 1982 when he took five for 63 in the second innings to bowl the Kiwis to only their second victory over the Aussies. That was something special and he went on taking wickets all over the world in all conditions. Even in Sri Lanka, a graveyard for fast bowlers, he had eight for 43 to win in Kandy and 10 for 102 in Colombo.

But the match he rates as the best showing by himself and the team came at Brisbane in the first Test of the 1985–86 series when New Zealand won by an innings and 41 runs.

'It was a near perfect performance by the team,' he said. 'Normally we caught about 60 per cent of our chances but in that match we were 100 per cent. There was a bit of cloud cover and some moisture in the wicket and everything went right.'

He had nine for 52 in the first innings and six for 71 in the second and followed that up with 11 for 155 in the third Test at Perth as New Zealand won again to finish with 33 wickets in the series at 12.1 each. That's some bowling.

New Zealand were always considered one of the junior Test nations but during Richard Hadlee's time they became a side to be reckoned with and they have never had a period before or since when they could claim that. He gave them a chance of winning because he was a great bowler by any standards and thoroughly deserved the knighthood bestowed in 1990. Has any one man done more to raise a nation's stature in the game? I don't think so.

Martin David Crowe (1982–95)

He made his Test debut at the age of 19 and after a sticky start went on to become the best of New Zealand's batsmen with 17 centuries and an average of 45.36 from 77 Tests.

Crowe spent a year on the MCC ground staff in 1981 where he was coached by Don Wilson and was in the Kiwis team to play Australia the following February when he came up against Lillee and Thomson at their ruthless best. In his first innings 'Tommo' hit him in the ribs and on the head and then he was run out for nine. Some baptism, eh? Against fast bowling like that he managed just 20 from his first four innings. In my opinion he was thrown into Test cricket too soon given the limited amount of first class cricket played in New Zealand and against deadly quicks on poor pitches he was on a hiding to nothing.

He came to the Yorkshire nets in the summer of 1982 before breaking the Yorkshire League batting record for runs in a season set by Billy Sutcliffe, making 1,349 at an average of 89.93 for Bradford where he also acted as groundsman at Park Avenue. I didn't know much about him but he used to bowl at me in the nets and he complained to me just recently that I wouldn't let him have a bat and kept him bowling all the time! But, like Richard Hadlee, it was a full season of county cricket which saw his talent bloom and he made 1,870 runs with six centuries in the summer of 1984 with Somerset. A tall, strapping lad, he had a big forward stride, played straight, had the ability to concentrate and was always eager to learn. The only downside to his time in the West Country is that he shared a flat with Ian Botham and found Beefy's high life too much for his constitution – he wouldn't have been alone there!

'It was a great education in more ways than one,' he told me in New Zealand during the spring of 2008. 'When I came home after playing every day I felt I understood my batting and I was ready for Test cricket.' He made 188 against the West Indies in Georgetown in April 1985 together with six failures against their powerful attack, but he started to put big scores together including another 188 in a win in Brisbane, 137 in Christchurch against Australia and 106 against England at Lord's in 1986.

When I came across him on England's tour of 1986–87 I found it extraordinary that he had got into a run of low scores. He told me that he didn't know where he was on the crease, didn't know what guard he should take, his confidence was down and he'd got himself into a low state of mind. He arranged for a strip to be cut on the Wellington College ground and I spent some time with him, just really trying to get him back to basics, to get him to concentrate on his assets like that big stride forward. To me batting is as complicated as a golf swing but if you let it get complicated in your head you've had it. Golfers have a phrase 'paralysis by analysis' and that can apply to batting as well. You've got to clear your head of all the theory and mumbo jumbo and concentrate on the simple fact of hitting the ball, either defensively or in attack. You can't do anything in golf or cricket if you can't hit the ball and you can't do anything if your mind's all fogged up. If you start analysing too much you can find maybe 13 or 14 things that are wrong but a good coach merely points out the things that can improve your personal approach. When coaching any batsman

I always try to keep it simple and focus on his strengths.

Between us we must have got something right because Martin got 143 in the third Test at Wellington in 403 minutes in the middle and went on to make New Zealand's record score of 299 against Sri Lanka in Wellington in January 1991, a match-saving innings. In England in 1994 he made 142 at Lord's and followed that with 115 in the next Test at Manchester. In all he made hundreds against all the Test-playing nations in all sorts of conditions. It was a pity that so many of his innings had to be made to save a game rather than win it, but in a small country it's really remarkable that they have produced so many good cricketers from a population of around four million. Martin Crowe was an outstanding example and did his country proud.

Glenn Maitland Turner (1969–83)

The shy young man from Dunedin who made his debut for Otago as a 17-year-old went on to become the only New Zealand player to score more than a hundred first class centuries. He was without doubt the best opening batsman the country has produced.

He owed a lot to Billy Ibadulla, the former Warwickshire player, who coached him at school and suggested he should try to earn a living in county cricket. At home there were a lot of doubters who had no idea about professional cricket and it took considerable strength of mind to make the trip to the other side of the world. Trials were arranged at Edgbaston and Turner worked a night shift in a bakery to raise the fare to England, but when he got there Warwickshire had their allocation of overseas players and set up further trials with Worcestershire, Surrey and Lancashire. Worcester snapped him up and he never got to The Oval or Old Trafford. After a year qualifying and playing in the Birmingham League he made his debut for his new county in the championship in May 1968 and quickly established himself as a batsman with a fantastic defensive technique; he was difficult to get out, had a strong mind and was someone who could bat all day but lacked the confidence to play shots.

His Test debut followed in the winter; he started with a duck against the West Indies and managed only 183 runs from his first half dozen innings. I first saw him at Lord's when I played against New Zealand in the first Test of the 1969 series. On a dry, turning pitch Derek Underwood lived up to his nickname of 'Deadly' by taking seven for 32 and bowling out the Kiwis for 131. Turner carried his bat for an undefeated 43 and he looked to me to have a lot of skill. When 'Deadly' got you on a 'bunsen burner' (turner) you'd got serious problems, believe me, but Glenn handled everything thrown at him. His first century came the following winter, 110 against Pakistan in Dacca, but he had gained a reputation as not much more than a blocker. He told me that the advent of the Sunday League in 1969 changed his game and turned him into the maker of so many handsome strokes. 'I had more in my locker than I thought,' is the way he put it. With the confidence to play more shots came more big innings: two double hundreds on the tour of the West Indies in 1971–72, carrying his bat again for 223 not out in Jamaica and 259 in Guyana, his highest Test score. He also passed 200 on two other occasions on the trip to reach his full potential.

Against England in 1973 he had a poor time because he came up against one of the best new ball bowlers I faced in English conditions, Geoff Arnold; I thought there was no one better. The following winter he was back on song with a century in each innings against Australia in Christchurch in a match where fewer than 1,000 runs were scored in four innings, 110 and 117 not out as the Kiwis won by five wickets. He was made captain in 1976 but it only lasted 10 Tests before a row with the New Zealand authorities over pay. The rest of the team had jobs outside cricket and received half pay when on national duty. But Turner was coaching in Otago and didn't get any money when he was away, only his match fees which didn't amount to much in those days. He found out that he was captain, the best batsman and the worst paid player and he didn't like that one bit. He felt he was being treated as a second class citizen and walked away from Test cricket for six years.

New Zealand's loss was Worcestershire's gain because in those six summers he scored 9,849 runs with 38 centuries for his county and although he was persuded back into the Test arena for two matches against Sri Lanka in 1983 the best was behind him. He should have played a lot more than his 41 Tests and would certainly have made a lot more than his 2,991 runs at an average of 44.64, but at the age of 30 he was virtually finished. If he had a reputation for being difficult with the authorities it should be remembered that the authorities are not always right. As the first true professional New Zealand cricketer he paved the way for so many of his countrymen to forge lucrative careers overseas and they should thank him for that as well as his distinguished batting.

Andrew Howard Jones (1987–95)

I want someone at number three who can play the new ball and handle the quicks and while Andrew Jones didn't have much style he certainly had guts and determination. Tall, focused and dedicated, he came late to Test cricket, making his debut against Sri Lanka as a 28-year-old in Colombo in April 1987. If no great stylist he was a bloody-minded batsman in the mould of David Steele and Peter Willey and I greatly admire that sort of player, one who's up for the fight, wants to get stuck in. I can tell you Test match cricket against very quick bowlers is no place for shrinking violets, they soon get found out if they haven't the stomach for it. He might not have pleased the purists with his constant moving about on the crease and playing the ball on the move but he was mighty effective and Jones has the best record of any New Zealand number three. All that moving about gave the impression he wasn't happy against fast bowling but in reality he was a batsman who was mentally strong and effective.

He got his runs, 2,922 of them at an average of 44.27, at the top of the order where the going is toughest and he had a good sense of humour as he showed in Australia in the winter of 1987. During and after the first Test in Brisbane he was mocked by the players on the field and in the newspapers by the Australian press who took the mick in their usual crass way. They thought he was a hopeless case and pilloried him in no uncertain terms. It wasn't very nice but if you want 'nice' don't go to Australia. The next Test followed in Adelaide and Jones made a fine 150 in only his third Test against a pretty good attack of Craig McDermott, Bruce Reid and Merv Hughes before he was run out. In those days at Adelaide when you left the field you went up the steps, through the members and on your right were the press sitting in the open. Instead of turning to the dressing rooms Jones went along the front row of the press box and gave every one of the Aussie newspaper writers the finger. I like that sort of mentality: it shows what a strong-minded individual he was. They didn't take the mick out of him again. He got 170 not out against India in Auckland and then three hundreds in consecutive innings against Sri Lanka in January 1991: 188 in Wellington where he shared a record 467 third wicket stand with Martin Crowe, and 122 and 100 not out at Hamilton in the next game. He made 143 on the hard, fast, bouncy pitch in Perth against McDermott, Glenn McGrath, Paul Reiffel and Shane Warne, and averaged over 50 against Wasim and Waqar at their best in New Zealand in 1994 – so there were no doubts about his ability to handle genuine pace.

I'm not interested in whether he was an ungainly player or not, I'm picking him because he's tough, up for the challenge and he can do the job.

Bert Sutcliffe (1947–65)

He became an iconic figure in New Zealand cricket in large part because of the vast amount of runs he made in the domestic game, but he came to wider notice on MCC's tour of 1946–47 when he made a hundred in each innings against them, 197 and 128, for Otago at Dunedin. Wally Hammond, the MCC captain and Sutcliffe's boyhood hero, said of his two innings, 'He didn't merely stay at the wicket. He hit and hit hard all round the wicket and I had to gesture the fieldsmen out into the deep for him. He was "farming" the bowling to protect his partners and directing the ball to the boundary as comfortably as a general sending out orderlies. In the second innings Sutcliffe went in and knocked up another century. It was a chanceless, brilliant piece of batting, as good as any I have seen.' That from a man who wasn't given to handing out praise lightly.

Tall and fair-haired, he made his debut in the first Test that winter (also Hammond's last) and put on 133 with John Reid in the first game of the series, his share 58. Many rated him the equal of Neil Harvey, the talented Aussie left hander, and his reputation grew after the 1949 tour of England when he made 2,627 first class runs, a total only bettered by Bradman among tourists. He also averaged 60.42 in the four Tests and made his first century in the second innings of the third Test at Old Trafford, when England used 10 bowlers to try and dislodge the Kiwis who drew all four matches in the rubber. Another hundred, 116 at

Christchurch, followed in March 1951, but there was a turning point in his career which I think affected him ever after. It came at Ellis Park, Johannesburg, on Boxing Day 1953 when Neil Adcock hit him on the head before he had scored. No helmets, remember, and it was such a sickening blow that he had to retire a little later on nine not out and was taken to hospital. It was a dreadful pitch which also saw Lawrie Miller taken to the emergency room but Bert returned with his head swathed in bandages to hit a courageous 80 not out which included four fours and seven sixes and put on 33 for the last wicket with Bob Blair. It was an innings which has become part of Kiwi cricketing folklore.

Up until that point he was the spearhead of a new dawn for New Zealand cricket. They had been seen as cannon fodder, just small fry who could be disposed of in three-day Tests and though Sutcliffe never played in a Test-winning side he provided the inspiration. You'd have thought that their nearest neighbours Australia would have given a helping hand in their development, but after playing one Test in 1946 it was another 27 years before they deigned to play them again. That didn't help one iota. Consequently Sutcliffe and a lot of others didn't get to play against the Aussies, which makes it difficult to judge his overall ability. My feeling is that after he was hit on the head he wasn't the same against genuine fast bowling. In India on lower, flatter tracks he remained a class act, making 137 not out in Hyderabad in the first Test in November 1955 and an unbeaten 230 in Delhi in the third.

He was obviously a player of outstanding gifts because after a poor tour of England in 1958 and one game at home he retired for six years and then, brought back into the side for trips to India, Pakistan and England, he got 151 not out in Calcutta. But in his last Test in May 1965 in a game

I played in he was again hit behind the right ear, this time by Fred Trueman at Edgbaston, had to retire hurt and called it a day for good. His tremendous batting at home, 355 and 385 (then the highest score by any left hander in the world) for Otago plus four other double hundreds mean you can't talk about New Zealand cricket without his name cropping up.

I don't doubt his courage for a single moment but against the sort of tremendous pace my teams are facing you're going to need more than bravery. He's in my squad but not as an opener. I don't think he's the best man to be in the top three against the other sides I've picked so I'd want him to bat down the order as the sixth batsman who would be exceptional on the subcontinent.

During the war he served in North Africa and Italy with the great Jim Laker and Peter Smith, the Essex legspinner, and perhaps that's where he developed his ability to play spin. Whatever the reason, his lovely stroke play and weight of runs make him a legend and he deserves a place in any New Zealand side.

Martin Paterson Donnelly (1937–49)

Although he only appeared in seven Test matches and played only 13 first class matches in his own country, Martin Donnelly remains a legend in New Zealand. He was quite a talented schoolboy cricketer and a rugby player good enough to win a cap for England against Ireland at Lansdowne Road. In 1933 he got a letter from Don Bradman, organized by his uncle Vic, 'looking forward to the young man taking his place amongst his country's champions'. It happened pretty rapidly. After only one first class game for Wellington when he made 22 and 38 he was picked for the 1937 tour of England at 19 years of age.

He made his debut in the Test that marked Len Hutton's first appearance for England and both scored ducks at Lord's in the opening game of the series, but he helped to save the match in the second innings. He went on to make an impression with an unbeaten 37 as Tom Goddard bowled out the Kiwis at Old Trafford, and a half century at The Oval. He scored 138 not out in his last first class match before the war for Wellington against Canterbury and 133 in his first in peacetime, for the Dominions against England at Lord's in August 1945. In his obituary *Wisden* said:

He scored magnificent hundreds in exhibition matches at Edgbaston and Scarborough in 1945, but topped them both in the match Denzil Batchelor called the perfect game, when the

Dominions beat England at Lord's with eight minutes to spare. Donnelly hit 133 in three hours. You sat and rejoiced, wrote Batchelor, hugging your memories to your heart and gradually letting the dazzle fade out of your eyes.

During the war he served as a tank commander in the desert and Italy and played a lot of inter-services cricket where his reputation grew. At the Gezira Club in Cairo, playing for the New Zealand Expeditionary Force team, he appeared in five matches and made 415 runs for once out, but it was when he went up to Oxford that he captured the English cricket public's attention. When news got about that he was batting in The Parks the lecture halls emptied, as *Wisden* recorded: 'Donnelly went up to Oxford to read history, and became a Dark Blue institution. His graceful batting was regarded by a generation of undergraduates as the best free show in town; as soon as the word went round that he was in, they would flock to watch.'

In that summer of 1946 he made hundreds for the Dark Blues against the Indian tourists, Lancashire, Leicestershire, Middlesex, Gloucestershire and topped them all with 142 against Cambridge at Lord's in the Varsity match. The following summer, the hot one of 1947, he passed three figures against Lancashire, the Free Foresters, Sussex and for the North v the South at Scarborough, but possibly his finest hour came in the Gentlemen v the Players match at Lord's when he made a magnificent unbeaten 162 which prompted C. B. Fry, who had watched all the greats, to comment that he was as good a left hander as any he had seen, including Clem Hill and Frank Woolley.

He played a season with Warwickshire in 1948 without hitting a hundred until September when he played for MCC against Yorkshire at Scarborough, and he made his highest score, 208 not out, an innings which had the Yorkshire crowd purring.

An astonishing 12 years after his previous Test he was in the New Zealand side that drew all four matches of the 1949 rubber, making 462 runs at an average of 77. It included a stupendous double hundred at Lord's, his first and only Test century. Of the series, *Wisden* wrote: 'Together with another left hander, Bert Sutcliffe, he taught the English public and cricket establishment to understand that here was a country of growing sporting significance, which should never again be palmed off with three-day Tests.'

He made his only hundred (120) in county championship cricket when he captained Warwickshire in June 1950 at Edgbaston against a Yorkshire side which included the young Fred Trueman and Johnny Wardle, and two games later he was gone from first class cricket, a victim of the lack of a professional game in New Zealand. Despite all his brilliance and charisma he simply couldn't earn a living at the game and became a marketing manager for Courtaulds in Sydney. What a loss to cricket. According to some observers he had a lot in common with Bradman: the hawk eye, similar build and a determination to establish psychological dominance over the bowler, although he never shared the Don's desire to bat for ever. Despite the brevity of his international career he has to be one of the best New Zealand batsmen of all time.

Charles Stewart 'Stewie' Dempster
(1930–33)

Stewie Dempster was a prodigy in junior grade cricket scoring nine centuries and a 99 in 10 innings as a 16-year-old and he carried that talent on to be rated among the top six batsmen in the world during the 1930s. Nobody dominated the club game in New Zealand as he did and in over 166 games he averaged 75.85, the nearest to him not topping 50, and he made 30 hundreds. Short, stocky and a tremendous driver through the off side, he made his debut in the Plunkett Shield for Wellington as an 18-year-old and was picked for the 1927 tour to England where he topped the batting averages with 1,430 runs at 44.68. There were no Tests – New Zealand were still three years away from full international status – but it was on that five-month tour that he said he learned his cricket. Stewie had never been coached and claimed that he learned all that he needed to know while standing at first slip as Jack Hobbs made 146 for Surrey against the tourists at The Oval. He must have learned pretty quickly because he got a hundred in the second innings of the same match.

In January 1930 he played in his country's first ever Test at Christchurch and in the second on his home turf in Wellington he made 136 and 80 not out, the first Test century by a New Zealander. He only had two Test innings on the 1931 tour of England but made 53 and 120 at Lord's while hitting his highest score, 212, against Essex at Leyton and finishing the trip with seven hundreds and 1,778 first class runs at an average of 59.26. He played in the Kiwis' inaugural Test against South Africa at Christchurch in February 1932 and the following year in his last Test innings made an unbeaten 83 out of a total of 153 in the same match where Wally Hammond scored the then world record Test score of 336 not out. It was the only time he didn't open the batting for his country and he had to come in at number four with two wickets down and no runs on the board because his train was late arriving in Auckland. As soon as the match was finished he boarded the steamer *Taimui* to sail for England and a job in Leicester arranged for him by Sir Julien Cahn as manager of one of his stores. He qualified for his patron's county, Leicestershire, and spent four years there, three of them as captain, making 4,659 at an average of 49.04 with 18 hundreds, twice scoring three on the trot, and also made 105 against Bradman's 1938 Australians as well as playing for the Gentlemen against the Players in 1937. That sort of average takes some doing on uncovered pitches and in a pretty unglamorous side, let me tell you. When you think that the greats of the game like Sutcliffe, Hobbs and Hammond were averaging in the mid fifties it shows just how good he was. Even after the war he was named in the party to play England in 1947 but an eye injury forced him to withdraw. It's extraordinary to me how little cricket they played. Just imagine what someone of his class would achieve if he was playing 13 Tests a year as they do now.

I've looked at John Wright, Bruce Edgar and other openers but I just have to pick Dempster because his record is too good to ignore. There's no doubt that anybody in New Zealand would pick him too because his legend lives on.

John Cowie (1937–49)

In looking for a partner for Richard Hadlee one name stands out, the man who took 45 Test wickets in only nine games spread over 12 years at 21.53 and who tops his country's bowling averages.

Jack Cowie was fast medium, swung it out and nipped it back sharply off the seam and after the 1937 tour of England the editor of *Wisden*, Wilfred Brookes, said of him, 'Had he been an Australian, he might have been termed a wonder of the age.'

He married his wife Nyrie on the day the boat set sail for England in 1937 and on that tour took 114 first class wickets at 19.95. But it was in the Tests that he stood out. In the first at Lord's he bowled Len Hutton on his debut for a duck and in the second innings the master batsman took 24 minutes over a single before Cowie had him again. Len commented, 'Terrific pace off the pitch, a forked-lightning offbreak and lift and swing away from the right-hand batsman.' He proved it again in the second match at Manchester when he had 10 for 140 in the match, including Hammond for a duck in the second innings. He finished the three-game rubber with 19 at 20.78. But the series wasn't a financial success for the Kiwis. It was a pretty wet summer and in those days the tourists used to take a share of the gate money rather than a set fee like they do now. So on the way home they undertook three games against the Australian state sides and when they arrived at Adelaide for the South

Australia match Bradman was down to play, a guarantee of a huge crowd to see the master in his only innings against New Zealand. He was 11 not out overnight and when Cowie and co. arrived next morning they saw the Don blasting the ball all round the Adelaide Oval rather than having a quiet net, obviously intent on doing the New Zealanders some damage. There were still long queues outside the famous ground when play started but Bradman nicked the second ball of the day to Eric Tindill, the wicketkeeper. He stood there and as he was given out there was a huge groan that was heard outside. The punters turned around and went home and Sammy Luttrell, the NZCC treasurer, told Tindill and Cowie, 'You two have cost us £1,000.'

In the only Test against an Australia missing Bradman, Cowie had six for 40 at Wellington in March 1946 and although it was another year until the next Test, in a rain-affected match at Christchurch he took six for 83 against an England side including Washbrook, Compton and Hammond in his last Test.

Although he kept fit by road running and neither drank nor smoked, he was 37 years of age when New Zealand toured England in 1949 but had five for 127 from 43 overs at Leeds before he broke down and couldn't bowl in the second innings. In his last Test at The Oval in August he had four for 123 from 28 overs, his last victim being Trevor Bailey.

Along with Eric Tindill, who also played rugby for New Zealand and was in the famous Prince Obolensky match at Twickenham on the tour of 1935–36, Cowie became a Test umpire and the two men stood together in the match against England at Christchurch at the end of February 1959. He was awarded the OBE in 1972 as much for his services to NZ soccer as cricket after serving on their

Football Association council for 14 years. He was yet another who suffered from the amateurism and lack of competitive games; otherwise who knows what he might have achieved. After Hadlee I don't think there has been better.

Richard Charles Motz (1961–69)
Bruce Richard Taylor (1965–73)

I need a couple of seamers to back up Richard Hadlee and
Jack Cowie and while there are a good few to choose from
they are all much of a muchness.

I'm going to go for the big, aggressive, broad-shouldered
Dick Motz who was a bit of a handful on his day, lively
without being an express bowler, hit the deck hard and was
always at you. I liked his attitude of wanting to knock your
block off and I feel that he's as good as any of the back-up
bowlers. He had five wickets in his first Test at Durban
against South Africa and six in the second in Johannesburg
and went on to become the first New Zealand bowler
to take 100 wickets when he had Phil Sharpe leg before at
The Oval in the last of his 32 Test matches.

It wasn't easy being a bowler in his time because the Kiwis
won only four matches in that period but he was no mug, as
he proved on that first tour in 1961–62 when he had 81 first
class wickets at 17.77 each and 19 in the five Tests at 26.57. I
know he could bowl because he did me for nought at Lord's
and nought at Trent Bridge on the 1969 tour and I'll never
forget it. At Lord's Ray Illingworth won the toss on a cloudy,
dark day and asked me what I thought. Well, the last thing I
wanted was to go out on one of those mornings just not
made for batting but when he asked what I would do if I
was captain I had to admit that taking first knock was
the best thing to do – I thought Derek Underwood would
bowl them out as quickly as they came in as the pitch,

which started dry and patchy, wore. I lasted 10 balls before Dick hit the ridge and the ball flew at my throat and all I could do was fend it off to be caught. Happily I made a few in the second innings and 'Deadly' did as predicted. At Nottingham I did better, I lasted 12 balls before he pitched one short, hit me on the arm and then my chest and dropped on to the stumps with just enough strength to remove a bail.

He had a good series against the West Indies at home in February and March 1969, taking 17 wickets in three Tests, but after his last game at The Oval it was discovered that he had been bowling for 18 months with displaced vertebrae in his back. What must that have been like? After he retired he became a publican and when I was commentating in New Zealand in the 1970s he popped up to say hello; a nice gesture from a man who'd been trying to knock my head off whenever we had met previously!

Bruce Taylor made his debut in Calcutta in 1965 in the second Test and made 105 from number eight with three sixes and 14 fours. He followed that up with five for 86 and in the next Test at Bombay had five for 26 and three for 76, quite a start to a 30-match Test career which saw him take 111 wickets at 26.6. He hit the deck hard rather than just put it on the spot like a lot of other medium pacers and he could move it both ways off the seam as well. Curiously he appeared to be a better bowler on good pitches and had 27 wickets in a four-Test series in the Caribbean in March and April 1972, and that against a side including at various times Garry Sobers, Lawrence Rowe, Roy Fredericks, Gordon Greenidge and Clive Lloyd. That haul included his career best, seven for 74 in Barbados, nine for 182 in the match. He must have liked the West Indies because he hit his second hundred in Auckland in the first Test against them in February 1969, 124 coming in 111 minutes with five sixes and 14 fours.

There are a lot of different names that crop up, Danny Morrison, Deon Nash, Bob Collinge, Chris Martin and Gary Bartlett (a chucker, no doubt about that), but I think that Motz and Taylor showed aggression, ability and guts and deserve to take their place in my side.

Christopher Lance Cairns (1989–2004)

Chris was definitely the best all-rounder New Zealand have had by far. A destructive batsman against the slow bowlers, he hit 87 sixes in Test matches, a total only bettered by Adam Gilchrist and Brian Lara, and with the ball he had a high action and moved the ball off the seam at what I would call a briskish pace.

A big, strapping lad, he never looked as though he was straining and with an economical action it appeared he was always performing well within himself. My feeling was that he didn't like the hard work of bowling and much preferred batting. He enjoyed the adulation of the crowd when he was smacking the ball out of the ground and thrilling the public with his big hitting but I always thought he could do with a squib up his backside when it came to the other part of his game. He was a good medium pacer but he could have been better and taking his 218 wickets at 29.04 didn't really reflect his capabilities.

He made his debut at Perth against Australia in November 1989 and in his second Test against Sri Lanka in Auckland had nine for 211 in a drawn match. He had eight for 138 in the second Test of England's tour in January 1992 in Auckland and the first of his five centuries (120) came against Zimbabwe in January 1996 at Auckland.

Potentially he was a world class player and for three years at the end of the 1990s and into the early part of the new century he hit the high spots. But he kept suffering illness and injury, missing matches, and it seemed his body didn't like hard work. The one thing he did have, though, was the ability to change the course of a game and that's priceless. He took six for 77 in the first innings of New Zealand's nine-wicket win over England at Lord's in the second Test of the series in July 1999, and five for 31 in the 83-run win at The Oval in the fourth a month later, adding a whirlwind 80 from 93 balls with eight fours and four sixes in the Kiwis' second innings. These performances as New Zealand won the series 2–1 made him one of *Wisden*'s five cricketers in 2000.

He enjoyed his best overall return in December 1999 at Hamilton in the first Test where he bowled his country to victory over the West Indies. He had three for 73 from 31 overs in the first innings, smashed 72 from 82 balls with nine fours and two sixes in the reply and then had seven for 27 as the West Indies were bowled out for 97. He followed that up with match figures of seven for 69 as New Zealand won by an innings and 105 at Wellington in a game where Courtney Walsh had none for 112 in 41 overs.

In March 2004 he gave South Africa some stick in Auckland with his highest score, 158 from 171 balls with 18 fours and seven sixes in another New Zealand win and signed off from Test cricket appropriately enough at Trent Bridge where he played county cricket for Nottinghamshire. It was a notable farewell too, with nine wickets for 187 in the match which England won by four wickets.

The only all rounder to compare with him is his dad Lance who was a giant of a man who carried a bat with cut-away shoulders which made him look like a caveman when he walked out wielding it like a club. Like father like son, he hit it a long way too.

John Richard Reid (1949–65)

No discussion of the best New Zealand side of all time could take place without mention of John Reid, an iconic figure who did just about everything in the team – captain, wicketkeeper, opener, middle order batsman, occasional bowler with 85 wickets and then selector. No doubt about it, he was a tremendous performer when it was really hard going and the Kiwis were cricket's whipping boys. I played against him in 1965 and he was a tough fighter, a real battler, at his best when things were not going well. He made his debut at Old Trafford against England in 1949 and played 54 Tests over the next 16 years, finally seeing his country to their first win in an official Test match after 26 years and 45 Tests when they beat the West Indies at Auckland in March 1956 in the fourth game of the rubber.

One of his finest matches came in the third Test of England's tour at Christchurch in March 1963 when he made 74 and 100 in a losing cause. Fred Trueman, who bagged seven for 75 in New Zealand's first innings, said they were two of the finest knocks ever played against him. He also had a glorious tour of South Africa in 1961–62, making 546 runs in five Tests at an average of 60.6. But overall his average was 33.28 and much as I would like to have him in my side I'm afraid Andrew Jones gets the number three spot and I don't see where else I could fit him in. I like

John Reid and I'm a great admirer of all he has done for his country but I can't let sentiment overrule my judgement so the best I can do is make him first reserve.

The Wicketkeepers

There are really only three in contention, Adam Parore, Ian Smith and Brendan McCullum. I've heard good things about Eric Petrie who was an absolutely top class glove man in 14 Tests between 1955 and 1966 but he only had a batting average of around 12 and that's no good in the modern game. Fast bowlers would be running up from fine leg tearing off their sweaters and caps at the prospect of bowling to duffers. The wicketkeeper has to contribute runs however good he is behind the stumps.

Adam Parore was a strong character who played 78 Tests and made an unbeaten 100 against the West Indies at Christchurch in February 1995 and 110 against the Aussies in Perth in November 2001, ending with a batting average of 26.28. He was pretty good and dependable in 12 years behind the wickets with 204 dismissals, the best by a Kiwi wicketkeeper.

A lot of people would go for **Brendan McCullum** because he has played some brilliant, exciting, swashbuckling innings full of spectacular shots, particularly in one-day matches when he opens the batting. A lot of people's view will be coloured by those exhilarating strokes with terrific hand—eye coordination and fast bat speed and his willingness to threaten bowlers with intent to cause serious damage. It's great stuff, no doubt about that, but for me he hasn't done enough in Tests to offset the superior glove work of Parore and Smith. To me he's still working out how to play in the longer game, still mulling over what approach to take; should he be conservative or brave? In limited overs cricket he can set the ball rolling at the top of the order but in Tests the scene is set and he can't decide what role to play. It could be that he will turn out to be another Adam Gilchrist but he hasn't done it yet and the jury is still out. It's all right smashing medium pacers round the ground and standing a couple of feet outside your crease to ordinary bowlers, but against the likes of Trueman, Lillee, Garner and the wealth of real bowling talent he'd be facing in my tournament I don't think he'd have much of a price.

Ian Smith played the first of his 63 Tests at Brisbane in 1980 and ended up with a batting average of 25.56. His moment of glory came at Auckland in the third Test of the series against India when, with New Zealand tottering on 131 for seven, he came in at number nine and blasted 173 off 136 balls, including 24 off one over from Atul Wassan, hitting 23 fours and three sixes. He made one earlier hundred, an unbeaten 113 against England at Auckland in February 1984, and also had the distinction of seven dismissals in an innings against Sri Lanka at Hamilton in February 1991.

There's not a lot to choose between them, it's the toss of a coin really, but I think I'm going to go for Smith, strong-minded and a good personality, never afraid of a challenge.

The Spinners

Because we are going to play matches on the subcontinent it's important to have two spinners in the squad. In the heat and humidity the pace bowlers will wilt and need a break and the pitches will turn. New Zealand are not exactly blessed in the spin department, mainly because of the pitches they play on which up until recently were principally the rugby grounds of Wellington, Auckland and Dunedin.

The first man I'm going for is **Daniel Luca Vettori** who became the youngest New Zealand player of all time when he made his debut as an 18-year-old against England at Wellington in February 1997. From that moment he's pushed on to become the best left arm spinner in world cricket, exercising great control, subtle variations in flight and changing his pace so well that there is sometimes a 20kph difference between deliveries. He spins it, keeps the batsman guessing about what's coming next and has an unflappable temperament while getting through a lot of overs.

It's nice to have the accolade of being the best left arm spinner in the game but now we've got covered pitches they rarely win matches outside the subcontinent. Pitches just don't break up and the only assistance the finger spinner gets is from the other bowlers' footmarks so it's difficult for them to take wickets at the same cost as the seamers who take theirs at somewhere in the low twenties, while spinners tend to cost 30 plus a wicket. But when there is turn Dan exploits it well and against Sri Lanka at Hamilton, a proper cricket ground, he took nine for 130 in only his fourth Test in a rare New Zealand victory. In Sri Lanka in 1998 he had 17 wickets at 21.2 in three games although they lost the series. Probably his best performance came in March 2000 against Australia in Auckland when he became the first Kiwi to take 12 wickets in a home Test with five for 62 and seven for 87 but they still lost by 62 runs. Again, in Wellington in December 2006 he had 10 for 183 in the second Test against Sri Lanka but New Zealand lost by 217 runs.

It's clear that despite some fine performances the finger spinners rarely win matches these days but they are still needed to change the pace of the game, give the batsmen something different to think about and rest the pace men. By the end of the 2008 home series against England Vettori had 245 wickets but at a cost of 34.8 each, which says more about the state of the pitches than it does about the quality of his bowling. In addition to his skill with the ball he has become a good enough late order batsman to pass 2,000 runs in Tests, something only Richard Hadlee and Chris Cairns have achieved among his countrymen. He's got a textbook defence with a big stride forward, better than most of their specialist batsmen, has a clear mind, sticks to the shots he is comfortable with and that's smart. He's very good against the spinners, letting it come to him rather than thrusting at the ball, shovels the ball through mid wicket with a strong bottom hand and sweeps well too. Since he became captain he's got a better batting average than any of the so-called proper batsmen and it's a clear case of a man making the most of his ability by using his brain.

Alongside Vettori I'm going to pick **John Garry Bracewell**, the offspinner, a spiky character who's done the double of 1,000 runs and 100 Test wickets. He rubs people up the wrong way but I don't mind that, I've done it myself once or twice, and I like his approach to the game, aggressive and combative. We're going to be playing against the best in the world who will be fiercely competitive so we'll need strong characters in the dressing room, opinionated players, not shrinking violets, and Bracewell is just the ticket.

He made his debut in November 1980 at Brisbane and in only his fourth Test, against India at Auckland, he had match figures of nine for 136. He suffered a fair bit from playing on those seamer-friendly rugby grounds at home; I know I didn't like them one bit – with dressing rooms like dungeons under the stand they weren't pleasant places to play. But Bracewell's offspin actually won matches for his country even in the 1980s when the art of finger spin was almost dead. He was the first New Zealand spinner to take ten in a match with 10 for 106 in the eight-wicket win over Australia in Auckland. His six for 32 in the second innings of that match in March 1986 helped New Zealand to be the first side to win two series against their neighbours in one winter. He had two for 81 and six for 51 against India in Bombay in November 1988 and made 52 and 32 in a match where only 894 runs were scored as the Kiwis won by 136 runs, a real match-winning performance, and six for 85 in 35 overs in the nine-wicket win over Australia at Wellington in March 1990. His only century came in another Kiwi victory, against England at Trent Bridge in 1986 when he made 110 and took three for 29 as New Zealand won by eight wickets. But perhaps his most extraordinary innings was making an unbeaten 83 from number 10 against the Aussies in Sydney in the second Test in November 1985 and putting on 124 for the last wicket with Stephen Boock.

Bracewell clearly has the stomach for a fight and that's

the sort of man I want, a real tough nut in my dressing room. Given the depth and quality of the rest of the sides it's going to be hard for the Kiwis, one of the younger Test nations, so they're going to have to battle hard. I can be sure Bracewell will be up for it.

New Zealand

Richard Hadlee

Martin Crowe

Glenn Turner

Andrew Jones

Bert Sutcliffe

Martin Donnelly

'Stewie' Dempster

Jack Cowie

Dick Motz

Bruce Taylor

Chris Cairns

Ian Smith

Daniel Vettori

John Bracewell

John Reid

Adam Parore

Brendan McCullum

India

Kapildev Ramlal Nikhanj (1978–94)

Kapil Dev, as he is always known, was voted India's Cricketer of the Century in 2002 but that had more to do with him leading his country to their World Cup triumph in 1983 and the growth in popularity of one-day cricket on the subcontinent than being a reflection of his contribution to the advance of India on the Test stage. I don't think you can separate Kapil and Sunny Gavaskar in this respect and it was a bit unfair on the little opener who had every right to feel aggrieved. But the limited overs contests are what produces the money in India. Whereas once there would be 100,000 inside and 10,000 outside Eden Gardens in Calcutta for a Test match now you can walk in, while tickets for one-day games go like hot cakes, they fill stadiums and the fans can't get enough of it.

My judgement is based on achievements in Test cricket and on that basis alone Kapil is outstanding, a fantastic cricketer. Over six feet tall with a beautifully athletic build, he had charisma and a lovely action, getting close to the stumps and swinging it away late, inducing the drive at a lively pace. The way he leapt into his delivery stride took him so far round you could see his back before he swivelled and let the ball go and he is far and away the best pace bowler India has ever produced. As a batsman he was a clean striker of the ball, making eight hundreds, and he loved attacking the bowling and could change the course of a match with his hitting. Of course, you can play like that when you're taking wickets by the bucketful as he did and his bowling gave him the freedom to bat the way he did.

His quiet debut was in sharp contrast to Sunny's explosive arrival on the scene, taking one wicket at Faisalabad as a 19-year-old against Pakistan in October 1978, and he'd only bagged half a dozen when he made 126 not out from 124 balls against the West Indies in Delhi in January the following year. In that six-match series he took 17 wickets which was good going on those hard, dry strips where the ball quickly roughs up and it's not going to seam. He pitched it up, swung it and bowled long spells, returning match figures of seven for 84 in Madras.

I played against him in 1979 and in the first Test at Edgbaston he got through 48 overs to take five for 146 as England piled up 633 for five declared and he ended that four-match series with 16 wickets. It's fair to say he didn't get much help and carried a heavy workload. People should remember what sort of team a bowler is playing in when assessing returns and it's not easy when you're a one-man band. But Kapil never bottled it, always kept going and I admire that sort of dedication.

Against Australia in the six-match series in India at the end of 1979 he had 28 wickets at 22.32 and got through 226 overs because although they didn't have dumplings bowling at the other end they weren't class either.

At the end of 1979 and into 1980 he enjoyed his best series at home when Pakistan played on Indian soil for the first time in 19 years, taking 32 wickets at 17.68 with match figures of nine for 121 in Delhi in the second Test, six for 63 in Kanpur in the third and 11 for 146 in Madras in the fourth – some bowling that on those pitches – to give his side a 2–0 win in the rubber.

In Australia in 1981 Kapil got through more than 36

overs to take five for 97 in Sydney in the first Test, hard work in that heat, and at Melbourne in the third emphasized his durability to take five for 28 and skittle the Aussies for 83, bowling 16.4 overs with a thigh strain to win the match.

I played against him again on England's tour of 1981–82 and in the first Test in Bombay he took five for 70 as we were bowled out for 102. It was blazing sunshine and a dry pitch but Kapil had bags of aggression, swung it in the morning, swung it after lunch and saw us off. Although not genuinely fast he could surprise you with a bouncer and was a very dangerous opponent, proving it again with six for 91 in Calcutta. After taking 24 wickets in Pakistan in 1982–83 India went to the Caribbean in the early part of 1983. The West Indies had Marshall, Holding, Roberts and Garner, India Kapil Dev. Not much of a contest that, was it? They were overwhelmed and lost the series 2–0 despite Kapil making his second Test hundred, 100 not out in the second innings of the draw at Trinidad in the second match of the five-game series. After a tour like that there was little expectation of success in the World Cup which followed and even when they reached the final at Lord's against the West Indies there was little hope, particularly after they were bowled out for 183. Kapil got through 11 overs, conceding only 21 runs, and Mohinder Armanath took three for 12 as the mighty fell with a bloody great thump and Kapil's place in history was etched in letters ten feet high.

To underline his liking for the West Indies he returned his best Test figures of nine for 83 in Ahmedabad in the third Test in November 1983, but still couldn't prevent his side losing by 138 runs as they were sent packing for 103. India lost the series 3–0 and Kapil the captaincy, but he was back in charge when Australia visited in 1986 and made 119 from 138 balls in the tied Test in Madras that September and in December put Sri Lanka to the sword in Kanpur with 163 from 165 balls, the best of his eight centuries.

In February 1994 at Ahmedabad he dismissed Hashan Tillekeratne to overtake Richard Hadlee's then world record of 431 wickets, but the late outswing had gone as it always does as age thickens the waistline and that all important swivel is lost, and he played only one more Test, against New Zealand.

He was up there with Botham, Hadlee and Imran, a superb all-rounder who did so much along with Sunny to take Indian cricket forward and the two of them are still fêted wherever they go in their country.

Sunil Manohar Gavaskar (1971–87)

Sunny Gavaskar's record will stand against anybody's and I rate him along with Barry Richards as one of the two greatest opening batsmen of my time. Remarkably consistent and run-hungry, he was technically correct with lovely balance and his footwork made great use of the crease. To that he added patience and great concentration – he had no weakness really. For a player who stood less than 5ft 5in tall he could get on the front foot so well and his driving was a delight. You might expect a small man to suffer from bouncers but, as he told me with a twinkle in his eye, being short made it easy for him to get under them. He could play on any surface against any bowling attack and if he got in it was odds on he was going to make a hundred. Like all opening batsmen he bagged a few low scores against the new ball but when he settled into an innings his conversion rate was excellent.

I've come to know him pretty well since we both retired, working with him in the commentary box all over the world, and he's got a very astute mind, a good sense of humour and has become a great friend. But underneath it all there's a bloody-mindedness and if he makes his mind up there's no shifting him; it must be a trait among opening batsmen.

His debut on the international stage in 1971 was nothing less than stunning with an amazing first series in the Caribbean at the age of 20. In the second Test in Trinidad he made 65 and 67 not out and hit the winning runs as India won for the first time in 25 starts against the West Indies. He went on to make 116 in the third Test in Guyana, 117 in Barbados and 120 and 220 in the last game of the series when they went back to Port of Spain, Trinidad; four Tests, 774 runs at an average of 154.8 – not even Bradman can match that.

His first taste of English conditions was not easy and there were only two half centuries in the series of 1971 which was marred by the incident at Lord's in the first Test when John Snow shoulder-charged him as he went for a single. Snowy was banned for a match and Sunny was brought down to earth in more ways than one. Derek Underwood was his nemesis on England's tour of 1972–73, getting him in four innings, three times cheaply. On the 1974 tour of England he had 101 and 58 at Old Trafford but a weak Indian side suffered three heavy defeats and were bowled out for 42 in the second Test at Lord's. Back on his favourite turf in the Caribbean in 1975–76 he had hundreds in back-to-back Tests in Trinidad, 156 in the second and 102 in the third where the Indians chased 406 to win by six wickets.

With experience he blossomed and became a real run machine in Australia in 1977–78 with 113 at Brisbane, 127 in Perth and 118 in Melbourne followed by 111 and 137 against Pakistan in Karachi in the third Test in November 1978. When the West Indies arrived in India the following month, he was made captain and scored 205 against them in the first Test in Bombay, 107 and 182 not out in the third in Calcutta and 120 in Delhi to aggregate 732 runs in six Tests at an average of 91.5. Phew, that takes some doing, but after all those runs and winning the series 1–0 he was stripped of the captaincy for the tour of England in 1979. Who can work out Indian politics? After hundreds galore and those results you'd think he'd have the job for life.

On that tour in the fourth and final Test at The Oval he played one of the most remarkable innings I've seen. England were in the driving seat for most of the match and after I made a hundred in the second innings we set them to make 438 in just over a day. Nobody expected them to get anywhere near it against our attack of Willis, Botham, Hendrick and Edmonds who'd bowled them out for 202 in the first innings. But Sunny and Chetan Chauhan put on 213 for the first wicket and Dilip Vengsarkar added another 153 for the second with Sunny who went merrily along never looking like getting out. He ended with 221 and the Indians were only nine short of what would have been a world record chase at the close with two wickets left.

It was a brilliant effort, all the more so because it was in foreign conditions. When you're playing at home you've got the crowd behind you, you know the grounds, you've got knowledge of the surface and how it will play and you're in your comfort zone. But when you're in someone else's backyard it's a different story and that's what sorts out the great from the ordinary and how players should be judged. Sunny did it around the world and that's what makes him outstanding and indicates his strength of character and eminence on the world stage. A week after that phenomenal effort at The Oval he's made captain again and they're taking on Australia at home. Sunny makes 115 at Delhi in the fourth Test and 123 at Bombay in the sixth and they win the series 2−0. The following month, November, they're playing a six-match series against Pakistan, he makes 529 at an average of 52.9 and they win the series 2−0. The Centenary Test against England is next in Bombay but guess what? Sunny's replaced as captain!

But he gets his stripes back for the tour of Australia in January 1981 and is involved in an incident which underlines his stubbornness and refusal to budge when he thinks he's right. In the second innings of the third Test at Melbourne he and Chauhan put on 165 for the first wicket when Sunny was given out leg before to Dennis Lillee. He doesn't like it at all, won't go and in the end tells Chetan to walk off with him. This is developing into an international incident but at the players' gate they are met by Wing Commander Durrani, the manager, who sends Chetan back to the middle and gives Sunny a rollicking. He has the last laugh, however, with the Aussies bowled out for 83 in their second innings to give India a 59-run win.

When Sunny gets a bee in his bonnet you'll know all about it.

In the drawn series with England in 1981–82 in India he makes 500 runs at 62.5 and in Faisalabad in January 1983 he becomes the first Indian opener to carry his bat, making an unbeaten 127 out of 286 in the third Test. But India lose the series 3–0 and Sunny is again replaced as captain. Knowing him as I do I think he was really pissed off at being made the scapegoat and he didn't have a good time of it on the Caribbean tour which immediately followed. He got 147 not out in Guyana against Holding, Marshall, Roberts and Garner, no mean feat, but his next best was 32 and he was well below par.

A major milestone came when the West Indies went to India in 1983 and in November in the third Test at Ahmedabad he passed my world record number of Test runs, 8,114, when he reached 83 in his 90. He ended that series with an unbeaten 236 in Madras batting at number four although he might just as well have opened because the Indians lost their first two wickets without a run on the board.

He had a big series in Australia in 1985–86 with 166 not

out in Adelaide and 172 in Sydney, but he was coming to the end of a marvellous career which finished in March 1987 in the series against Pakistan where he twice failed to add to his tally of 34 centuries, getting out for 91 in Madras and then making a brilliant 96 on a turning pitch at Bangalore.

Sunny was given life membership of MCC in recognition of his feats but turned it down because of an incident at Lord's in 1987 when he was playing for the Rest of the World against an MCC XI to commemorate the club's 200th year. The team were travelling by coach and when it pulled up outside the Grace Gates the players got off and went into the ground. Sunny, who was 80 not out overnight, had forgotten his blazer and went back aboard the coach to get it but when he tried to get in the gateman turned him away because he didn't have a pass. He got back on the bus and read his paper until panic set in and someone came to find him. He was quite content to sit there knowing that without him there was no game. But he never forgave the snub and turned down life membership.

Years later I was with him at a cocktail party in the Maharajah of Gwalior's palace when Dennis Silk, then president of MCC, and I managed to talk him round and he finally accepted the honour. It was ironic really that he had to be persuaded to take it while I was turned down by MCC's cricket committee three times before it was finally offered. Sunny deserved the accolades, he was the absolute tops.

Sachin Ramesh Tendulkar (1988–)

Sachin has made a bigger impact on the world stage than any other cricketer, fêted throughout India, rich beyond the wildest dreams, his name immortalized in the record books. But when I first saw him on his Test debut in Karachi in 1988 when he was just 16 years and 183 days old the pads looked too big for him and he really did seem to be a boy among men. And what a baptism, playing against Pakistan, the arch rivals, on foreign soil with so much national pride at stake. I know Asian players start younger and finish earlier than in the rest of the world but I really did wonder whether this was one youngster too young, a thought that was reinforced when Waqar hit him in the face and drew blood. But I needn't have worried as he quickly proved to have an excellent technique and good footwork; deep down inside he's a tough cookie and he's got a really sharp cricket brain into the bargain. That he has shown no particular weakness against any type of bowling probably prompted Sir Donald Bradman to comment that Tendulkar reminded him of himself after watching him in Australia where he played an innings still talked about Down Under, 114 on a lightning-fast pitch at Perth as a 19-year-old in February 1992.

His first Test hundred came in the second innings of the second match of the 1990 series against England at Old Trafford in August when he was still aged only 17 years and 122 days and there have only been two younger centurions,

Mohammed Ashraful of Bangladesh and Mushtaq Mohammed of Pakistan. It won him the man of the match award and secured a place as one of *Wisden*'s five cricketers of the year. The Almanack recorded:

What made his first so special were the circumstances in which he made it, as a seventeen-year-old coming to the rescue of his country. Yet those who had seen him stand up to a barrage of bouncers from the Pakistani fast bowlers at Sialkot the previous winter would have had no doubts about his genius, or his capacity to set an example to colleagues old enough to be father figures. He had already shown his character in the first innings at Manchester when, after waiting nearly an hour for his first run, he went on to regain his one-day touch. Tendulkar remained undefeated on 119, having batted for 224 minutes and hit seventeen fours. He looked the embodiment of India's famous opener, Gavaskar, and indeed was wearing a pair of his pads. While he displayed a full repertoire of strokes in compiling his maiden Test hundred, most remarkable were his off-side shots from the back foot. Though only 5ft 5in tall, he was still able to control without difficulty short deliveries from the English pacemen.

As his career blossomed it ran parallel with the advent of satellite television across the subcontinent which made him instantly recognizable to millions of people. The previously fuzzy pictures were now pin sharp and shown all over India, whereas in earlier times there were only radio and newspapers which reached a tiny proportion of the population. It also coincided with a relaxation by the authorities on the size and type of logo players could wear on their kit and bats, which opened the door to some huge sponsorship deals. When I got my hundredth hundred at Leeds in 1977 Slazenger paid me £13,000 to endorse their products. With the change in the rules the Madras Rubber Factory bought a batmaking company and Sachin carried their logo on his bats in a deal worth millions and he now endorses all manner of products. Worldwide television has been responsible for raising the profile to such giddy heights and advertisers and sponsors couldn't have a better conduit than Sachin.

While he knows his own worth, and there's nothing wrong with that, he remains a modest, polite, likeable lad with none of the airs and graces someone of his status is prone to. There's no side to him at all despite all the accolades, the hero worship and the money his feats on the cricket field have brought.

He was already an established Test performer when he became Yorkshire's first overseas player in 1992, a huge job in a county where it had become an unwritten rule that you had to be born there to wear the White Rose. A lot of people were opposed to the change but it had to come because other counties had been using two overseas players for years and wiping the floor with Yorkshire. Think of Rice and Hadlee at Nottinghamshire and Richards and Garner at Somerset, and Yorkshire trying to get by on home-grown talent. Sachin was a terrific signing and although some people say he didn't do much I don't agree. It has to be remembered he was playing in a poor side in foreign conditions and he made an important contribution to the four games that were won that summer. In addition he was a great ambassador for the club and hugely popular with everybody, members, sponsors, office staff and team-mates.

He became a superstar at home as one-day cricket became the number one recreation. The World Cup win in 1983 started it off and Sachin was a dab hand, opening the batting and scoring hundreds. In my youth, growing up in a coal mining town before the days of TV, the only place to go was the cinema. For the Indians it became one-day cricket; they can't get enough and it has replaced Test matches as the prime attraction with Sachin top of the bill.

It hasn't all been plain sailing and he's had to work hard to perfect his skills against the best in the world. When preparing for Shane Warne's arrival in India in early 1998 he went to Madras and got Laxman Sivaramakrishnan, the Indian legspinner, to bowl at him from around the wicket into specially prepared rough outside leg stump. He knew that was what he was going to get from Warne and was ready. He made 155 not out in the second innings of the first Test in Madras and took the world's number one to the cleaners. *Wisden* wrote:

On the first day, Tendulkar had been as much a victim of Warne's guile as of his own daring. He drove his first ball with scorching power past the bowler. But the fifth dipped as he rushed forward, and turned to take the edge of his flailing bat; Taylor completed a marvellous slip catch. In the second innings, however, when Tendulkar scored his third and highest century in seven Tests against Australia, he was as severe on Warne as on the rest. Warne followed up his first-innings four for 85 with a deflating one for 122. Tendulkar's belligerence was awesome and his shot-placement enthralling.

Two days before the Headingley Test in 2002 I invited all the Indian party to my house in Yorkshire for lunch, which my wife Rachael had specially catered to ensure they had the sort of food they like. Some wanted to watch old films of cricket, others went on the putting green but Sachin and Rahul Dravid and the bowlers spent time with me in the conservatory where I told them that it was no use taking wickets at 45 apiece. I said if they did that the batsmen would have to score 901 runs to win the game and nobody can do that. It may seem self-evident now but I don't think they'd considered such a simple fact. I also told them that they had to think positively from the word go, it was pointless going to Leeds and thinking about a draw, that wouldn't happen, as it's usually a result pitch. They had to bowl a consistent off stump line and be very positive. They won by an innings, the first time they had enjoyed such a margin of victory overseas since beating a weakened Australia in 1977–78. Sachin made 193 and Tanya Aldred wrote in *Wisden*:

Tendulkar, Yorkshire's prodigal son, despite his year here as a 19-year-old had never made a first-class century at Headingley. Now, in his 99th Test, as visitors quaffed champagne in the hospitality box Yorkshire had named after him, he did it, overtaking Don Bradman's total of 29 Test hundreds as he stroked the ball round the ground. But the highlight of the match was not the moment of his longed-for century; it was the silly session late on Friday afternoon when, as the skies darkened, he and Ganguly saw four lights on the scoreboard, disdained them, and ran amok, scoring 96 off the first 11 overs of the third new ball. Together they added 249, an Indian fourth-wicket record against England.

It was sensational stuff and I'm happy to have played a small part in it because the Indians are really nice guys, love their cricket, are always keen to spend hours talking about the game and constantly striving to improve.

Things were not always easy for the little genius. In Australia in 2004 he had a bad run and when I met him in my hotel in Adelaide where the Indians were staying, he was very down. In the first three Tests of the series he was averaging only 16.4. As a good friend for some years I had a little chat with him and suggested, based on my own experiences, that all that was necessary was to spend time at the crease and to cut out the risky shots. I later slipped a note under his door reminding him 'form is temporary, class is permanent', a cliché, I know, but nonetheless true. I hope it helped him out of the lean spell and, according, to *Wisden*, he heeded my advice. The Almanack recorded:

From the moment Tendulkar was given out lbw to his third ball at Brisbane, he had had an awful series, with both his driving and self-belief gone astray.

Tendulkar had thought through his problems to the point of cutting out one of his most distinguished strokes, abandoning the cover-drive and instead just waiting for the chance to hit to leg. He maintained this policy for ten hours 13 minutes and 436 deliveries, scoring an unbeaten 241, his highest first-class score and perhaps the highest ever made by a man still nowhere near his own top form. Twenty-eight of his 33 fours and 188 of his runs came on the leg side.

Afterwards the records kept coming: he passed Sunny Gavaskar's Indian record of 10,122 runs in the third Test against Pakistan at Bangalore in March 2005 when making 41 in the first innings, and overtook Allan Border's 11,174 in the second innings against Pakistan at Delhi in the first Test in November 2007 when making 56 not out. He was fastest to 8,000 runs in three fewer innings than Garry Sobers and reached 11,000 runs in 36 fewer innings than Border.

Through it all he remains the same unaffected lad I first met and is a credit to his country and the game. He deserves his fame and fortune and along with Brian Lara he's the best batsman I've seen since Garry Sobers and Viv Richards.

Rahul Sharad Dravid (1996–)

There are no options for the number three spot; Rahul
Dravid is the best by far. One of the sweetest natured, nicest
young men you could ever wish to meet, it's hard to imagine
that he's also one of the toughest men in the world to get
out. His defence was so good when he started out they
nicknamed him 'The Wall' and it's as true now as it was then
that if you don't get him early you're in for a long wait
because he doesn't give it away. Not a flamboyant strokemaker like Tendulkar or Lara, he doesn't seek to dominate
the bowlers but does it my way, wearing them down until
they are thoroughly dispirited. He's got a great technique,
putting in a big stride to get to the pitch of the ball and
plays every delivery strictly on its merits, very much an old-
fashioned type of batsman who makes few mistakes.
Nothing outrageous, doesn't use a heavy bat and you won't
upset him with sledging or trying to slag him off – he's
imperturbable and in his own private cocoon when he's at
the crease. I think he's one of the few modern players who
would have been able to perform on uncovered pitches
because he's technically so sound, has patience and concentration and feels no pressure, all characteristics required
to perform at the top level in that long-gone era.

In his first Test, at Lord's in June 1986, Dravid made 85
batting at number seven and his first Test hundred, 148,
came in Johannesburg in the third Test of the 1996–97
series. He's had a century in each innings twice, against New

Zealand at Hamilton in the second Test in January 1999, 190 and 103, and at Calcutta in the second Test against Pakistan in March 2005 he scored 110 and 135. He'll always be remembered for the record partnership with V. V. S. Laxman when India followed on and beat Australia at Calcutta in March 2001, his 180 a crucial contribution to a 376 stand for the fifth wicket. They batted the whole of the fourth day together, making 335 from 104 overs and when he was run out he'd batted for seven hours 24 minutes.

The key to assessing a batsman is whether he gets runs when it matters, to either save a game or win it; draws are relevant in Tests because if a side goes one down it takes a hell of a lot of doing to get back on terms. Rahul passes that exam easily; his 75 at Port Elizabeth in the second Test of the 2001 series held off South Africa and his 115 at Trent Bridge against England in 2002 earned the draw which allowed his country to go on and win the series. In the next match, at Headingley, his 148 was a vital part of a victory by an innings and 46 runs. In the chapter on Sachin Tendulkar I tell the story of how the Indian party had lunch at my house; as Dravid got on the bus after the second day my wife called out, 'Well played, Rahul,' to which he replied, with a smile, 'It was your lunch that did it, Mrs Boycott.' It was a formidable innings and *Wisden* said: 'Dravid was immaculate from the start, watching each ball like a seamstress and ignoring the ones which thudded into his shoulder, helmet or chest.' For sure it was his patience which paved the way for Tendulkar and Ganguly to run amok later and it was a fine example of his virtues. More came at The Oval in the final Test of the series when he underlined his ability to wear the bowlers down rather than take them apart and *Wisden* reinforced my view:

Dravid ground on and on, false strokes as rare as a steak tartare, to become the first Indian to make centuries in three consecutive Test innings in the same series since Sunil Gavaskar in 1970–71. He also took his crease occupation for the series past 30 hours – an entire Test match. What he didn't do was dominate, or even accelerate. If Headingley was his arthouse classic – an innings the connoisseur knows will not be bettered – this was Dravid's blockbuster: grander in scale and spectacle, but a colder, more deliberate affair which never set the pulse racing.

He made it four consecutive hundreds with another in the first Test against the West Indies in Bombay the following month but his sublime effort came in the second Test of the series in Australia which I saw in November 2003. *Wisden* was again spot on with its account which, in part, read:

It was as much a triumph of the Indian spirit, exemplified by none better than Dravid, who was on the field for most of the five days, batting 835 minutes and scoring 305 runs. He was last out in the first innings and there at the end to secure victory. It was a monumental effort, the finest performance by an Indian batsman in an overseas Test, because he made the difference. The victory was all the more incredible because India had not won a Test in Australia in 23 years.

He simply played everything on its merits, leaving every ball that carried the threat of an edge alone, while taking advantage of every scoring opportunity. After he played himself in, his cover-driving was sublime, and the only time he was in danger of getting out was when he top-edged a hook off Gillespie. But it sailed over backward square leg and brought up his hundred. He batted all but six minutes of ten hours and hit 23 fours and a six in 446 balls; it was at the time his highest first-class score, and a Test record for India abroad.

He had plenty of other big scores and was the fastest man to pass 9,000 runs in Test cricket taking 176 innings, one fewer than Ricky Ponting and Brian Lara. Given the heavy weight of his scoring it is a puzzle that he has been out in the nineties eight times, a figure exceeded only by Michael Slater (nine) and Steve Waugh (10) among leading batsmen. With the frequent failure of India's openers Dravid has had to face the new ball so many times, so his hatred of going in first can only be psychological. He prefers number three and in my side he's a shoo-in.

Vijaysingh Madhavji Merchant
(1933–51)

Along with Sidhu there are really only two players in contention to be Sunny's partner at the top of the order because none of the others have records which stand much scrutiny. Vijay's 10 Tests were all against England but spread over a period of 18 years starting with India's first official match in December 1933 and ending at Delhi in 1951 when he was 40 years of age.

A child prodigy, he made masses of runs in the Ranji Trophy, had a first class average of 71 and there is no doubt he was a class player. At only 5ft 7in tall he was a brilliant square cutter and hooker and, for a little man, drove beautifully as well. In that first series against Jardine's tourists his best was 54 at Calcutta, but he made his first century at Old Trafford, Manchester, when the Indians made the first tour of England in 1936 and followed on. Merchant and Mushtaq Ali put on 203 for the first wicket and India forced a draw in the second game of the three-match rubber. He followed that with 52 and 48 at The Oval and made sufficient impression to be one of *Wisden*'s five players of the year.

It was 10 years before he played another Test, the first of the 1946 series, at Lord's, and made another hundred at The Oval in the third match, 128 in five and a quarter hours, which was enough to earn a draw in a rain-ruined game. He suffered from ill-health in later years and missed tours to Australia and the West Indies before making his final appearance in the first Test of England's 1951–52 tour under Nigel Howard at Delhi against an attack which contained the young Brian Statham as well as the canny Derek Shackleton. His seven and a half hour innings of 154 meant he finished with a Test average of 42.71, no mean feat given he was playing against vastly more experienced bowling than he met in domestic cricket. He has to be judged, like Barry Richards, on very few Test matches but, as with the South African, I feel he has the class I need.

Navjot Singh Sidhu averaged 42.13 from 51 Tests and is someone I've come to know very well due to our commentary stints on ESPN. I call him 'the mad Sikh' (in the nicest possible way, of course) because of the crazy things he comes out with on air which have made him a cult figure on the subcontinent. As an opener he was all dour defence against the quicks but once he saw a spinner he was off down the pitch and wallop, he was on the aerial route. He was capable of the long innings as shown by his 11-hour 13-minute 201 against the West Indies in Trinidad in 1996–97, but he is more celebrated for the way he took apart the world's two greatest spinners Muttiah Muralitharan and Shane Warne. At Lucknow in the first Test against Sri Lanka he made 124 with nine fours and eight sixes and Murali's five wickets cost him 162 as India won by an innings, and he had 99 in the next match in Bangalore with nine fours and two sixes as Murali took four for 179 in another lost cause. The offspinner came in for more rough treatment when India went to Sri Lanka in August 1997, his two wickets in Colombo in the first Test costing 174, with Navjot hitting 111 with 13 fours and two sixes.

When Australia toured in 1998 he had 62 and 64 in Madras, 97 in Calcutta and 74 and 44 in Bangalore, cracking

47 fours and seven sixes in the series and being particularly severe on the Aussie legspinner.

He was deeply offended by Mohammed Azharuddin after the Indian captain won the toss and decided to bat at Manchester in the third ODI of 1996. He was strapping his pads on when the rest of the team laughingly told him he wasn't playing, something Azharuddin had forgotten to tell him. Embarrassed and humiliated, he packed his bags and flew home, deeply hurt. When I was in the Indian dressing room a couple of years back the story was being recounted when he went to the bathroom. I said, 'You better send someone with him or he might climb out of the window and go home.' He can laugh about it now.

Not many Indians have wanted to open the batting, they prefer the comfort zone of the middle order when the ball is old and soft. Although Vijay started at number six he became a class act against the new ball so, with apologies to my good friend Navjot, I'm going with him.

Vijay Samuel Hazare (1946–53)

He was already 31 years old when he made his debut against England at Lord's in the first series after the Second World War. He went on to play 30 Tests and made a pretty good fist of it, scoring seven centuries. Like so many we can only guess what he might have achieved in internationals if the hostilities had not taken six prime years out of so many cricketing lives.

Hazare was coached in Maharashtra by Clarrie Grimmett, the great Australian spin bowler, and in his autobiography he says that Grimmett was against any alteration in his stance:

Purists would grumble at my stance. My hands are said to be too far apart on the handle of the bat to permit a free swing. And they say that as my bat is held firmly between the pads, almost locked between them, my strokeplay must suffer. Grimmett must have seen both these peculiarities of mine. Yet, beyond making a few corrections, he strongly advised me against changing my grip and stance.

If he wasn't much of a stylist he certainly didn't give it up easily and made a huge contribution to the emerging cricketing nation.

During the war years when cricket was at a standstill, much of the credit for keeping the game alive in India goes to Hazare, who with Vijay Merchant took part in run-scoring duels that drew crowds of 20–30,000 to Bombay's Brabourne Stadium.

Perhaps his greatest moment came in Adelaide on the 1947–48 tour when he became the first Indian to score a hundred in each innings of a Test, 116 and 145, and although they got a 4–0 walloping against the likes of Miller, Lindwall and Bill Johnston he finished with 429 runs in the series. Against the West Indies in 1948–49 he made 543 runs at an average of 67.87 with 134 not out in Bombay to save India from defeat when they followed on, and 122, again at Bombay, in the fifth Test when, chasing 361 in 395 minutes, they finished six runs short with one wicket left. Dramatic stuff.

He topped the batting again when England went to India in 1951–52 with 164 not out in Delhi, his highest score in Tests, and 155 in Bombay. But on the dreadful pitch at Kanpur, a brute of a turner and a spinner's dream, he bagged 'em as Malcolm Hilton and Roy Tattersall bowled them out as fast as they came in.

He was nearly 37 years of age when the Indians came face to face with Fred Trueman on the 1952 tour and were blown away by his sheer pace. It's not overstating the case to say they were terrified and stories soon grew, one of them being that an Indian batsman, wanting the sightscreen moved, when asked where he wanted it said, 'Between me and that mad bugger Trueman.' Certainly that's an invention because there were no sightscreens at Headingley but it illustrates just what a state the Indians were in against such searing pace. Yet among all the havoc Hazare stood firm and in four Tests made 333 runs at 55.5, with 89 and 56 at Leeds, where India at one stage were four wickets down and not a run on the board, and 69 and 49 at Lord's. It would certainly have been a 4–0 whitewash if the last game at The Oval had not been washed out with only 10 hours 35 minutes' play possible. I bet the Indians were never more pleased to see rain. I take my hat off to Hazare who stood firm and set a fine example to his young, inexperienced team.

In the first official Test by a Pakistan side he made 76 in Delhi and 146 not out in Bombay in 1952–53 but then took on one tour too many when he led the side to the Caribbean and managed only 194 runs in the five Tests.

From the Australian tour in 1948 till Pakistan visited in 1953, he averaged over 70 and a lot of people think leading the side at a time when Indian cricket was particularly turbulent took its toll on this silent, thoughtful man. Merchant later said Hazare could have been India's finest batsman, were it not for the captaincy: 'It was one of the tragedies of cricket.' I don't totally agree with that although it is a fact that in 14 matches as captain he averaged 39.72 while averaging 54.91 in his other 16 games. It was a case of some bugger had to do it and it fell to him to carry the burden.

Javagal Srinath (1991–2002)

Finding a new ball partner for Kapil is fairly easy because there's not much choice; India have hardly been blessed with a surfeit of quick bowlers down the years. Javagal was probably a bit quicker than Kapil and their bowling averages and strike rates are very similar: Kapil's average 29.64 against 30.49, Kapil took a wicket every 63.9 balls, Javagal one every 64. There's no comparison, of course, in the rest of their statistics with Kapil playing in 131 Tests and taking 434 wickets, Srinath in only 67 Tests for 236. Neither is Srinath likely to capture the imagination like Kapil nor get the recognition of the man who won the World Cup, but he was an uncomplaining, hard-working bowler who gave everything.

He let it go from wide on the crease and batsmen were forced to play at it because he could nip it back sharply quite regularly and when it went straight on they were likely to edge it. I felt he didn't bowl the one that went straight on often enough and that he tended to pitch it a little too short. I know it's natural for bowlers from the subcontinent to bowl short of a length; they don't want to be pitching it up and getting driven on those dry, grassless batting pitches where there is little seam movement. But if he'd got it up another couple of feet and made the batsman come forward more, I think he would have got a stack more wickets.

Like Kapil he carried a heavy workload with not much at the other end and never saw a green top or a pitch with much moisture in it, so, in the main, it was a pretty thankless task getting the new ball for India, particularly at home.

The burden was increased by the growth of one-day cricket and in addition to the Tests Srinath played in 229 of them, four more than Kapil – that's the equivalent of nearly 46 Tests! Little wonder he retired at 33 years of age.

Among his outstanding performances with the ball was six for 21 at Ahmedabad against South Africa in the first Test in November 1996 when he bowled India to a 64-run win and finished with eight for 68 in the match. His best match figures, however, were not enough to stop Pakistan winning the first game of the Asia Test Championship in February 1999 at Calcutta where he took five for 46 and eight for 86 in the 46-run defeat. His accuracy and resolve were shown at Port Elizabeth in the second Test in November 2001 when, after taking six for 76 in the first innings, he got through 17 overs to take two for 28 and prevent a South African victory.

Srinath took wickets regularly rather than in spectacular bursts right from his first cap in Brisbane in November 1991 to his last appearance against the West Indies in Calcutta in November 2002, and is second only to Kapil among India's pace bowlers in number of wickets taken.

The All-Rounder

Every side needs a good class all-rounder but finding one in India is hard work. They haven't produced anybody who can remotely compare with Imran, Botham or Miller and you can't count Kapil Dev because he was primarily a bowler and didn't make anything like the amount of runs you look for from a class all-rounder.

India have relied on spinners who can bat a bit and the best of these is **Mulvantrai Himmatlal Mankad**, known throughout the cricket world by his schoolboy nickname of Vinoo. He produced some outstanding performances in a not very good team; during his 44 appearances India won only five games and he had a hand in all of them. A right hand bat who opened as well as batting up and down the order, he was a very effective orthodox slow left armer who returned some spectacular figures.

He made his debut at Lord's in the first Test after the Second World War but came to prominence on Lord Tennyson's goodwill tour of India in 1937–38 when he topped the batting and bowling averages, 62.66 with the bat and 14.53 with the ball. His lordship is reported to have said Mankad was already worth his place in any world XI. On that 1946–47 tour he did the double, making 1,120 runs and taking 129 wickets, something no tourist has done before or since and a performance good enough to make him one of *Wisden*'s five Cricketers of the Year.

In Australia in 1947–48 Mankad made three ducks but

Graeme Pollock. The first name you write down when picking any South African side.

Above: Barry Richards: only four Tests before the curtain came down.

Left: Mike Proctor, a real match winner wherever he played.

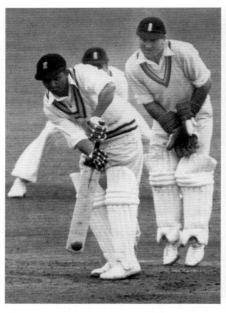

Vijay Hazare. Not much of a stylist but he didn't give up easily.

The young Sachin Tendulkar, who went on to make a big impact on the world stage.

Sunil Gavaskar, one of the two best openers of my time, consistent and run hungry.

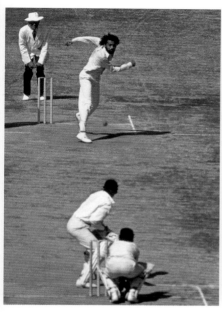

Chandrasekhar. He might have had a withered right arm, but crikey, he could bowl all right.

Bishen Bedi. Poetry in motion, perfectly balanced and a joy to watch.

Kapil Dev. Far and away the best pace bowler India has ever produced.

Prasanna, a little fellow who could spin and had subtleties of flight.

Imran Khan. He's number one, it, Mr Pakistan to cricketers all over the world.

Javed Miandad. A tough, spiky individual who loved getting up the opposition's noses.

Wasim Akram. Aggression and the ability to swing it and seam it from left arm over the wicket made him special.

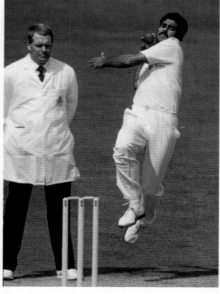

Waqar Younis. The other half of a lethal partnership with Wasim Akram.

Sir Garfield Sobers, the greatest cricketer there has
ever been, blessed with so much natural talent.

Sir Viv Richards. The swagger, the chewing gum,
the faint smile; enough to give bowlers the jitters.

George Headley. They called him 'The Black Bradman' after his mastery of Clarrie Grimmett.

Malcolm Marshall, one of the three best fast bowlers I ever faced.

Lance Gibbs. The ideal foil to fiddle a few out, 309 of them!

Curtly Ambrose. Terrific stamina brought him 405 wickets at 20.99 each.

Martin Donnelly. Only appeared in
seven Tests but remains a legend
in New Zealand.

Bert Sutcliffe and Jack Cowie. Bert became an iconic
figure in New Zealand and was rated by Wally Hammond,
while Jack's nine Tests were spread over 12 years.

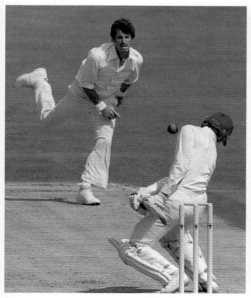

Sir Richard Hadlee. He kept you under pressure
all the time with hardly anything to hit.

Martin Crowe. In my opinion, he was thrown
into Test cricket too soon.

Muttiah Muralitharan. Ever since I first saw him, I've thought he throws it. If it's all right for him, why bother bowling properly?

Martin Donnelly. Only appeared in seven Tests but remains a legend in New Zealand.

Bert Sutcliffe and Jack Cowie. Bert became an iconic figure in New Zealand and was rated by Wally Hammond, while Jack's nine Tests were spread over 12 years.

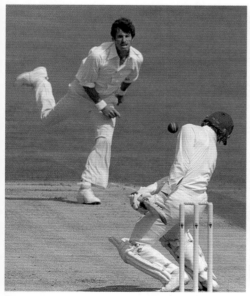

Sir Richard Hadlee. He kept you under pressure all the time with hardly anything to hit.

Martin Crowe. In my opinion, he was thrown into Test cricket too soon.

Muttiah Muralitharan. Ever since I first saw him, I've thought he throws it. If it's all right for him, why bother bowling properly?

also two centuries, 116 and 111 at Melbourne in the third and fifth Tests, and took 12 wickets in a series where the Indians were blown away 4–0. He also caused a stir in the second match at Sydney when, without prior warning, he ran out Bill Brown at the non-striker's end for backing up too far, something that was considered 'not on'; for years after to 'Mankad' somebody was a euphemism for unsporting behaviour.

On England's tour of India in 1951–52 he excelled as a spinner for the first time with 34 wickets in the five Tests at 16.97 each. At Madras in the last game of the rubber he had eight for 55 (four of them stumped) and four for 53 as India won their first match in 25 starts as a Test nation.

He missed the carnage at Headingley in the first game of the 1952 tour of England because he was the pro at Haslingden in the Lancashire League and they refused to release him, but in the second Test at Lord's he scored 72 and 184 and bowled 97 overs in the game, taking five for 196 from 73 overs in England's first innings of 537 which led to an eight-wicket England win.

He also had a major role when Pakistan played their first official Test at Delhi in October 1952, taking eight for 52 and five for 79 as India won by an innings. But despite the odd win India were a poor side and Mankad had a tremendous workload mainly because there was no one else. But he completed the Test double of 1,000 runs and 100 wickets in 23 matches, just two fewer than Ian Botham. That's pretty good considering how highly Both is regarded.

Mankad's two magic innings came at the end of 1955 with 233 against New Zealand in Bombay in December and the next month in Madras in the fifth Test he set the world record opening stand of 413 with Pankaj Roy, Mankad's the lion's share with 231.

I think the only other spinner who can come anywhere near him with the bat is **Ravishankar Jayadritha Shastri** who made his debut as a 19-year-old when he was flown out to New Zealand as a replacement for the injured Dilip Doshi in February 1981 and took six for 63 in the match. Ravi had a high action, didn't spin the ball a lot and lacked the subtlety of Bishen Bedi. His 151 wickets cost more than 40 apiece but he averaged 35.79 with the bat and I thought he played the quicks particularly well. He was often used as a stand-in opener and I think he was miles better at it than some they have tried over the years; three of his 11 centuries came from the top of the order, 206 against Australia at Sydney in January 1992, his best, 187 against England at The Oval in the third Test in August 1990 and 128 against Pakistan at Karachi in January 1983. He also shares the distinction with Garry Sobers of being the only man to hit six sixes in an over when he belted Tilak Raj, Baroda's left arm spinner, out of the Wankhede Stadium in January 1985 on his way to an unbeaten 200 for Bombay.

Ravi wasn't really a match-winner with the ball but somewhere along the way I might have to consider the heresy of leaving out Bedi to get in someone who can make runs. That wouldn't be Bishen's fault but down to India's inability to produce a genuine all-rounder. In the end I give the vote to Vinoo Mankad in my squad of 14 players because he could win matches.

The Offspinner

I need an offspinner and, for me, the choice is between Prasanna, Venkataraghavan and Harbhajan Singh.

Erapalli Anatharao Srinivas Prasanna was a real artist, a little fellow who could spin it and had subtleties of flight. He got a great loop on the ball, meaning that he got the ball up into the air and it dropped sharply, drawing the batsman forward only to find he hadn't reached the pitch of it. He made his debut in 1962 at Madras against England, taking one wicket in India's win, and went to the West Indies in 1961–62 but only played in one test. He then went back to university and was off the scene for the best part of five years. When I first came across him in the first Test of the 1967 tour of England at Leeds he was playing in only his fourth match. I made my highest score of 246 not out in that game (and was dropped for slow scoring) and Prasanna returned none for 182, but it wasn't easy against him and I thought he was a clever bowler who maybe deserved a better return than that. When he went on the 1967–68 tour of Australia he had 25 wickets at 27.44 each in the four Tests, all of them lost by India. When they went on to New Zealand in February he became the key bowler, taking 24 wickets in four Tests at 18.79 each and producing match-winning performances in three of them: six for 94 in the second innings of the first Test at Dunedin, match figures of eight for 88 in the third at Wellington, and eight for 84 in the match at Auckland, the fifth.

He liked the Kiwis all right and had his best figures against them at Auckland in January 1976 when he took three for 64 and eight for 76 to win the match and had nine for 111 to win the fourth Test against the West Indies in Madras the previous year. This was the beginning of a golden era for Indian spinners with **Srinivasaraghavan Venkataraghavan** arriving on the scene and often being preferred, sometimes for political reasons, to Prasanna. In his fourth Test Venkat had match figures of 12 for 152 from 112 overs, never bettered them in his next 53 Tests and didn't take ten in a Test again.

He played county cricket for Derbyshire so I played against him quite a few times and thought he bowled pretty flat and into my pads, more to stop me scoring than to get me out. Pretty negative stuff, I thought; while Prasanna would always be trying to lure you into a false shot, Venkat was content to stop the runs. A genuine spinner has to give it some air and they have to accept that sometimes batsmen are going to get after them, they have to be philosophical about that and of the two Prasanna is the more likely match-winner.

Harbhajan Singh comes on the scene in a completely different era when the complexion of not only Indian cricket but the whole of the game has changed. In the earlier era there were only the spinners, no seamers to speak of and it was often a case of someone getting through a couple of overs to take the gloss off the new ball and on they came. They didn't just bowl on turning pitches, they had to get through all the donkey work as well and it's much harder to win a Test if the spinners have to take all 20 wickets.

Now India have some young, aggressive seamers who are pretty decent, knock over two or three at the top of the order, and plough through a lot of the hard work, bowlers like R. P. Singh, Irfan Pathan, Zaheer, Sharma, Mohammed Asif. They make it a lot easier for the spinners who can bowl at new batsmen who haven't had time to settle in. Harbhajan has put in some mighty impressive performances, notably the two home Tests against Australia in 2001 when he had 13 for 196 as India won after following on in Calcutta and 15 for 217 in Madras when India won by two wickets. They're phenomenal performances and only Narendra Hirwani, the legspinner, can better those figures in Calcutta.

I also honestly believe that the modern offspinner is given extra help by being able to bowl the 'doosra' – the one that goes the other way – and it's been a big factor. To produce such a delivery the bowler has to open up chest on and bend his elbow – that is, throw it, as I'm convinced they do. Now that the ICC has made it legal it's been a big thing for offspinners, certainly made the game more interesting and been a huge factor in their success. If Prasanna had been allowed to bend his elbow and bowl the 'doosra' he'd have got a bucketful of wickets and I know he could do it because he demonstrated it to Sunny Gavaskar and myself in a television studio. But in the days when throwing was outlawed he wouldn't have dared to try it. Times may have changed but I'm still picking Prasanna as my offspinner.

Anil Kumble (1990–)

He's unique among current spinners because he bowls it flatter and quicker than anyone, with an armoury comprising a topspinner which bounces, a type of flipper which keeps low and skids on, googlies and although not a big spinning leggie it's there. His arm is high so that sometimes it is beyond the perpendicular which makes it harder to produce legspin but he's so quick through the air that on good pitches a lot of batsmen have started to play him as though he is a medium pacer. He's never been one to flight the ball and instead relies on his many variations combined with unerring accuracy. He's a great professional, simply loves bowling and gets through a lot of overs with no fuss, no histrionics, a captain's dream because no matter how tough the going he'll bowl. If the pitch turns or gets worn he's dynamite and I reckon if you can't read him he's nigh on unplayable. He's too quick with so much variety that you can't get down the pitch to him and in India where the soil doesn't bind together for too long he's in his element. He doesn't need the usual spinners' attributes of flight and guile because he has his own methods and if it turns he can attack and destroy sides. The best compliment I can pay him is that he's the biggest match-winner India have had since Kapil Dev and has fantastic figures to prove it. He's taken wickets all over the world on all kinds of surfaces and he's out on his own in front of the four from the golden era.

Kumble is only the second man after Jim Laker to take all

10 wickets in a Test innings when he bowled out Pakistan at Delhi in February 1999, taking 10 for 74 and 14 for 149 in the match, his best figures, and he showed rare courage when bowling against the West Indies in Antigua in May 2002 with a fractured jaw. In a match where all 11 Indians bowled in the West Indies innings, only the third time in Test history that's happened, *Wisden* said:

The most memorable image of a batsman's match was provided by a bowler, Kumble. Sheathed in head bandages like some battle-front survivor, he returned to the action on the third evening with a broken jaw. It had just been announced that he was flying home for surgery, but when he saw Tendulkar turning the ball he hurried out, went straight into the attack, and bowled 14 consecutive overs, in which he dismissed Lara and had Hooper caught off a no-ball. Only the close of play halted him; next day, he departed, and was sorely missed.

He played a leading part in winning three Tests for India, and I like match-winners. The first was at Headingley in the third Test of the 2002 series when he had match figures of seven for 139 in a victory by an innings and 46, at Multan in a win by an innings and 52 over Pakistan he had six for 72 in the second innings, and in Kingston, Jamaica, in July 2006 he bowled out the West Indies, taking six for 78 as they fell 49 runs short in the fourth Test.

Kumble went past Glenn McGrath's 563 wickets at The Oval in August 2007 and in the same match thoroughly enjoyed making his first Test hundred after 17 years and 118 matches. Third in the all-time wicket-takers' list behind Shane Warne and Muttiah Muralitharan, he's far and away the most successful Indian bowler of all time with 10 wickets in a match on eight occasions and five in an innings 35 times. And look at the overs he's got through, 6,447 in 124 matches, that's nearly 52 a Test, with a wicket every 64 balls. No one can accuse this lad of getting his wickets the easy way.

Bhagwat Subramanya Chandrasekhar (1964–79)
Bishen Singh Bedi (1966–79)

Chandra was a remarkable character with his long, bouncy run-up, quite different to most wrist-spinners who tend to toss it up, and from his high action it came at you quite quickly. His right arm was withered by polio when he was five years old and he couldn't throw with it but crikey he could certainly bowl. He'd stick the ball in his right hand and deliver topspinners, googlies and the occasional leg-spinner from the back of the hand and if there was anything in the pitch he'd find it. Because of his pace he wasn't always the most accurate but there was such a mixture of deliveries if you couldn't read him, and it wasn't easy because of his hand, you didn't always manage to put the bad ball away.

He made his debut against England in January 1964 in Bombay but made his first real impact on the same ground that October with eight for 123 in the win over a strong Australian team which included Lawry, Simpson, Burge and Booth. But like all the Indian spinners of the time he suffered from lack of support from seam bowlers. A perfect example came against the West Indies in 1966 at Bombay where Chandra took 11 for 235 in the match and got through 93 overs while the seamers managed four overs in the whole game. What a thankless task and needless to say India lost. It was a familiar scenario for all of them in a supposedly golden age of spin and explains why such clever bowlers paid rather more for their wickets than they would have done with some decent seam support.

Chandra's reputation was made at The Oval in 1971 when India beat England on their own midden for the first time in 22 Tests spread over 37 years. England were on top for most of the game and expected to set a stiff target for the Indians in their fourth innings but Chandra took six for 38, England were 101 all out and India knocked off the 174 for victory with four wickets in hand.

His fame grew with a match-winning performance against an Australian side weakened by the Packer revolution in December 1977 when he took six for 52 in both innings at Melbourne in the third Test to bring India their first victory Down Under by a margin of 222 runs and he had 28 in the series at 25.14 each. The Aussies may have lost a few players but any win in their backyard is fine.

Bishen Singh Bedi came into the side in 1966 at Calcutta against the West Indies and now the Indians had two fine spinners but still no seamers. Loose-limbed, graceful, poetry in motion, that was Bish, perfectly balanced and a joy to watch. Bowling with wonderful variety of flight and degrees of spin, he put a great loop on the ball which teasingly dropped shorter than you expected. He had a faster ball, a curved arm ball and a faster arm ball, a wonderful repertoire for all pitches and situations. If you hit him for four he'd applaud the shot but I wasn't sure if it was to get you to try and play the same stroke again; he was always setting traps for the unsuspecting. He could get you out without hurting you and it was almost a pleasure to go if he'd beaten you with a magic ball.

He got me out in the third Test at Birmingham in 1967, a strange dismissal for me, stumped for 25. I'd been dropped for the second Test for slow scoring in the first and I was terrified to play a maiden over and fretting if I missed a chance to score. That's why I was going down the pitch to him after an hour in the middle and people must have thought that 'st Engineer b Bedi' was a misprint, surely caught behind was more likely.

Against Australia in India in 1969–70, Bish had 21 wickets at 20.57 and in the Delhi Test returned five for 37 and four for 71; when England toured in 1972–73 he had 25 at 25.28 each and on the 1976–77 England tour 25 at 22.96 including six for 71 in India's only win in Bangalore. In that last series there was huge controversy during the third Test in Madras when Bish, by now captain, objected to John Lever and Bob Willis using gauze patches soaked in Vaseline to keep the sweat out of their eyes. Bish and one of the umpires claimed that it was being used to keep the ball shiny and there was an inquiry and telegrams flying backwards and forwards between the Indian board and the old Test and County Cricket Board. It seemed England's explanation had been accepted when Bish said he'd noticed the same thing earlier in the series and the whole thing blew up again. He's never been slow to speak his mind and even now as a grandee of Indian cricket controversy is never far away.

There was another row in the West Indies in April 1976 when, on a relaid pitch at Kingston, Jamaica, in the fourth and final Test the Indians took a terrible battering from Michael Holding and Wayne Daniel. Vishwanath had his finger dislocated and broken, Gaekwad was hit on the left ear and in hospital for two days and Patel had stitches when he top-edged a shot into his mouth. No helmets in those days and a ridge on a fast bowler's length made the ball rear frighteningly and dangerously. The Indians, of course, had nothing to hit back with, Madan Lal and Armanath weren't going to put the wind up anybody, and bowled only 15 overs out of 140; that's how stupid the golden age of spin was. Bedi declared in the first innings as a protest against the intimidatory bowling and in the Indian second innings everyone thought Bish had declared 12 in front in protest again at the persistent short pitched bowling and it took some time before an explanation was made that the three injured batsmen couldn't take part and Bish and Chandra had injured their hands in the field. A lot of people weren't convinced by a scorecard which registered five 'absent hurt'.

In my book Bish was a fine bowler and I never use that word carelessly. A great character who will talk about cricket until the cows come home and loved every minute on the field.

Syed Mujtaba Hussein Kirmani
(1976–86)

India have had about four keepers who could be considered
top class, Kiran More, Nayan Mongia, Faroukh Engineer
and Syed Kirmani. The glove man has got to be able to
make a few runs so I looked first at **Faroukh Maneshka
Engineer**, ebullient, enthusiastic, always with a smile on
his face and a bit of a swagger as he crossed between the
wickets. A bit of a character, he made his runs at 31.08
which isn't fantastic and not that much different from the
others; the best of them came when he opened the innings.
The third time he went in first he made 94 before lunch
against the West Indies at Madras in the third Test in
January 1967, finished with 109; that was against Wes Hall,
Charlie Griffith, Garry Sobers and Lance Gibbs, so it was
pretty impressive stuff. In 1971, batting down the order, he
did quite well at The Oval with 59 and 28 not out as India
won in England for the first time, and in five Tests at home
against England he topped the batting averages with 415
at 41.5, making 121 and 66 going in first in the final Test
in Bombay. He opened in only one of the three Tests in
England in 1974, at Lord's, and made 86 and nought but I
feel he was at his best at the top of the order. With attacking
fields set for the new ball and plenty of space, he naturally
went for his shots and worked the ball through mid wicket
brilliantly. He'd either be out very quickly or very quickly
seize the initiative from the bowlers and put his side on top
and could play with exhilarating style. But I think he should

have got more runs when he was batting down the order and two hundreds in 46 Tests isn't much to shout about. There's no way he's going to open in my team so I'm going to go for the man who is generally accepted to be the better wicketkeeper, Syed Kirmani.

Though not rated as a batsman he too made a couple of centuries and averaged 27.04, so there's not that much difference there. But Sunny Gavaskar swears by him as the number one wicketkeeper, a job he held for 12 years keeping to those fabulous spinners. That couldn't be easy, given the variety and the number of overs they got through and requires intense concentration as well as superb fitness. He had great hands and grew up with Chandra in Karnataka province which was a big help given that bowlers like Chandra can often fox the wicketkeeper as easily as the batsmen.

Kirmani made his debut at Auckland in 1976 taking over from Faroukh, had six dismissals in his second Test at Christchurch that February and finished with 198 from 88 matches, 160 caught and 38 stumped, a high percentage of stumpings for a modern wicketkeeper and testament to the quality of the Indian spinners. He made 101 not out batting at number five against Australia in the sixth Test in November 1979 when India won the match and the series, and 102 batting at number eight against England in Bombay in November 1984, the only match India won in that five-game series. I don't think there will be many objections to Kirmani being given the gloves.

The Extra Batsman

In picking the extra batsman I considered four who've made a stack of runs in their careers.

The first of these is **Pahlan Ratanji Umrigar**, universally known as Polly, who held every record in Indian cricket when he retired in 1962, most Tests, most runs, most hundreds, records that stood for 16 years until Sunil Gavaskar set new standards.

Polly had a lot of success on the subcontinent right from his debut against the West Indies in Bombay in the second Test in December 1948 and made the first of his 12 centuries in his eighth Test innings, 130 not out, against England batting at number seven in Madras in the fifth Test in February 1952, India's first victory over England for 20 years. But it was a different story later that year when India came to England and were blown away by the sheer pace of Trueman and the artistry of Bedser, Umrigar managing just 43 in seven innings. It was understandable because they had never seen pace like it and I remember Fred telling me that when Umrigar was batting at Leeds he could see Tony Lock at leg slip between Polly and the stumps. No doubt one of Fred's exaggerations but indicative of the fear which ran through the side.

Polly had a hard time on the next tour of England in 1959, struggled again and had seven poor innings and one good one when he made 118 at Manchester in the last Test of the series. Most of his hundreds were made on the slower, lower pitches of the subcontinent including his 223 against New Zealand in Hyderabad, the first Test double century for India. He also made hundreds in the Caribbean, 130 in Trinidad in 1952–53 and 172 not out on the same ground in April 1972, but Port of Spain in those days was a spinners' pitch and very similar to Indian conditions. For all his runs I worry about his ability to handle real quality pace bowling and there's going to be plenty of that around, so for that reason I'm looking elsewhere.

One guy who can play the quicks is **Dilip Balwant Vengsarkar**. Tall, slim and orthodox, he had great technique and used his height to get on top of the pacemen. He made his debut against New Zealand at Auckland in January 1976 and opened the batting in 11 of his first 13 innings before settling in at number three, and it took him 16 Tests before he made a hundred against the West Indies in Calcutta in December 1978, 157 not out. He followed that with a pair in Madras and then another century, 109 in Delhi. In July 1979 at Lord's he followed a first innings duck with 103, and in subsequent series at the famous old ground in June 1982 and 1986 he also made hundreds, 157 and 126 not out respectively, the last of them helping India to win at headquarters for the first time in 11 attempts. Incredible record that. He also made 61 and 102 not out at Leeds on the 1986 tour as India won again and had five centuries in eight Tests with 164 not out against Australia in Bombay and 153 and 156 against Sri Lanka in Nagpur and Cuttack. Seventeen hundreds in 116 Tests and an average of 42.13 doesn't really do justice to his talents.

I saw **Mohammad Azharuddin** burst upon the international scene with three hundreds in his first four Test innings on England's tour of 1984–85, and he was just amazing. Slim, with boyish good looks, he was tall and talented and could play the ball early or late with great timing and wonderful wrist work. Spectators just loved him and his ease and poise at the crease. He was brought in for the third Test of that tour and made 110 at Calcutta, 48 and 105 in India's defeat in Madras and 122 and 54 not out in the draw at Kanpur. What a start to a fantastic career which had 22 centuries from 99 matches and an average of 45.03. He made hundreds against all the major Test-playing nations and missed out on a double hundred twice, leg before for 199, his highest score, against Sri Lanka in Kanpur in December 1986 and 192 against New Zealand at Auckland in February 1990. It was a pity his career ended amid the match-fixing scandals of 2000.

But the man I'm going for is **Vangipurappu Venkata Sai Laxman**, someone, like Doctor W. G. Grace, who is widely known just by his initials. I see him as a right handed David Gower, whom he reminds me of in so many ways. He stands up at the crease, there's limited foot movement but the key is his weight is always going forward into the shot. He takes the ball at the top of the bounce with sublime timing. Just like Gower, the bowlers always feel they have a chance with him because he's not always to the pitch of the ball, giving it more time to move and do something, but VVS is very straight on front or back foot. You don't see any clever-clogs shots, reverse sweeps or slogs, because he is so good he doesn't need to. I've seen bowlers produce nigh on identical deliveries, pitching in the same area and VVS play two completely different shots to different parts of the field. What's more, he gets runs under pressure and there's no better example than when he turned the second Test of the series with Australia on its head in March 2001. Following on 274 in arrears VVS made an almighty 281 in 10 and a half hours with 44 fours and even clobbered Shane

Warne, bowling around the wicket into the rough, with shots against the spin. That takes some doing, I can tell you – the great legspinner finished with one for 152 from 34 overs. On the 2003 tour Down Under he made 148 at Adelaide in the second Test and 178 at Sydney in the fifth.

The Aussies have been the best side in the world for the thick end of 20 years so anyone who makes runs against them has to be a bit special. Well, VVS has made five of his 12 hundreds against them and I judge people not by how many runs or hundreds they've got but whom they made them against and in what circumstances. That's why VVS is my man.

India

SQUAD	RESERVES
Kapil Dev	Ravi Shastri
Sunil Gavaskar	Venkat (Srinivasaraghavan Venkataraghavan)
Sachin Tendulkar	
	Harbhajan Singh
Rahul Dravid	
	Faroukh Engineer
Vijay Merchant	
	Pahlan Umrigar
Vijay Hazare	
	Dilip Vengsarkar
Javagal Srinath	
	Mohammad Azharuddin
Vinoo Mankad	
	Bishen Bedi
E. A. S. Prasanna	
Anil Kumble	
Chandra (Bhagwat Chandrasekhar)	
Syed Kirmani	
V. V. S. Laxman	

Pakistan

Mohammad Imran Khan (1971–92)

You can't talk about Pakistan cricket without invoking his name. He is the number one, it, Mr Pakistan to cricketers all over the world. In his country's short history they have turned out some very talented players, individually gifted, quiet, well-mannered, kind and generous people. But collectively, at best they've been like unruly children and at worst a rabble, fighting each other instead of the opposition. I always felt that if someone could come along and harness all that talent they would be capable of beating anyone in the world but so often they were riven by in-fighting, intrigue, interference by ex-players, politicians and just about anyone with an axe to grind. It became a free for all.

'Immy' was the best ever at holding it all together and the exception to everything that had gone before, so professional, disciplined, totally committed and clear thinking. He had such desire, such a forceful personality, was so tough, that I admire him tremendously. Off the field he was cricket's heart-throb and made girls as weak at the knees as the batsmen who faced him with a wonderful physique which was the result of hard training. On the field he was a charismatic captain who led by example. No one in cricket worked harder than he did and by his effort and all-round talent he persuaded others who saw him train and practise that they couldn't give anything less than their best because they knew he wouldn't accept it. He had that priceless ability to get the best out of people and a great cricket brain; he knew what he expected of himself and others. That was good for Pakistan.

We always talk about Sir Richard Hadlee, Kapil Dev and Sir Ian Botham as the great bowling all-rounders of the 1970s and '80s but Imran tops the lot. Just look at his record and remember he was bowling on those flat, barren pitches in Pakistan where a sheep couldn't find a blade of grass.

He made his Test debut at Birmingham against England in 1971 when he was run out for five, didn't take a wicket in 28 overs and wasn't picked again for three years. While up at Oxford University he made his reputation as a batsman with a hundred in each innings against Nottinghamshire in The Parks in 1974 and another that summer, 170 against Northamptonshire on the same ground. He played in all three Tests in England in 1974 but did nothing special with 92 runs and five wickets.

In the first two Tests on the Australian tour of 1976–77 in Adelaide and Melbourne he totalled 86 in four innings and had six wickets for 354 runs before the party moved down to Sydney for the last game in the series. I was in Australia at the time playing for Waverley and because our ground was being dug up we were practising at the SCG at the same time as the tourists. I knew Mushtaq Mohammad, the skipper, and Asif Iqbal, the vice captain, from county cricket and they asked what I thought of their bowling. I told them that Sarfraz Nawaz, who played for Northamptonshire, was bowling an 'English line', too straight for Australia, and should bowl outside off stump. At that time 'Immy' was nothing more than a lively medium pacer and I told 'Mushy' that he had the physique to bowl genuinely quick and he should use him to go flat out in short spells and be a real strike bowler. They tried it in Brisbane against Queensland and in the Test in Sydney Imran, bowling like lightning, had six for 102 and six for 63, in the second innings getting through 19.7 eight-ball overs in a spell broken only by the tea interval. Sarfraz finished with six wickets in the match for 119 and Imran had 12 for 165 as Pakistan won for the first time Down Under. I was in both dressing rooms and the Aussies were amazed at his stamina and resilience. Rod Marsh said, 'He just didn't get tired. You'd hit him for four and he'd come back at you faster than ever.'

I think I might have had a part in the transformation but I don't know why I should be doing Imran any favours because he stopped me making a century against all first class opposition when he bowled me for 89 at The Parks in May 1974. This proved to be the nearest I came to completing the clean sweep, the highest score I made against the Dark Blues in eight attempts!

Imran went to play in Kerry Packer's World Series Cricket for two years but came back with 123 against the West Indies in Lahore, 16 wickets at 19.5 in the three Tests in Australia in November 1981 and had match figures of 14 for 116 against Sri Lanka in Lahore in March 1982. He first captained Pakistan on the tour of England in 1982 and although they lost the three-match rubber 2–1 he was outstanding with 21 wickets at 18.57 and 212 runs at an average of 53.

Back home in 1982–83 he had 13 wickets in three defeats in the Tests against Australia, then came India the same winter. This was World War Three to both countries and Pakistan won the six-match series 3–0. Imran had three for 19 and eight for 60 in Karachi in the second game and in the next, at Faisalabad, six for 98, five for 82 and 117, incredible stuff. In the six Tests he took 35 wickets at 12.91 each and finished the winter with 48 victims. At the age of 30 he was a god.

Astonishingly, the selectors removed him as captain and appointed Zaheer Abbas in his place for the 1983–84 tour of Australia, but the president of the Pakistan Board of Control sacked the selectors, reinstated him and allowed Imran to pick a new team. That's how big he was. In the event he was suffering from a stress fracture of the left shin, wasn't really fit and missed the first three Tests. In the fourth, in Melbourne, playing as a batsman, he made 83 and an unbeaten 72.

In the winter of 1984–85 he played for New South Wales and helped them win the Sheffield Shield, taking 25 wickets in six games at 19.52 including nine for 100 in the one-wicket win over Queensland in the final at Sydney.

When Sri Lanka went to Pakistan in 1985–86 he claimed nine for 95 at Sialkot in the second Test and, even on a big spinners' pitch in the next at Karachi, he had five for 64 in the match to finish with 17 wickets at 15.8 each. In the West Indies in October 1986 he took 18 wickets in the three-match series at 11.11 each but wickets were hard to come by in India in 1987 where four of the five games were drawn, Pakistan winning in Ahmedebad, but there was compensation with 135 in the first Test in Madras.

He produced the series-winning performance on the 1987 tour of England with 10 for 77 in the innings and an 18-run victory at Leeds in the third Test and made sure England didn't get back into it with eight for 190 in the fourth at Birmingham and a century, 118, at The Oval, both matches being drawn.

In the Caribbean in 1987–88 he had 23 wickets in the three-Test rubber at 18 each and there were a few who could play in that West Indies side like Desmond Haynes, Gordon Greenidge and Ritchie Richardson to name but three.

Wherever Imran played he led from the front and produced match-winning performances not just from himself but from those around him. To average 37.69 mainly from number seven in the order and take 362 wickets at 22.81 says it all.

Hanif Mohammad (1952–69)

The 'Little Master' as he is known became a legend in his own lifetime and will always be synonymous with Pakistan's birth as an international cricket nation. But to fully understand his enormous contribution it's important to put his 3,915 Test match runs at an average of 43.98 in the context of the times. Partition in 1947 was followed by years of bloodshed and I've seen those old black and white films of thousands of people trudging towards their new homeland with animals, children and possessions. There were murders galore and amid the turmoil of the times survival was the name of the game.

For a teenager to even think about playing cricket in those circumstances beggars belief but only five years after the split with India, in October 1952, the 18-year-old Hanif marked his Test debut against them in Delhi with a half century in an innings defeat. He made four hundreds in the other first class matches on tour which is a tremendous performance for a kid just finding his feet. It's difficult to grasp at this distance in time what growing up in that turbulent era must have been like, let alone playing Test cricket.

After that five-match series Pakistan came to England in 1954 and Hanif was faced with green, seaming grass pitches for the first time and an England attack made up of Statham, Tyson, Bedser, Appleyard, Laker, Wardle and Bailey. I wouldn't have found it easy to play against that lot on a flat one. By the time he was 20 years of age he'd nine

Tests under his belt. At the same age I'd only just started playing for Yorkshire seconds and he was facing an attack like that on uncovered pitches – definitely a steep learning curve.

Back at home in the second Test against India he made the first hundred on home soil by a Pakistan batsman, 142 on the matting pitch at Bahawalpur. In Dacca, before it became part of Bangladesh, he made 103 against New Zealand, but the Test innings he will always be remembered for came in January 1958 on Pakistan's first tour of the West Indies. Trailing by 473 on the first innings, Hanif made an incredible 337 when Pakistan followed on, spending 16 hours 10 minutes at the crease, to earn a draw. Monumental concentration and stamina from the 24-year-old who was only 27 runs short of Len Hutton's record Test score when he was caught behind.

He held the record for the highest first class score until Brian Lara surpassed his 499 made for Karachi against Bahawalpur in January 1959. He batted 635 minutes and hit 64 fours and was then run out going for the 500th run. Ten and a half hours and then run out going for a single? It wouldn't have happened to me, I can tell you.

Hanif was without any doubt the best batsman of the fledgling nation with a fabulous defence, intense concentration and bottomless reserves of stamina. He proved his credentials again at Dacca in the second Test of 1961–62 against England, spending just short of 15 hours at the wicket as he made a century in each innings, 111 in 497 minutes in the first followed by 104 in 396 minutes.

The uncovered pitches in England and Trueman, Statham and the very quick David Larter of Northamptonshire confined him to 177 runs on the 1962 tour but he was captain and wicketkeeper in the one Test against Australia in Melbourne in 1964, taking over from the injured Abdul Kadir behind the stumps and making 104 and 93 with the bat to earn a creditable draw. On the tour of New Zealand which followed he scored 100 not out in Christchurch in the third Test and when the Kiwis went to Pakistan he made an unbeaten 203 at Lahore in the second Test of 1965.

Hanif finally came to terms with English conditions in 1967 with a patient, unbeaten 187 at Lord's in just over nine hours, made out of 354 with the next highest score 76 from Asif Iqbal, an innings which went a long way to making him one of *Wisden*'s five Cricketers of the Year in 1968.

In the last of his 55 Tests at Karachi Hanif played with his two brothers, Sadiq and Mushtaq, in the same side against New Zealand, only the third time three brothers have played in a Test and only the second occasion they have been on the same team. Dr William Gilbert Grace played with his older and younger brothers Edward and George against Australia at The Oval in 1880, and in 1892 in Cape Town Frank Hearne played for South Africa while his brothers George and Alec played their only Tests for England, with cousin Jack in the team for good measure.

Hanif Mohammad was there at the emergence of the nation on the international stage and with 12 members of his family having played first class cricket he can justly be called the father of Pakistan cricket.

Fazal Mahmood (1952–62)

Fazal would have been a certainty for India's tour of Australia in 1947–48 but with partition looming he stood down and made his debut along with Hanif in Pakistan's first ever Test in Delhi in October 1952.

They called him the Asian Alec Bedser and Fazal is the best right arm fast medium bowler the country has ever produced. He had a solid build and, like Alec, had a great command of line and length and bowled leg-cutters and nip-backers to great effect. On matting he was devastating and after an ordinary start in that first Test at Delhi he was a different proposition on the jute matting of the University Ground at Lucknow in the next game. He bowled Pakistan to their first win by an innings and 43 with five for 52 in the first innings when India were sent packing for 106 and seven for 42 in the second. Match figures of 12 for 94 in your second Test, not bad going. But on grass at Bombay he had none for 133 in the match from 46.2 overs to prove it's a funny old game.

It was on the 1954 tour to England that he really made his name with a fantastic performance in the fourth and final Test at The Oval. Pakistan hadn't looked like beating England in the first three matches but had lost only once, going down by an innings and 129 at Trent Bridge. But against a batting line-up which had Len Hutton, Reg Simpson, Peter May, Denis Compton and Tom Graveney as the first five, Fazal had six for 53 as England were bowled out for 130. Then, needing 168 to win, he took six for 46 from 30 overs of high class seam bowling to bring Pakistan a 24-run victory. It was a magnificent performance, and not surprisingly *Wisden* made him one of the five Cricketers of the Year for 1955. The 1–1 draw in the series really put Pakistan cricket on the map.

In October 1956 Australia made their first trip to Pakistan for the inaugural Test between the two sides and a team boasting Colin MacDonald, Neil Harvey, Ian Craig, Keith Miller, Richie Benaud, Ray Lindwall and Alan Davidson were routed for 80 on the matting at Karachi with Fazal taking six for 34 from 27 overs. They did better second time around, Benaud top scoring with 56, but in the conditions Fazal was far, far too good for them, returning seven for 80 from 48 overs as Pakistan won by nine wickets.

There was a chastening experience on the tour to the Caribbean in 1957–58 with Fazal bowling 179.2 overs in the first four Tests, taking 12 wickets for 646 which included two for 247 during Garry Sobers' world record 365 not out at Kingston where he put on 446 for the second wicket with Conrad Hunte as West Indies declared at 790 for three. You'd think that was enough to break any man's spirit and make him give up but Fazal showed his immense resources by coming back in the last match of the series at Port of Spain to have six for 83 and two for 35 as Pakistan won by an innings and one run.

It had taken a lot to recover from that Kingston hiding and in 1958–59 they made him captain when the West Indies toured Pakistan and the home side won the first two matches in Karachi and Dacca. Fazal took four for 35 and three for 89 in the first game and six for 34 and six for 66 in the second to prove his credentials as a match-winning bowler. When Australia came back for three Tests Fazal missed the second but had five for 71 in the defeat at Dacca and five for 74 in the draw in Karachi.

After a drawn five-Test series in India where both sides were scared of defeat because of the national shame it would have brought, Fazal lost the captaincy. He was beginning to lose a bit of nip off the pitch and wasn't selected for the tour of England in 1962, but was eventually flown in as a replacement for injured bowlers. He got through 60 overs to take three for 130 at Trent Bridge in the fourth Test and two for 202 from 53 overs at The Oval where the legend began.

But he'd done his bit. His performances with the ball won Test matches and along with Hanif they were the great players of their era in a team struggling to get a foot on the world stage as Sri Lanka and, to a much lesser extent, Bangladesh were to do later. Pakistan owes Fazal, who died in 2005, a great debt.

Wasim Akram (1985–2002)
Waqar Younis Maitla (1989–2003)

Wasim was the first on the world stage, making his debut in January 1985 in the second Test against New Zealand in Auckland, and it didn't take him long to show how good he was. It may have been an inauspicious start with two for 105 but in his second Test in Dunedin he took five for 56 and five for 72, 10 in the match for 128 from 59 overs. He was only 19 years old.

He didn't do much to catch the eye in the next half dozen or so Tests but he was learning his trade and still picking up wickets including six for 91 against the West Indies in Faisalabad.

What made him special was his aggression and his ability to swing it and seam it from left arm over the wicket and, being tall and well built, he got bounce. He took shortish, quick steps in his run-up followed by a fast, whippy action that almost made him bowl through the delivery stride. What made him even more special and very dangerous was that he learned to bowl around the wicket with devastating pace and accuracy. It was phenomenal the way he could move the ball in and out from wide on the crease and he destroyed England's middle order in the World Cup in Melbourne. I remember Allan Lamb getting an absolute cracker which swung in at pace, pitched middle and hit off, the stuff of legend. You couldn't just prop forward to him either because he'd pin you; he was miles too quick for that.

Wasim developed into a fantastic cricketer and added to

his talents with the first of three centuries in Adelaide against Australia in the second Test of the 1990 series, making 123 to follow figures of six for 92 and five for 98 in the first Test in Brisbane in January. On the back of bowling like that Pakistan should have been winning but too often the batsmen weren't up to it and his efforts went to waste.

Against the West Indies on home soil in November the same year he had 21 wickets in three Tests at 14.19 and in the Test in Lahore came on second change and took four wickets in five balls, one of only three men to record the feat in Test history. To do that on the flat, dry pitches in Pakistan is special. You're OK with the new ball but after that it's bloody hard work, especially for the seamers.

Together with Waqar, Wasim destroyed England at The Oval in 1992, returning nine for 103, his partner six for 89, and he went on taking wickets all over the world. In three Tests in New Zealand in February 1994 Wasim took 25 wickets at 17.24 including his best of seven for 119 in Wellington. But perhaps his most astonishing feat came against a pretty strong Zimbabwe side which included the Flower brothers, David Houghton, Alistair Campbell and the Strang brothers at Sheikhupara Stadium in October 1996. He hit an unbeaten 257 with 12 sixes and 22 fours, an innings I'm not likely to forget because every time we meet in commentary boxes round the world he asks me what my highest score was. When I tell him his best score was only 11 more than mine he adds the killer: 'Yes, Geoffrey, but I also got 400 wickets.' I suppose that just shades it!

His liaison with Waqar puts the pair right up there alongside, if not in front of, other great fast bowling combinations like Trueman and Statham and Lillee and Thomson. Waqar started four years later with four for 80 on his debut, aged 18, against India in Karachi in November 1989, and in the three-match home series with New Zealand the following year had 29 wickets at 10.86 each, including seven for 76 in Faisalabad, his best Test figures.

His stats are absolutely out of this world with a wicket every 43.49 balls, a terrific strike rate, and in tandem with his partner, it was one of the great sights in cricket to see them in action. Waqar had a long run-up, accelerating slowly before the legs started pumping and there was a sense of expectation that something extraordinary was about to happen every time he let the ball go.

To add to their repertoire they were just about as deadly once the shine had gone and masters of reverse swing with the old ball. Waqar could deliver very fast, inswinging toe-crushers and although all batsmen knew the yorker was coming they couldn't do anything about it. He also had a sharp bouncer to keep the batsmen honest and if that wasn't enough he could also straighten the inswinger a fraction off the pitch or even shape the ball out a little. There was no fuss, no histrionics, no cussing or sledging, he just got on with the demolition job. I was so impressed with them that I remember saying during the 1992 series that this pair could bowl out England 'with an orange', and they did.

In the winter of 1992–93 Waqar took 19 wickets at 22.5 in a three-Test series in the Caribbean and at home against Zimbabwe, still a decent side, in December 1993 had 27 wickets in three Tests at 13.81 including his best match figures of 13 for 135 in Karachi. In two Tests in Sri Lanka he had 14 wickets at 16.5 and 16 at 21.12 in the three-game series in South Africa including 10 for 123 in the match at Port Elizabeth where it's pretty flat. It was fitting that Wasim should take his 400th wicket in the same match where Waqar reached 300, the first Test against Sri Lanka in Colombo in June 2000, because they were exceptionally good and along with Imran the real strength of my Pakistan team.

These three provide the real quality firepower needed against the best in the world and they don't come much better than this trio.

Mohammad Javed Miandad Khan
(1976–93)

What ever you think about Javed, you can't ignore Pakistan's leading Test match run maker, a superb batsman with wonderful hands. If you wanted to learn to play with soft hands he was the man to watch, he never went hard at the ball, was never rigid in his strokeplay. If you can bat with relaxed hands and you've also got that nimble footwork of his you're three parts of the way to being a great batsman.

He was a tough, spiky individual who loved getting up the opposition's nose. He'd call for two when there was never a second run, he'd irritate fielders and upset the bowlers and it's fair to say that his behaviour didn't win him many friends. There was also the suspicion that he got away with murder on home turf before neutral umpires because Pakistan officials were afraid to give him out LBW. I don't know about that but it's a fact that he was playing his 50th innings in his 35th Test before a bowler won a leg before verdict over him in Pakistan, to Sri Lanka's Ravi Ratnayeke in Sialkot in October 1985. For good measure he went the same way in his next Test innings, this time to Ashantha de Mel in Karachi.

He made a century (163) on his debut as a 19-year-old against New Zealand in Lahore in the first Test of the 1975–76 series, and in his home city of Karachi, in only his third innings, scored 206, the first of six double centuries. The first hundred came off only 77 balls and he had a hundred before lunch batting at number four! That's not bad for a teenager.

I first came across Javed in 1977–78 when I was a seasoned Test player and he was a youngster. He could be difficult even then, but I got on well with him because I think there was a mutual respect. If you were straight with him, no problem, but if you tried to take a yard he'd want three back. He was always up for a fight with anyone looking for confrontation. He never saw batting as an aesthetic pursuit, 'play up and play the game' was not for him. He saw the whole thing as a battle and there were a couple of incidents on that tour where I had to calm things down. Our bowlers were fed up at having LBW appeals turned down, Javed taking the mickey out of fielders and generally getting up everyone's nose. In the fierce heat on flat pitches where it's not easy to get anyone out it was clear to see how Javed could wind them up, and in Australia on the 1981–82 tour things boiled over in the first Test in Perth when Dennis Lillee lost his head, deliberately impeded him as he went for a run and then aimed a kick at him. Javed raised his bat like a club and would no doubt have clobbered him if the umpire hadn't stepped in to keep them apart. Lillee claimed he was provoked by abuse from Javed but he was suspended for two one-day internationals as a result.

The secret of his huge aggregate of 8,832 runs at an average of 52.57 is that when he got in he made *big* scores. Nine of his 23 hundreds were worth more than 150, the best at home being 280 not out at Hyderabad against India in 1982–83, the highest abroad 271 in Auckland against New Zealand in 1989–90. He was also the first Pakistan batsman to make a century in each innings of a Test match since Hanif Mohammad in 1962 when he made 104 and 103 not out at Hyderabad against New Zealand in 1984–85.

His runs alone would make him worth his place but add in that love of a fight, his desire to take bowlers on at their own game, be it sledging, stares or finger pointing, whatever, Javed's adrenalin was pumping and he gave as good as he got, and sometimes better. I've always been a big fan of his batting and got on well with him.

Abdul Qadir Khan (1977–90)

Pakistan haven't had too many legspinners with Intikhab Alam and Mushtaq Ahmed having quite good records but I go for Abdul Qadir because I feel he's got a bit more in his bag of tricks.

I played in the series when he made his debut, the first Test of the 1977–78 rubber at Lahore, where he returned one for 82, but in the second match in Hyderabad he routed us, taking six for 44 from 24 overs. He didn't get me though; I told him he wouldn't get me out and added that I wouldn't be padding him away either. I also got the umpires to agree that if the ball pitched outside the leg stump and hit me playing back they wouldn't give me out leg before. It was a bit of psychology on the officials and a bit of kidology on the bowler although I felt pretty confident against legspin because I had practised at Johnny Lawrence's 'indoor school' (a freezing cold converted greenhouse) every winter from the age of nine. Johnny was that very rare commodity in Yorkshire, a right arm wrist-spinner, who became my coach and mentor. He had played with success for Somerset so I was taught to understand the art: watch the hand carefully and never trust entirely what you see. I made 79 out of 191 all out in the first innings before Derek Randall ran me out (getting his own back for 1977 at Nottingham, I always joke with him) and an unbeaten century in the second as Mike Brearley and I put on 185 for the first wicket to comfortably save the game.

Abdul, who bowled in plimsolls in that first match, had boundless energy with good days and expensive days but he could be a match-winner and that's what Imran saw in him. It takes a special talent to bowl leggers and a special captain to understand the cause and effect of what the bowler is trying to do.

He was hugely successful on the dry pitches of his native land and no one has more wickets for Pakistan in home Tests than his 168 at 26.82 apiece from 40 games. Overseas his figures were less impressive: 10 for 406 in England in 1982, 12 for 732 in four Tests in Australia in 1983–84 and he was sent home for disciplinary reasons from the New Zealand tour of 1984–85. In England in 1987 he had 11 in the series at 40.9 each; in all 68 wickets from 37 overseas Tests but despite the lack of wickets he always wanted to bowl.

Back on home soil the following winter, 1987–88, he destroyed England with nine for 56 in the first innings of the first Test at Lahore and four for 45 in the second as Pakistan won by an innings and 87 runs. Only Imran has better match figures in Pakistan history than his 13 for 101, ending the three-match series with 30 wickets at 14.56 each. The only side he never did much against at home or away was India and that had as much to do with their greater know-how against spin as anything else.

Saeed Anwar (1990–2001)
Mushtaq Mohammad (1959–79)

Finding an opening partner for Hanif poses a bit of a problem because most of the Pakistan batsmen don't want to face the new ball and it's easy to see why. On their flat, dry, grassless mud pitches the shiny, hard ball zips through with pace and bounce and it's the best time to get people out. After 25 overs the ball tends to get dirty, scuffs up, there's little seam movement, no swing and it bounces about stump high so it's a lot easier and they're all queuing up to bat in the middle order. Even Hanif floated up and down and that's why no one ever seems to stay in one place. Sometimes you think they've drawn the names out of a hat rather than pick specialists in each position.

Going in first is bloody tough, take it from me, and you've got to want to do the job; batting later is not so bad because you can get forward to most bowlers and still have time to rock back to pull, hook, cut or just duck. That's why Pakistan players have had so much trouble overseas when they come across bouncy or seaming pitches; these are conditions they rarely see and they're in trouble. It's the nature of their upbringing – where we grow up and learn our cricket dictates how we play.

I considered Mudassar Nazar, a careful player, good at wearing bowlers down with super concentration and stamina, the sort to give an innings a good platform. He rarely played an extravagant shot and if it wasn't pretty to watch it was effective. But if I have Hanif I prefer the opposite type as a partner and although a strokemaker like Majid Khan did open the innings I am going for someone who preferred to do the job all the time.

Saeed Anwar, a left hander, is the ideal complement to Hanif. The left–right handed combination poses problems for bowlers who have to keep changing their line of attack and he was a lovely, fluent strokemaker. In many respects he was like David Gower – poise, grace, timing and always giving the bowlers a chance. But both got a lot of runs and kept the scoreboard moving and with Hanif occupying the crease for long periods it's essential to have someone at the other end who is going to play a few shots. So for me it's Saeed who gets the vote.

Looking at the middle order it's very, very difficult to choose between Majid, Zaheer, Mushtaq, Inzamam and Mohammad Yousuf but in the end I have to make a judgement based on how I've seen them play, their records and the needs of my squad. They are all top batsmen but after Hanif, Saeed and Javed, I go for Hanif's youngest brother, Mushtaq. I've only one spinner, Abdul Qadir, in my line-up, so I need a batsman who can do a bit with the ball and Mushy is a cricketer I like a lot. Stocky, versatile, smiling and cheeky, he's a lovable guy and he had a 20-year career with Pakistan, a nation which didn't get many Tests in its early years and was mostly confined to three-match series.

As a legspinner he had strong, flexible wrists and it was hard to pick his googly; as a batsman he had plenty of concentration and could change gear according to the state of the game, playing carefully or attacking.

When he was given his first cap in March 1959 in the third game against the West Indies in Lahore, Mushtaq was the youngest ever Test player at 15 years and 124 days, batted at number eight and made 14 and four. Picked as a batsman he found Wes Hall and Sonny Ramadhin too good and he missed the next three Tests. But batting him at number eight – give us a break! Although people mature quite quickly in Pakistan someone made a mistake.

In India in 1960–61 he played in all five Tests and made 101 at Delhi in the fifth in only his eighth innings and in February 1962 scored 109 against England in Karachi while still not much more than a kid. In England in 1962 he hit 55 and 100 in the fourth Test at Trent Bridge to prove his ability in different conditions but for me he didn't bowl enough for Pakistan. They usually had two spinners in the side and clearly the specialists had first choice of when to bowl; Mushy was only used as a last resort. To me that was a mistake. He was better than that and should have bowled a lot more. He was a big spinner of the ball, had a topspinner and a good googly. That googly was so hard to spot. I remember in one game against Yorkshire at Bradford Park Avenue, George Sharp, the wicketkeeper at Northamptonshire where Mushy played his county cricket, moving outside off stump anticipating the legspinner only for the googly to go the other way and on for four byes. In that 1962 series the Pakistani spinners took four wickets, England's 20, yet Mushy bowled only nine balls in five games. Someone got it horribly wrong.

He didn't appear again in the Test side until the 1967 tour of England by which time he had started to bowl a bit more and took nine wickets in the series at 17.44 apiece including four for 80 at The Oval. It seemed he only got an over or two when others failed but his skill with the ball could be a match-winner and he proved it against New Zealand in February 1973 when he followed up a double hundred by taking five for 49 to bowl out the Kiwis in their second innings and bring victory by an innings and 166 runs.

The runs still came, 121 in the third Test against Australia in Sydney in January 1973, 157 against England in Hyderabad in the second Test of the 1972–73 tour and he was made captain for the two Tests at home with New Zealand scoring 101 in the win at Hyderabad and 107 in the draw in Karachi.

He led his country on the tours to Australia and the Caribbean in 1976–77 and produced a match-winning performance in the fourth Test against the West Indies at Port of Spain, Trinidad, making 121 and 56 and taking five for 28 and three for 69 in a 266-run win.

Just as he was getting his feet under the table along came World Series Cricket in 1977–78. Mushy joined Imran, Majid, Zaheer and Asif in signing for Kerry Packer amid uproar as the establishment accused the Australian entrepreneur of trying to destroy the game. Opinions were sharply divided; there were those who said international cricket was not a closed shop and any player could play for anyone they chose, and others who said Packer was tearing up the fabric of the game and striking at the very heart of cricket. The burly Australian with his 'pyjama game' was castigated and criticized the world over and by the time England arrived in Pakistan for the 1977–78 tour Packer was anxious to build bridges and try and pour a bit of oil on the very troubled waters. In an attempt to prove he was not trying to split cricket Packer agreed to release players when they were not required for World Series games and Mushy, Imran and Zaheer flew back to Pakistan to play in the third Test in Karachi. I was captain and our players were not best pleased. Meetings were held and votes taken and even the milder, quieter players like Bob Taylor and John Lever were vehemently against the Packer players being allowed to play. If England's 'defectors' Derek Underwood, Denis Amiss and Tony Greig had been allowed back into the side some of them would have been out of a job; the feeling was that you couldn't have your cake and eat it. After the unanimous vote I told the Pakistan officials and selectors that if their three Packer players were picked there wouldn't be a third Test, we wouldn't play. There were all manner of phone calls back and forth and while the Test and County Cricket Board welcomed the players' support against Packer they pointed out that they had a contractual obligation to the Pakistan board so we must play. I think Doug Insole, the chairman of the England committee, believed I was behind it and tried to pressurize me into getting the team to play, talking about leadership and the role of the captain. He implied if I wanted to keep the job I'd have to make them get on the field. I said, 'No, I agree with the team,' and after talking to the mild-mannered Kenny Barrington, who was part of the management team and the sort of man who wouldn't say boo to a goose, Insole realized the depth of feeling in the dressing room.

On the day before the game we stood in the empty stadium and I told the Pakistan officials point blank, 'If they play, we'll be going home.' So they didn't pick them.

In 1978–79, even though by now World Series Cricket was under way, Packer released players when they were not in action and Mushy was back as captain, joined by Majid, Zaheer, Imran and Asif for the home series with India and everything in the garden was rosy. Morals and scruples just didn't come into it. On the tour of New Zealand only Mushy was available for the first Test but the others turned up for the second and third matches. Hard luck on those who lost their place, wasn't it?

It's interesting that when Pakistan went to Australia for two Tests in March 1979 they played their Packer contingent but the Aussies didn't pick theirs. It was a different issue for them because the schism had occurred on their own doorstep and was a much bigger bone of contention, not least because England were out there playing an Ashes series at the time.

The feelings still ran deep and tempers were short between Pakistan and the Australians. *Wisden* records that in the first of the games in Melbourne 'two Australian players and one Pakistani were cheated out'. In one bust-up Rodney Hogg was run out after leaving his crease before the ball was dead and although Mushy asked the umpire to revoke the decision he refused and a disgusted Hogg took a swipe at the stumps as he departed. Graham Yallop, the captain, said afterwards that the biggest surprise in the whole incident was that Hogg left one stump standing in the ground.

Mushy had finally had enough and bowed out after that series, completing 20 years as a Test cricketer while he was still only 36 years of age.

Wasim Bari (1967–84)

I go for Wasim in front of keepers like Imtiaz Ahmed, who had a batting average of just under 30, because he was the tops with the gloves, a real expert behind the stumps. Alan Knott told me Wasim had great hands and, watching him, it was lovely the way the ball just disappeared into his gloves. There was no shouting or carrying on, he just got on with the job. It's not rowdy wicketkeepers who never shut up that bother me, it's the bloke who catches every nick and with bowlers like Wasim, Waqar and Imran in my side that's the sort of man I want, someone who holds on to everything that comes his way.

He made his debut at Lord's in July 1967, was virtually a fixture in the side for 17 years and in 81 Tests had 228 victims, some 81 more than his nearest rival Moin Khan.

At Leeds in July 1971 he achieved the then world record of eight catches in a Test match, holding five in the first innings (I was the fourth after making 112) and three in the second and they made him captain for the three-match series against England in 1977–78. It was a pretty thankless job with all the big names like Majid, Imran and Asif defecting to World Series Cricket, but I was impressed with the way he went about his business during a turbulent time for Pakistan cricket. I was vice captain on that tour and took over for the third Test in Karachi after Mike Brearley had his arm broken between Tests by Sikander Bakht, and I spent some time with Wasim when we were invited to tea with the President, General Zia. It was a bit of a dash, a quick wash, a change of shoes, blazer on over whites and into the heavily guarded car for the drive to the presidential palace, but the General, who was also the head of the Pakistan cricket board, was really clued up and interested in Wasim's view of the situation. Not long after, the General was blown up in a mystery explosion aboard a military plane and no one knows what really caused it; was it by accident or design?

Wasim showed his calm, intelligent approach to problems on and off the field and never allowed them to interfere with his excellent work on it. In February 1979 in Auckland in the third Test against New Zealand, he caught seven of the first eight to create a new world record in the first innings but had to give up the gauntlets due to injuries to his thigh and ankle. Who knows, he might have created a new record for dismissals in a match but, as it was, Bob Taylor equalled his achievement in the Jubilee Test against India at Bombay a year later.

Batting mainly down the order, his average was only 15.88 and I accept the current thinking that a wicketkeeper must be able to contribute runs, but when they are as good as him behind the stumps I'm prepared to make an exception. You've got to go with the best in a specialist position and I think the only exception is Australia's Adam Gilchrist with his astonishing batting average.

Majid Jahangir Khan (1964–83)
Asif Iqbal Razvi (1964–80)

For the one remaining batting place you could really spin a coin because there's not that much to choose between any of the candidates. Looking at Majid Khan I got the impression that he wasn't that interested most of the time but deep down he was a very composed, quietly confident individual with a great technique. Softly spoken, unassuming, he was never rushed or hurried into anything and while he had that inner self-belief he was never conceited.

Majid had a distinctly moderate start to an international career in which he became renowned for his princely driving and domination of bowlers. He made his Test debut at the age of 18 against Australia in Karachi in October 1964, batting at number eight but opening the bowling. The following winter against New Zealand he took the new ball in all three Tests without much success, one wicket in each of them, but in the second match, in Lahore, he made 80 and 44 coming in at number seven. He had a rough time in England in 1967, making just 38 runs in six innings. Pakistan prides itself on picking youngsters who mature early as if it's some big deal, but it's very rare for them to find their feet. Indeed, Majid had a poor time in England in 1971 as well, playing in only two of the three Tests and averaging 35.9. So you think, he's been around the Test scene for seven years, played in 11 Tests, made one half century and taken 12 wickets, nothing remarkable; has it been too much, too soon? The old saying is that if you're good enough, you're old enough and I don't have a problem with that but you can play kids too soon as well as too late. Up to this point the highlight of his life was making 147 in 89 minutes against Glamorgan at Swansea with 13 sixes, an innings powerful enough for the Welsh county to sign him up.

Going up to Cambridge University in 1970 was, I think, the making of him. He made 200 in his first Varsity match that year and a couple of seasons later led the Light Blues to their first win over Oxford for 14 years. He developed as a person in that rarefied environment where the pressure was so much less intense and instead of being a bit player in the big league he was now the star.

He came back to Test cricket for the tour of Australia in 1972–73 and in the second Test at Melbourne, now batting at number four, made 158 in such majestic fashion that Dennis Lillee promised to knock his trademark floppy hat off his head. Majid is reputed to have replied that if he could do it he could keep it. The metamorphosis was remarkable and now he really started to perform: 110 against New Zealand in Auckland, 99 against the Kiwis in Karachi, the same year, 1972–73, and on the tour of England in 1974 he opened the batting with 48 and 18 at Leeds and 98 and 18 at The Oval. Against the West Indies the following winter he made 100 in Karachi, and in the same Pakistan summer 98 in Hyderabad and 112 and 50 in Karachi against New Zealand. In the Caribbean against Roberts, Croft and Garner and still opening he hit 530 in five Tests, averaging 53, and that's some going out there, I can tell you. He had really started to blossom as a player when along came World Series Cricket, but with Packer releasing him along with others he still made runs in the Tests, 119 not out at Napier against New Zealand and 108 against Australia at

Melbourne (followed by a pair in Perth) in the winter of 1978–79.

But after opening in the first three Tests against India in 1979–80 he dropped down the order and the batting seemed to be up and down. An unbeaten 110 against Australia in Lahore in February 1980 was his last Test hundred and signalled a decline in performance. The gloss had worn off and in four Tests against the West Indies in 1980–81 he averaged 22, followed by three Tests in Australia with an average of 23. The final blow came in England in 1982 when his cousin Imran was captain and didn't pick him for the first two Tests. Majid played at Leeds, making 21 and 10 in a defeat and there is a major fall-out between the two. They have never spoken a word to each other to this day and if Immy comes into any room where Majid is, the son of Jahangir Khan will up sticks and leave. The ill-feeling runs that deep.

Asif Iqbal made his debut in the same game as Majid, again played as a bowler, he shared the new ball with him and batted at number 10. It's so difficult to believe that two such glorious stroke makers could have been picked as bowlers and left to languish among the tailenders. It just looks crazy with hindsight.

Asif was a wonderful attacking batsman, light on his feet and quickly down the pitch to the spinners, or even friendly medium pace; he could make fielders look silly so good was he between the wickets and when the field was brought in to try and stop the singles he'd pierce it almost at will. He used a long-handled bat and carved up bowlers with it and he earned his nickname of 'the Smiling Assassin'. The open stance which became more open with the passing of the years was used to good effect and he shot to prominence on Pakistan's tour of England in 1967. Batting at number nine in the first Test at Lord's, he came in with his side 139 for seven and put on 130 with Hanif, finishing with 76. He opened the bowling in all three Tests and got me out in the second at Trent Bridge. We bowled them out for 140 and there was a violent thunderstorm about an hour from the end on the first day when I was four not out. Pitches were uncovered in those days and next morning he slid one past me and bowled me for 15. What a death getting out to a medium pace dobber and I wasn't best pleased when I found out he was really a batsman. I always tell him that he was only a variation on my medium pace but without the cap.

At The Oval in the last game Pakistan were 53 for seven when he came in and made 146 in 200 minutes with 21 fours and two sixes and although it didn't save them from defeat it was a brilliant innings.

He came back to England in 1971 and made an unbeaten 104 at Edgbaston in the first Test batting at number six, and in New Zealand in February 1972 he scored 175 at Dunedin in the second Test and 102 against England in Lahore in the first Test of the 1972–73 tour. After a poor series in England in 1974 (53 in five innings) he had his best period, making 166 against New Zealand in Lahore in October 1976, 152 not out in the first Test at Adelaide against Australia in December 1976, 120 in the third at Sydney in January 1977 and 135 against the West Indies in Kingston in the following April.

Just as he was in his pomp Packer's World Series started and although he missed a few Tests he still made good hundreds: 134 not out against Australia in Perth, 104 against India in Faisalabad and 104 in Napier against the Kiwis.

They named him captain for the six-Test series in India in 1979–80 but the rubber was lost 2–0, Asif making only 267 from nine innings, and he packed up after the last match in Calcutta. It was a sad end to a fine international career. There's nothing to choose between them but I'll go for Majid because he gives me the option of having an additional opener.

Syed Zaheer Abbas Kirmani (1969–85)
Inzaman-ul-Haq (1992–2007)
Mohammad Yousuf (1998–)

Known on the English county circuit simply as 'Zed', Zaheer Abbas was a tall, lean, graceful player who could play off front and back foot transferring his weight easily, a very important part of a batsman's footwork. He never seemed to whack the ball but caressed it with wonderful wrists and timing which enabled him to score quickly. I played against him a fair bit and I always thought that if he got in there was an inevitability about the hundred that would follow.

He made his debut at 22 years of age against New Zealand in October 1969 in Karachi, making 12 and 27, and wasn't picked for the next two matches. When Pakistan were next in Test action, in England in 1971, suddenly, out of the blue, he bats at number three and makes 274, his highest Test score, in the rain-ruined first Test at Edgbaston with 38 fours. A terrific knock for someone of his years and he went on to average 96 for the three-match series. But in his next 13 Test innings against Australia, New Zealand and England he managed an aggregate of only 229 runs.

Then in England in 1974 he makes 240 in the third Test at The Oval and averages 54 for the rubber. Again he follows that with a run of low scores and accumulates just 60 in five innings against New Zealand in 1976–77. No one thought he'd do much against Lillee, Gilmour and Walker on the trip to Australia because of that high backlift but he confounded everybody with 85 and 101 in the first Test at Adelaide, and 90 and 58 at Melbourne to average 57.16 over the three matches. Another poor series followed, 131 in six innings in the Caribbean against Roberts, Croft and Garner, before he signed for World Series Cricket. In October 1978 when released by Packer he made 583 in the series against India, then a record for a three-match series, including an unbeaten 235 in the second Test at Lahore and averaged 194.33!

In the six-Test series against India in 1982–83 he had 650 runs at an average of 130 with 285 in Lahore, 186 in Karachi and 168 in Faisalabad. He captained his country on the 1983–4 tour of Australia and his last Test hundred came against India in Lahore, an unbeaten 168.

He was a bit of a mystery. He seemed to blow hot and cold. When he made runs, he made them big time but he had these dips in form. He was such an eye-catching batsman that those who saw him play in county cricket with Gloucestershire will be convinced he was one of the best in the world. Their judgement is coloured by some of the marvellous, breathtaking innings they saw. A lot of people called him the 'Asian Bradman' and others rank him alongside Viv Richards. Those big double hundreds and a few not outs whack the average up. But I worry about those lean periods.

I always think of Inzamam-ul-Haq as the sleeping giant mainly because he was a big bloke and usually looked half asleep. I've seen him getting ready to bat, sitting in a comfy chair with his pads on, bat resting against one arm and his gloves on the other, looking as though he had settled in for a kip.

He had 14 ducks to his name, far more than any other top order Pakistan batsman, and that was probably because he took a while to wake up when he got to the crease. Once he was roused he was one helluva player.

I don't think I've ever seen any professional sportsman

who looked less like an athlete than Inzy. He used to drive Imran to distraction with his lack of fitness and Immy had him lifting dumb-bells and doing exercises in the dressing room to try and get him fitter. He had an abhorrence of exercise unless it was out in the middle when none of that seemed to matter and he played some really big innings.

Although Immy despaired of Inzy's fitness he never doubted his ability from the moment he first saw him in the nets and Immy was proved right time and again. He had a lean spell in his first seven Test innings starting in England in 1992 but made 75 in the defeat in Port of Spain, Trinidad, and 123 in Antigua in the third Test of the 1992–93 Caribbean tour. He made an unbeaten 200 in the Asia Test Championship final against Sri Lanka in Dhaka in 1998–99 and in the only Test played before the 2002 series with New Zealand was abandoned because of terrorist bombs made the highest score on home soil, 329 at Lahore in May with 38 fours and nine sixes in 579 minutes.

In the home series against England's Ashes-winning side in November 2005 he made 53 and 72 in Multan, 109 and 100 not out in Faisalabad and 97 in Lahore, and in the Faisalabad game went past Javed's record 23 centuries for his country. In that series he was run out twice and if he had a weakness it was his running between the wickets. You can forget Denis Compton and me; he was abysmal. You just weren't sure whether he was going to run, he never called and you had to be a mind-reader when you were out in the middle with him. Immy was always going on at him about his calling but it just went in one ear and out the other. His runs spoke for him: 401 in the three-match series in India in March 2005 including 184 in the third Test at Bangalore and when he retired after the match with South Africa in Lahore two years later he had made just three fewer than Javed's record 8,832 runs for his country. I think he was a good player with a sound temperament and you couldn't upset him out in the middle. Universally liked, he was always good natured and I only ever saw him lose his temper twice.

The first time was in Toronto where Pakistan used to play India in five one-day games in a nice little tree-lined ground, the sort you might find in the English countryside. The crowd though couldn't have been more different; they were hostile and insulting and when Inzy was on the boundary were calling him 'potato', flicking orange peel at him. Finally he flipped. He called for the twelfth man, asked him to bring out his bat and waded into the crowd to send his tormentors packing as they saw the burly figure of Inzy coming at them waving his bat above his head. I know it happened because I was commentating on television for ESPN who had the series beamed back to the subcontinent.

The other occasion when Inzy lost control is the by now infamous Test at The Oval when Pakistan forfeited the game after accusations of ball tampering by the umpires. I feel part of that problem was the language. The Pakistanis don't always understand if you speak quickly and they don't like being shouted at, bullied, put down or dealt with in an offhand way. It's a throwback to the days of the Raj when they were treated like third class citizens and if you speak down to them they get offended very quickly. It's significant that although Inzy was suspended for four one-day matches as a result of the fiasco he returned home a hero to the people.

I can't ignore Mohammad Yousuf who started life in the Test team as a Christian called Yousuf Youhana before changing his name in 2005 when he became a Muslim.

He's got a fantastic record over the last few years and in my book is the only player in the world to rival Ricky

Ponting as the world's number one. He's got a simple method, very like the Australian's, in that he likes to get forward with a big stride and get slightly outside the line of the ball to play his shots in an arc from mid off to the leg side. He doesn't like to drive through the off side unless the ball is very full and although the aesthetic cricket strokes are those lovely drives through the covers, like Michael Vaughan's, they're the ones that put you most at risk because that's where the slips and wicketkeeper are waiting to punish any error of judgement. If the ball is short Yousuf has the balance to rock back and pull but, like Ponting, is not a great hooker. The Aussie captain has become such a feared batsman because he is so effective. While not belligerent like Matthew Hayden, he still makes his runs at a good rate, very successfully. Yousuf picks length like all great players and makes very few mistakes and though big hitting is eye-catching, the key is to put your side in a position from where you can win the match and that's what Ponting and this guy can do. While Ponting is the Australian banker Yousuf is the man Pakistan turn to for that high level of consistency. He looks inoffensive, there's no great presence, no huge physique, just an enormous number of runs.

He had three fifties in his first half dozen Test innings, starting with the second Test against South Africa in Durban, and the first of 23 centuries came against the West Indies in Bridgetown, Barbados, a patient 115 that took just two minutes under six hours. He followed up with another in the next match in Antigua, spending five and a half hours over 103. A double hundred came in the second Test against New Zealand in Christchurch in March 2001, 203 in eight and a half hours, another against Bangladesh in Chittagong in January 2002, this one, not surprisingly, a lot quicker in five hours 25 minutes. His best came against England at

Lahore in November 2005, 223 in just over 10 hours and was the starting point for an extraordinary year in 2006 in which he beat Viv Richards' 30-year-old record for the number of centuries and aggregate of runs scored in a calendar year. He makes hundreds like shelling peas: 173 in the first Test against India at Lahore, 126 in the third, both in January. In the first Test against England at Lord's in July he made 202 and in August had 192 at Leeds in the third and 128 at The Oval in the fourth. Against the West Indies in Lahore in November in the first Test he had 192, followed by 191 at Multan in the second and one in each innings, 102 and 124, in the final match in Karachi. In the last game he overtook Viv's 1,710 and finished with 1,788 from 11 Tests with nine centuries. He also beat Sir Donald Bradman's record of six centuries in consecutive Tests with seven hundreds in those three Tests against England and four against the West Indies.

As a Muslim he prays five times a day but I think it's the bowlers who should be doing the praying. At just turned 33 years of age he has it in him to become the most successful of Pakistan's batsmen and in my middle order I'm going for him and Inzy.

Shoaib Akhtar (1997–)

I need to have a back-up fast bowler because pace is so important. I know Shoaib is a bit of a risk, a bit of a show pony. He breaks down too often or he's suspended and he always has trouble with authority, we all know that. But good fast bowling wins Test matches, brings that touch of apprehension to certain players and Imran would be the only guy who could handle him. It's a pity they played in different eras because when you do get Shoaib on the park he's very quick and he loves being the centre of attention. I sometimes think he's in the wrong profession and would have done better on the stage or in films but there's no doubt in my mind that it would have been better for him and better for Pakistan if he had played under Imran all his career – *he* wouldn't have stood any nonsense on or off the field.

Imran would have harnessed that tremendous ability, moulded his character and it's obvious that Shoaib needs someone like that; he's proved time and time again he can't handle himself, he's no idea. Immy was a great leader of men; if he rated you he'd go out on a limb to support you against anybody and stake his own reputation on you. But if you crossed Imran or didn't pull your weight you'd be done for and lucky if you ever played again. It's a bit like Brian Clough when he took over, briefly, at Leeds United. He had Eddie Gray, a fantastically talented Scottish ball player, in his office and complimented him on his skills. 'But,' he added, 'you're always injured and never get on the park. If you'd been a racehorse, they'd have shot you.'

Shoaib hasn't grasped that and if he's not careful by the time he finishes he won't have done justice to his talent. He doesn't realize that to be able to bowl genuinely fast is a great gift. You're the ace, the name on everybody's lips, the king. History only records match-winning performances and no one cares or remembers the nearlys or the maybes. I don't feel we've seen him fulfil all that potential. Terrific pace, lightning fast, aggressive, all these things, but that's not enough without control and accuracy. I always say it's no good being the fastest in the world if you're sending down long hops and half volleys, they're not going to trouble quality batsmen. Yes, you can terrify tailenders but at the top level if you miss by three inches that's fine. Great bowlers, and I use the word properly, are systematically accurate at bowling at you to hit the heart or ribs, the most difficult ball to play and I should know after 25 years of it. That sort of delivery, just short of a length, means you have to play it or get out of the way and if you play it you have to keep it down. There's no such thing as perfect bounce on a turf pitch and if the ball hits a harder bit of ground or hits the seam it's suddenly four inches higher than expected; try playing that at 90mph! That's the area the great quicks have been brilliant at exploiting, they don't waste their time and energy bouncing it miles over your head. The crowd may love it but it's a waste and too often Shoaib goes down that road. He's the showman still obsessed with speed, he wants to be the fastest in the world and hasn't harnessed other skills to his pace. I think he could and should have done more and realized like Waqar, Wasim and Imran that pace alone is not enough. The Rawalpindi Express has too often been the Rawalpindi rickshaw as his total of 46 Tests in 10 years suggests. He's going to be a reserve bowler in my team and I go with him because, and only because, I have Immy as captain to make him toe the line.

Pakistan

SQUAD	RESERVES
Imran Khan	Asif Iqbal
Hanif Mohammad	Zaheer Abbas
Fazal Mahmood	Shoaib Akhtar
Wasim Akram	
Waqar Younis	
Javed Miandad	
Abdul Qadir	
Saeed Anwar	
Mushtaq Mohammad	
Wasim Bari	
Majid Khan	
Inzaman-ul-Haq	
Mohammad Yousuf	

Sri Lanka

Muttiah Muralitharan (1992–)

Nearly all Sri Lankan cricket centres around the pheno-
menon of Murali, the leading wicket-taker in Tests, and it is
an astonishing fact that of the 52 matches won in their brief
history up to the end of March 2008 Murali played in 47;
that's how much he means to their cricket.

They played the first of their 177 matches against England at Colombo in 1982 but my memories of the island go
back further when Ceylon, as it was then, was the stop-over
point for MCC teams heading for Australia. On my first
visit in the winter of 1965 I played in the first match against
the President's XI but ended up horribly ill after catching
some sort of bug. I had a terrible time and spent a week in
hospital in Singapore (as recounted in my chapter on Don
Bradman) where they nearly paralysed me. So I don't think
I'll forget my first trip to the beautiful island in the Indian
Ocean.

The second visit was no less memorable for different
reasons. This was on an MCC goodwill tour to Sri Lanka,
Malaysia, Bangkok and Hong Kong in 1970 and in the
only first class match I was bowled in the first over by the
biggest, most blatant chucker of all time, a chap named
Tikiri Kehelgamuwa who went on to become a police chief
and still dines out on the story of how he 'bowled' Geoffrey
Boycott for a duck. In Bangkok there was a lady doing
the scoring and when I was out I was credited with 116 but
I knew I'd made 151 – I always knew how many runs I'd

made, I counted every one of them. I told her she'd given a third of my runs to somebody else but she wouldn't have it.

From those humble beginnings it was 13 Tests before the Sri Lankans won their first match, against India in Colombo in September 1985, and 20 before they won a game overseas, in Pakistan in March 1986. Nothing much to shout about in 37 Tests until Murali made his debut against Australia in August 1992. His first 10 Tests on home soil produced 40 wickets. However, there were doubts about his action and when he went to Australia in 1995 the growing whispers about its legality were given substance when umpire Darrell Hair called him seven times in three overs for throwing in the Boxing Day Test in Melbourne. At Brisbane in January 1996 in the one-day game against the West Indies (part of the triangular tournament) Ross Emerson, who was standing in his first international, repeatedly no-balled him which led to a political storm. Things came to a head in January 1999 when Emerson again called him at Adelaide in a one-day game against England in the Carlton & United triangular series. Arjuna Ranatunga took his men off the field, causing a 14-minute delay which only ended when the Sri Lankan board told the team to continue with the game.

Let's be clear. Ever since I first saw him I've thought he throws it. I've never had any doubts about that and neither have a lot of other former players. This is not a personal thing but a professional judgement. Murali is one of the nicest lads you could wish to meet and from his origins in the backwoods of Tamil hill country, where his father was a confectioner, he has achieved immortality as the man with more Test wickets than any other in history. As a purveyor of the ball he is without parallel; his enormous spin and accuracy are two things that combine to make life difficult enough for any batsman. Add on the 'doosra', the one that moves from leg to off with no discernible change in action, and if you can't 'read' it you're done for. Most batsmen can't pick him so they have little chance of survival let alone runs – the same was said of Sonny Ramadhin, the West Indian, and Australia's John Gleeson, both of whom could make the ball go the other way. But they did it with their fingers and Murali does it with an extraordinary rotation of the wrist, almost the reverse of the googly for a legbreak bowler. There's no doubt he's a genius at it but the question remains, is it legitimate?

The International Cricket Council looked at video evidence which was inconclusive before the University of Western Australia in Perth became involved with Dr Marc Protus, Professor Bruce Elliott and Dr Paul Hurrion carrying out a series of tests using high-speed cameras to film Murali's action in laboratory conditions. In 2002 their findings that tolerances of five degrees of flexion for spinners, 10 degrees for fast bowlers should be allowed, were ratified by the ICC. But more doubts surfaced in 2004 after he introduced the 'doosra', which means in Urdu 'the second one', while taking 28 wickets in a three-match home series against Australia and was reported by the match referee Chris Broad. More research in Western Australia showed that his arm flexed 13 degrees when he bowled it; the boffins came up with so-called evidence that the naked eye could not detect flexion at anything under 15 degrees and that 99 per cent of bowlers threw it. The ICC, desperate for a solution, grasped this idea with both hands and it became part of their rules.

Ever since he was first no-balled in Australia, politics have played a more important part than cricket logic. The Aussies were scared stiff the Sri Lankans would go home in 1999 and then they would face legal action for breach of contract with the television companies, sponsors and radio stations. Millions of dollars were at stake so they had the Aussie board by the short and curlies. To Sri Lankans Murali is a national treasure and any slur upon him is a slight on their national identity. Murali is half their team and without him there is less revenue, less interest from TV and sponsors. He is the match-winner, the star turn and as important to their cricket as Don Bradman was to the Aussies.

The compromise was to turn to the scientists in Perth to examine Murali's action. They found that he had a flex of 13 degrees but by getting him to run up straighter, point his left arm to fine leg and get in closer to the stumps they reduced it to 11 degrees. You wouldn't need a boffin to tell you that but it went round the world that it was OK. To me it's utter balls. Tell me I'm cynical; Murali flexes at 11 or 13 degrees and the limit is set by the ICC at 15 degrees, just fancy that. So all those people like me who said he threw it were proved right. Now all the so-called experts are saying is that it doesn't really matter because everyone else threw it as well. That is just to trivialize the situation.

In 2004 when I was working for Channel 4 TV they carried out what was nothing more than a PR exercise at Lord's with Murali bowling on the Nursery ground with a plaster cast on his bowling arm. People said, 'He can't throw it if he's in a plaster cast, can he?' But there was no batsman and these weren't match conditions. What happens in the heat of battle when things are getting tight – who's there to carry out the measurements then? Those 11 or 13 degrees can become a lot more when the chips are down.

Michael Atherton maintains that it doesn't matter whether he throws it or not because he's 'good for the game'. That's dangerous thinking for two reasons. Firstly it does a disservice to all those who have gone before with legitimate actions, and secondly, if it's all right for him to throw it why bother trying to bowl properly when you can chuck it and take wickets? In 50 years time we'll be down to baseball pitchers and overarm bowling will be out of the window. Others who were put out of the game because of supposedly faulty actions like Geoff Griffin, Geoff Cope and Harold Rhodes would have every right to feel aggrieved, as would Tony Lock who was very ordinary once he had to change his action. The England and Wales Cricket Board even wrote to their umpires when Murali signed for Lancashire to tell them not to call 'no ball' if they were worried about his action but to make a private report. That's overwriting the laws of the game which they have no right to do. Just because Murali is an icon of Sri Lankan cricket it's OK, is it? I don't think so. A fear of litigation and the damage to international cricket is what has driven the whole affair and I don't care what anybody says, it's not right.

Having said all that, he has produced amazing figures, none better than the 16 for 220 at The Oval in August 1998 from 113.5 overs of magic. But the doubts remain however scientists dress it up and they're never going to go away however many wickets he takes. While the greats of the game like Bradman, Hobbs, Sobers, Warne, Hammond et al. have earned respect, Murali won't have that same cachet outside his own little island.

Sanath Teran Jayasuriya (1991–2007)

Jayasuriya has been the most influential figure in Sri Lankan cricket after Murali and without any of the controversy that dogged the spinner. He captured the imagination and if he didn't exactly revolutionize opening batsmanship he took it to a new level. People tend to remember him as a one-day specialist but that was his natural way and he took the same attitude and freedom of strokeplay into Test matches. His type of up-front batting against the new ball was risky but exciting; when it came off it thrilled spectators everywhere but more importantly took the game away from the opposition so quickly. Bowlers who were used to being in control with the new ball suddenly weren't too sure where to bowl or what fields to set and it was a whole new feeling for the pacemen who were now running up and thinking where and how far's he going to hit this. He had very little backlift, took the ball early at the top of the bounce with exquisite timing and didn't really try to keep it on the floor, quite happy to sweetly hit it over or through the field. The key was that his balance and his body weight were always going forward into the shot for maximum effect, like a boxer punching his full weight, although there was little footwork. He used a lot of bottom hand – in fact the top one never worked in the classical way because the bat was always at an angle and if you gave him room to get his arms free he'd kill you. He might have a waft and get out but he could and did make bowlers and fielders look silly with his wonderful talent and great array of shots. If you were in the crowd you didn't want to be going for a cup of tea when he was in because he could take your breath away. Although he only averaged around 40 in his 119 Tests it was his style that was so important. I've said before that bowlers win matches but batsmen put you in a position to go for victory and he did that beautifully at The Oval in August 1998 with 213 from 278 balls with 33 fours and a six, leaving Murali with a full day to bowl out England.

Everyone thought he was going to make the world record individual Test score at Colombo in August the previous year when he made 340 in the highest Test innings of 952 for six declared against India, putting on 576 with Roshan Mahamana for the second wicket, and in Faisalabad in October 2004 in a 201-run win over Pakistan he struck 253 from 348 balls, runs made out of 401 scored from the bat, the next highest score being 59 from Sangakkara.

Perhaps the nicest thing was the way he did it. There was none of the chest-out aggression you would see from, say, Viv Richards but a quiet, smiling demeanour and he some-times looked almost apologetic after taking bowlers to the cleaners. I think he's been fantastic for cricket and would be an asset to any side.

Marvan Samson Atapattu (1990–2007)

Marvan Atapattu was the perfect foil for Sanath Jayasuriya, a strong-minded individual who was quite content to occupy the crease while his partner provided the fireworks at the other end. He made his Test debut against India at Chandigarh in November 1990 and his career started with five ducks and a single in his first six innings. But he went on to play in 53 consecutive Tests and made 5,502 runs at an average of 39.02. His career was embroiled in controversy after a large sum of money was found in a safe in a hotel room he occupied but he was cleared of any suspicion of betting, and he finished with Test cricket after falling out with the selectors who he called 'muppets headed by a joker' before announcing his retirement during the Test with Australia at Hobart in November 2007.

The left hand, right hand combination worked well and with Jayasuriya he shared 4,469 runs, the third most prolific opening partnership after Greenidge and Haynes (6,482) and Hayden and Langer (5,665). It included the Sri Lankan record for the first wicket, 335 against Pakistan at Kandy in June 2000.

When he got in he made double hundreds, two of them against Zimbabwe when they were a half decent side, followed by 207 not out against Pakistan in Kandy in June 2000, an innings which took 652 minutes. He made 54 and 120 against South Africa on the same ground the following month and in February 2001 made 201 not out in the win over England at Galle, this one taking 684 minutes. He made 185 at Lord's against England in May 2002, 118 and 50 not out in the Caribbean at Gros Islet in June 2003 and three hundreds in four innings in March and May 2004, 118 against Australia in Colombo, 170 against Zimbabwe in Harare and 249 against the same opponents in Bulawayo.

Predominantly a back foot player, he gave the impression he was easy prey for bowlers who pitched the ball up but he had patience and concentration and was not easily ruffled, very much an old-fashioned type of opener who wore the opposition down. That's what you need when you have someone prepared to take the bowlers on at one end, some-one to dig in and occupy the crease for long periods at the other. Atapattu provided that perfect contrast in style. He wasn't afraid of anything or anybody and to my mind is the ideal partner for Jayasuriya.

Denagemage Proboth
Mahela de Silva Jayawardene (1997–)

A textbook player, I think he's the sort who would have made runs in any era. Elegant, good looking, Mahela Jayawardene bats in the classic manner, good off front and back foot and nimble-footed against the spinners. He has the best record of any of the pure Sri Lankan batsmen with 7,478 runs from 95 Tests, making a century about once in every four games and that's top notch. He made his debut as a 20-year-old against India at Colombo in August 1997 and came in with the score on 790 for four! He was on a hiding to nothing but made 66 and had two other half centuries before he passed the three-figure mark for the first time in only his fourth Test, against New Zealand in Colombo in May 1998, making 167.

Only five men have been younger when making a double hundred than his 21 years 273 days when he batted superbly to score 242 against India at Colombo the following February. But oh, how he loved batting against those South Africans, making a stack of runs against them: 167 in the innings and 51 runs win at Galle in July 2000, 237 on the same ground in August 2004, topping the lot with the highest score by a Sri Lankan, 374 with 43 fours and a six in nearly 12 and a half hours in the middle at Colombo in July 2006 in a win by an innings and 153, taking part in the world record partnership of 638 for the third wicket with Kumar Sangakkara.

He hit three centuries on the trot: 195 against England in

Colombo in the second Test in December 2007, 213 not out in the third at Galle, a terrific knock, and 136 in the Caribbean at Guyana in March 2008. He made 123 in the one-wicket win over the long-suffering South Africans in August 2006, and reached 7,000 runs in his 150th Test innings. But perhaps two of his best performances came in a rearguard action at Lord's in May 2006 when he played a real captain's role with 61 and 119 in 366 minutes to save the game, for which he justifiably won the man of the match award.

A handsome lad who's done a lot for cancer charities, I think he's the type who'd make runs anywhere against any type of bowling under any conditions.

Kumar Chokshanada Sangakkara
(2000–)

Sangakkara is a top player who's got better the more responsibility he's been given batting higher up the order, which is extraodinary really because it's tougher against the new ball. But I think he prefers the ball coming on to him, a bit like Alec Stewart, rather than come in against the spinners as you tend to do lower down. Now his wicketkeeping has improved he's become a big bonus for Sri Lankan cricket and an important part of their side. To bat at three and do well with the gloves is a tall order but he's as good at it as there has ever been and the only person who stands comparison with him is the now retired Adam Gilchrist. But where 'Gillie' could take an attack apart Kumar is a more subtle accumulator and a much more rounded left hander. He cuts and pulls well, drives beautifully and there are no real weaknesses in his game. Add to that a feisty nature and he becomes a real handful. Give him any lip and you'll get it back threefold and I like that in a player, a real competitor who's up for the battle – it's no coincidence that the Aussies respect him more than any of the other Sri Lankans who tend to be nice, quiet, reserved lads, something Sangakkara certainly isn't.

By April 2008 he'd played in 90 Tests, 73 of them as wicketkeeper, and made 6,127 runs at an average of 55.19. The first of his 16 centuries came against India at Galle, 105 not out in a 10-wicket win in August 2001, and the first of six double hundreds, 230, in an eight-wicket win against

Pakistan at Lahore in March 2002. In May 2004 he made 270 in Bulawayo against Zimbabwe, taking part in a 438-run stand for the second wicket with Marvan Atapattu, and thumped the hopeless Zimbabweans again with consecutive double hundreds, 200 not out and 222 not out in Harare and Bulawayo in July 2007. A tremendous effort in a lost cause in Hobart in November 2007 saw him make 192 out of fewer than 400 runs scored from the bat in the second innings and he was absolutely top notch in the 88-run win over England at Kandy the following month with scores of 92 and 152. He passed 6,000 Test runs in 116 innings and only Bradman (68), Sobers (111) and Hammond (114) have achieved the landmark in fewer. Pretty distinguished company that.

Sangakkara just seems to get better and better and of current players only Mike Hussey, Jacques Kallis and Mohammad Yousuf have a better Test average than his. In complete contrast to his on-the-field aggression he is studying law and is a real student of the art of batting which probably explains why he continues to improve. I like his style.

Pinnaduwage Aravinda de Silva
(1984–2002)

A small, unprepossessing man, Aravinda de Silva had none of the lithe grace of a Sobers or the menace of Viv Richards when he came out to bat but he was a top player, make no mistake about that. He made his debut at Lord's against England in August 1984 and the following 92 Tests were played while his country was in its infancy as an international side. To have scored 20 centuries and totalled 6,321 runs was no mean feat in a weak team that won only two of its first 32 Tests.

There was nothing about this chubby fellow that said he was going to destroy the bowling. He picked your pocket rather than mugged you with clever manipulation of the ball into gaps, and you'd suddenly look up and see he was 30 or so and wonder where he had made those runs because he didn't appear to have played a shot in anger. A lovely timer of his strokes, he was good on the cut and pull and a graceful driver and without being in the 'great' class of batsmen he was in the next echelon. Although it plays no part in my selections, it's worth noting that he was also brilliant at the one-day game and made an unbeaten 107 when Sri Lanka beat Australia to win the World Cup final in March 1996, to prove you don't have to smash it miles to make runs in any form of the game. He had good hands and, brought up on the slower pitches in his part of the world, he played the ball late and used his wrists to manoeuvre the ball where he wanted it.

De Silva made a major contribution to his country's first Test win, making two and 78 not out against India at Colombo in September 1985, and the first of his hundreds came at Faisalabad the next month, 122, in his fifth Test followed by 105 at Karachi in November. At Brisbane in December 1989 he hit 167 in 491 minutes to win the man of the match award in a draw and his highest score, 287, was in the first Test at Wellington against New Zealand in February 1991, followed by 123 in the third at Auckland. When Sri Lanka won for the second time, beating England at Colombo in March 1993, he made 80 in the first innings and scored 78 and 31 when they beat Australia for the first time in September 1999 at Kandy.

He had three hundreds on the trot, 168 against Pakistan at Colombo in April 1997 in the first Test, 138 not out and 103 not out in the second, also in Colombo, and he made it four in five innings with an unbeaten 110 against India in Mohali in November the same year. He scored 106 at Galle in February 2001 in the innings and 28 runs win over England and in his last match cracked 206 from 234 balls with 28 fours and a six against Bangladesh in Colombo in July 2002. He was quite a player and he'll do me nicely at number five.

Warnakulasuriya Patabendige Ushantha Joseph Chaminda Vaas (1994–)

I'm a big fan of the left arm seamer who for 13 years has bowled all over the world and been a great credit to his country. Bowling on home pitches lacking any real pace and not receptive to seam is hardly an incentive for a medium fast bowler, but Chaminda has kept running in tirelessly and you have to admire his tenacity, spirit and competitiveness. It can be soul destroying when your home games are played on such unresponsive pitches and it's easy to lose heart. But not him. He's ever willing, whatever the pitch or the state of the game, and that's an admirable attitude which shows his strength of character.

He gets in close to the stumps, bowls wicket to wicket and swings the new ball in late to the right hander. If you don't get your feet moving or play with the bat hidden behind the front pad you're in trouble and it's not surprising that 96 of his 343 wickets have been leg before, that's 27.98 per cent, a pretty high figure for a seamer.

Without Chaminda and Murali Sri Lanka would have no bowling strength to speak of. They've got through zillions of overs, Chaminda putting in 3,718 in 104 Tests, more than four times the workload of any other of their seamers. So many bowlers have come and gone after a few Tests but he's remained a fixture in the side and he doesn't go down sick if he doesn't like the look of the pitch. He won't be rated in the 'great' class but he's always had fire in his belly and Sri Lanka owe him a huge debt.

Among his outstanding feats were 14 for 191 against the West Indies at Colombo in the home series in November 2001 (only Imran Khan has better match figures for a seamer on the subcontinent) and 10 for 90 in Sri Lanka's first overseas victory at Napier, New Zealand in March 1995. In September 1999 he had six for 58 in the match at Kandy as Australia were beaten for the first time, 16 wickets in three Tests against England in February and March 2001, six for 29 in the 313-run win over South Africa in Colombo in August 2004 and six for 22 in the 240-run win over the West Indies in July 2005. In the most recent two-Test tour of the Caribbean he took 12 wickets for 237 despite the fact that his career is on the downward curve now.

He has taken 174 wickets at home and 169 on tour which shows his worth in all conditions. His only real failures were on the two tours to England where he managed nine wickets in six Tests at a cost of 699 runs. He's the first seamer on the team sheet and he'll take a hell of a lot of replacing when he finally retires.

The Rest

The seven I've picked are top class players, outstanding in their own right, but when it comes to finishing off the squad it's not easy because they are all much of a muchness and it's difficult to separate them. That's not to disparage them but they don't shout their class like the others. It was particularly tough on those who played at the start of the country's journey in Test cricket when they were inexperienced in the varying conditions around the world and up against some of the best players. So I've looked at those who made a major contribution when the team were struggling to keep their collective head above water, and tried to assess their value, and how they would have gone on in the current side which is at ease in the Test arena. I've gone for these six to complete my party.

Roy Dias played in the inaugural match against England at Colombo and started with a duck but in the second innings top scored with a classy 77 against an England attack of Willis, Botham, Emburey and Underwood. In Pakistan he was outstanding with 98 at Faisalabad and 109 at Lahore where Imran Khan bowled like the wind to take 14 wickets in the match for 116 runs. Technically sound with lovely timing, his average of 36 in 20 Tests would be worth a lot more today. In Sri Lanka's maiden Test victory, and series win, over India at home in 1985–86, his contribution was decisive. Two half centuries in the second Test helped set up a win, then with Sri Lanka on the brink of defeat in the final Test, Dias rescued them with a superlative 106, to earn a draw.

Asanka Gurusinha, a technically accomplished cricketer, was the rock on which the Sri Lankan batting was founded for 11 years from 1985. His gutsy, battling character earned the respect of opponents around the world, never more than when he batted for three hours to make an unbeaten 52 in a Sri Lankan total of 82 in Chandigarh in November 1990; at Melbourne in the Boxing Day Test of 1995 he scored 143 while the rest of the team mustered 144 between them. He started Test cricket as a teenager keeping wicket as well as being a top order batsman, but retired prematurely a year after the 1996 World Cup triumph after refusing to return home for training from a season of club cricket in Melbourne.

Tillakaratne Dilshan, earlier known as Tuwan Moham-mad Dilshan before he converted from Islam to Buddhism, burst on to the international scene with an unbeaten 163 against Zimbabwe in his first series during November 1999. Comfortable against fast bowling, with quick feet, strong wrists and natural timing, Dilshan has plenty of talent. But the bright start to his career was followed by a frustrating 15 months when he was moved up and down the order, and in and out of the side. After a lean series against England in 2001 he was dumped for two years. He came back mentally stronger and determined to play his own naturally aggressive game. This approach was immediately successful with a string of good scores against England and Australia, but he needs to cut out some of the rash strokes.

Ashantha de Mel was Sri Lanka's leading pace bowler following their elevation to full Test status. In Sri Lanka's inaugural test against England in 1981–82 he took a highly creditable four for 70 and one for 33 with his lively fast medium away swing. In the following tour of Pakistan he toiled willingly, taking 11 wickets. In the one-off Test against India in 1982–83 he became the first Sri Lankan fast bowler to take a five-wicket haul, with five for 68 in the second innings. A serious knee injury brought his career to a premature end after the 1987 World Cup, but he went on to represent Sri Lanka at bridge, including an appearance at the Commonwealth Games!

Rumesh Ratnayake made his debut as a teenager in New Zealand and with his whippy action generated a fair amount of pace and bounce. He was the key figure in Sri Lanka's first victory when he took four for 49 and five for 76 at Colombo to bring a 149-run win over India. Niggling injuries reduced his effectiveness but he worked hard in generally unresponsive conditions. On his day he remained a quality pace bowler. On the tour of Australia he produced a top class display of swing bowling in his only Test, at Hobart in December 1989, with six for 66. At Lord's in August 1991 he gave another accomplished performance of pace and swing taking five for 69, and then saved the side from defeat with a bright half century.

Lasith Malinga has a slingshot action that can produce a fantastic yorker and, when he drops it short, a difficult bouncer, and there's no doubt he produces genuine pace. He's not aesthetically pleasing but bowlers with his sort of delivery are sometimes difficult for batsmen to figure out because they don't have any natural rhythm. He lets it go from so low that on the tour to New Zealand in April 2005 the batsmen asked the umpires to change their black trousers because they couldn't see the ball against the background. He started off with a bang with match figures of six for 92 in his first Test against Australia in Darwin in July 2004, getting rid of Darren Lehmann and Adam Gilchrist in one over. But he's been troubled by overstepping and is inconsistent. When he gets it right he's a firecracker and he's already fourth in his country's list of wicket-takers with 91 from 28 Tests.

There are some other lads who may develop into useful players like **Farvez Maharoof**, a remarkable schoolboy batsman who did well at U19 level. I think they rushed him into the Test team too soon and he needs time to find his feet because it's a big step from age-limit cricket to playing with the big boys, as a lot of England players have found out. I can't talk about Sri Lanka's cricketers without mentioning **Arjuna Ranatunga** who was their Captain Fantastic for 10 years and won a place in the nation's heart when he lifted the World Cup. As skipper I think he's up there with Imran Khan as a true leader of men, his personality and presence a huge influence in the dressing room. He won 33.82 per cent of the 56 Tests he captained them in, a really tremendous record, and if I was picking captains he'd be straight on the team sheet. But sadly, although I like him and everything he stands for, I've got to leave him out.

Sri Lanka

SQUAD	RESERVES
Muttiah Muralitharan	Farvez Maharoof
Sanath Jayasuriya	Arjuna Ranatunga
Marvan Atapattu	
Mahela Jayawardene	
Kumar Sangakkara	
Aravinda de Silva	
Chaminder Vaas	
Roy Dias	
Asanka Gurusinha	
Tillakaratne Dilshan	
Ashantha de Mel	
Rumesh Ratnayake	
Lasith Malinga	

Zimbabwe & Bangladesh

I'm not going to pick a side for Zimbabwe or Bangladesh because there's no way either of them could compete with the other eight countries. I've maintained for some time now that Tests involving these two nations are an embarrassment. Nobody wants to see it and the vast accumulation of runs against them does nothing for the game. My mum would have scored runs and taken wickets against Bangladesh and as for the present Zimbabwe side, she'd have wanted to bat and bowl at both ends!

I've worked in Bangladesh; they are smashing people, there is some ability there and they deserve better. It destroys morale and talent to keep getting hammered. It ruins confidence and holds back their advancement. I believe they should be playing against sides of equal or slightly better ability. It's the stick and the carrot. Too much stick is no good for anybody and there has to be a chance of some success or what point is there in playing?

The figures now are totally meaningless against these two countries and it's stealing money off the public and the television companies to call them Tests. I realize both countries want to keep their status because it brings in TV money but surely you don't keep countries playing out of their depth just so they can make money. Cricketing ability must be the benchmark. Their officials all say they don't think it would do any good to relegate them from the Test arena. But, in the words of Mandy Rice-Davies in the famous court case, they would say that, wouldn't they? I honestly believe that the ICC should be ashamed of itself for allowing this devaluation of Test cricket to continue. Doing nothing is the politican's way and it's totally unacceptable. To look at it positively, the ICC could arrange overseas tours for these two countries to play the state sides in Australia, provinces in South Africa, the islands in the West Indies, the states in India and the English counties. In that way they would be able to grow, become accustomed to conditions overseas, learn from others and have a chance of winning a couple of games which would do wonders for them and put a stop to this meaningless cricket.

It's a fallacy to compare them to Pakistan when they came into Test cricket in 1952. They may have been a new country following partition in 1947 but they weren't new boys. Some of them were highly experienced and had played for India. The captain, Abdul Hafeez Kardar, had already toured in England with India in 1946 and played with Warwickshire and Oxford University. Fazal Mahmood was an experienced bowler with a lot of first class cricket under his belt and Hanif Mohammad came from a very gifted family. New Zealand and the West Indies also had a first class system in their domestic cricket before they came on the international scene in the 1930s and a lot of their players had been turning out in the leagues over here. But Bangladesh and the majority of the current Zimbabwe side are absolute novices, although one-day cricket is more of a lottery and I accept they have had their moments.

Bangladesh has won just one of its first 53 Tests, against Zimbabwe at Chittagong in January 2005, and Zimbabwe are not much better with four wins in the last 35 Tests up to May 2008, three of them against Bangladesh. In June 2001 they still had a decent team with Stuart Carlisle, the Flower brothers, Heath Streak, Guy Whittall and Andy Blignaut when they last beat a proper side, India in Harare.

Cricket is the number one sport in Bangladesh, with golf, tennis, soccer nowhere; I've no doubt they will become a force in world cricket. But it probably won't be in my lifetime or for a generation or so. A major problem is that they don't produce any fast bowlers so their batsmen, pretty talented against spin, never get used to facing real pace and are found out as soon as they come up against it.

When I made similar comments in my Lord Cowdrey lecture at MCC a couple of years back a lot of people in Bangladesh and Zimbabwe were upset at the headlines in the media. But the newspapers and commentators didn't point out the positive things I proposed to advance their cricket. I felt then, and I do now, that Bangladesh should be helped to make progress in the manner I've outlined. The simple fact is they were given full Test status too soon.

Zimbabwe is an entirely different matter. They had a half decent side at one time but since then have gone backwards and there's no sign of things getting any better. When I was a naïve young lad setting out on my first tour of South Africa in 1964–65 the President of MCC (who ran the tours in those days) gave us a little lecture before we set off about apartheid and told us not to get involved. We were guests in their country, it was nothing to do with us, etc., etc., and it was stressed that sport and politics were separate and don't mix. Forty years later and after all that's happened in the world the ICC are still peddling the same rubbish and using it as an excuse to do nothing about Zimbabwe. I'm not naïve any more and it is just too simplistic to take this approach, it's a cop-out. Bad management and corruption have ruined the Zimbabwe team and forced some very good players to walk away, some to careers elsewhere in cricket like Andy Flower to Essex, Murray Goodwin to Sussex and Neil Johnston to Western Province; others, like Henry Olonga, Guy Whittall and Alistair Campbell are lost to the game. The ICC, comprising the chairmen of the 10 Test-playing nations, do nothing because they're obsessed with money and self-interest and not acting for the benefit of world cricket. They are never going to relinquish their power and position and it would be far better in my book if the game and its future was in the hands of an independent organization like MCC, the law makers, who promote and develop cricket extensively throughout the world out of their own pockets without seeking profit.

Epilogue

To try and name a team to play against all opposition in all parts of the world from my selections is an impossible task. Everybody has their own opinion and judgements are bound to be coloured by players they have seen, which favours those of the television era who have been watched by millions all over the world. When *Wisden* named their five Players of the Century, voted for by a panel of 100 experts, they picked Sir Donald Bradman, Sir Jack Hobbs, Sir Garfield Sobers, Sir Viv Richards and Shane Warne. But the only one they all agreed on was the Don, who collected all 100 votes.

All are unarguably great players with fantastic achievements but I think some opinions tend to be biased in favour of the modern players.

In my squad there are seven who would form the spine of my team: Hobbs; Hutton; Bradman; George Headley, the West Indian they called 'the black Bradman'; Garry Sobers, the best all-rounder; Alan Knott, the finest wicketkeeper; and Sydney Barnes, who has to be the greatest bowler of all time, with figures to back up that claim. I don't think there's much argument about the core of my squad, but it's when you get to making up the rest that the debate starts.

Inevitably it all comes down to personal opinion about who would be successful in the various conditions found in Test-playing countries, from the flat, nothing pitches in

Pakistan to the fine strips in India which always turn on the third day and in Sri Lanka early in the match.

To start with, I need another batsman at number five. Most people would go for Viv, but what about Graeme Pollock, who averaged over 60 in the few Tests he played; Wally Hammond who out-Bradmanned Bradman in 1928 in Australia and held the world-record score; Brian Lara, twice holder of the highest Test score; or Everton Weekes, who older West Indians will tell you was the best ever? How the hell do you separate them? You may as well stick a pin in. Any of them will do for me, but for Tests played in the subcontinent I'd pick Everton, because he averaged 111.28 from five Tests in India in 1948–9, far and away the best in that country, and because older players who know what they are talking about rate him so highly. As one said, 'If you think Viv was good, you should have seen Everton.'

When it comes to the spinners, everyone would go for Shane Warne and so would I. But not in India, where he took wickets very expensively – 34 at 43.11 each in nine Tests – and wasn't the match-winner he was elsewhere. Leg-spin is not a big problem in Asia; they play it brilliantly, letting the ball come to them and using their flexible wrists to control the ball. I'd have no hesitation in telling Shane, 'You're not playing in India, Pakistan or Sri Lanka'; and though he probably wouldn't speak to me for a week, if I explained why I'd pick Jim Laker in front of him, he might just calm down – but I doubt it!

Jim took wickets on wet and dry pitches, and although he only played two matches in India with a Commonwealth side in 1950, I'm pretty sure he would have been a success out there. His fabulous feat in taking 19 wickets at Old Trafford in July 1956 for England against Australia was on a wet, drying pitch but a lot of people forget that he had already taken all 10 against them on a dry strip for Surrey at The Oval the previous May, 10 for 88. The soil doesn't bind in India and although they are good pitches at the start for batting they gradually break up and I'm confident Jim would have done well.

I'd prefer him to Murali because, quite frankly, I've always thought he throws it and in any case the Indians can read him and have taken a lot of runs off him, with Sachin Tendulkar averaging 111.86 from six Tests in Sri Lanka. It's a personal choice and I'm sticking with Laker.

For my left arm spinner I'm going to go with Wilfred Rhodes because he can also make a lot of runs. Derek Underwood has sound claims with 54 wickets at 26.51 in 16 Tests in India, but 'Deadly' can't bat and although we want to take 20 wickets we need to have the runs on the board. In my view it's vital to have one spinner who can bat.

Dennis Lillee, Malcolm Marshall and Fred Trueman were the three greatest genuine fast bowlers of my time and I'm going to have them in my squad. On fast, bouncy pitches I'd probably play all three but for matches in Asia I would pick Imran Khan. In the modern era, reverse swing has become an important part of the game and it's fair to say that Immy knows a fair bit about it and was a leading light in its development as a major weapon. I'd get pace with the new ball, reverse swing with the old ball and he can bat a bit too.

So for games in Asia I've got my first five batters, Sobers at six, Imran at seven, Knotty at eight, Rhodes at nine and Barnes at ten. Sobers and Imran can swing the new ball, Barnes was brilliant with it and if he didn't get it he got peeved and sulked, so I could have two spinners, Laker and Rhodes, plus Barnes to bowl fast cutters or I could leave out a spinner and play another fast bowler. If I had to pick one out of Lillee, Trueman and Marshall to bowl on the sub-continent, then it would be Malcolm. In India I think his ability to swing it, bowl cutters, up his pace and skid it through would get the vote, and 36 wickets in nine Tests at 24.61 in India and 10 at 21.45 in Pakistan support his case.

Four of my top five haven't played on the subcontinent where conditions are so very different from the rest of the world, so would they have come out on top?

I can't imagine telling the world's press that I'm leaving out Bradman because I'm not sure if he can handle spin in India. I think that'd be on the *front* page of the papers, never mind the sports pages, and the great man might have had something to say about it himself! His extraordinary hand–eye coordination, his nimble footwork and mental strength make it a certainty he would have made runs anywhere and you'd have to be very brave or very stupid to suggest leaving him out. When Jack Nicklaus was asked what was his favourite golf club, he said, 'Between the ears,' and I think it was the same thing with the Don.

Only my first seven would play in every match, with the others coming into the team to match the conditions in various parts of the world.

In the end it all comes down to opinions and in picking my best squad it's mine that count.

Statistics

All figures calculated to 15 April 2008.

England

L. E. G. AMES

First-class Matches (1926 to 1951)

593 matches   37248 runs   43.51 avge   295 HS   102 hundreds   703 ct   418 st

Test Matches (1929 to 1938–9)

47 matches   2434 runs   40.56 avge   149 HS   8 hundreds   74 ct   23 st

S. F. BARNES

First-class Matches (1884 to 1930)

133 matches   719 wkts   17.09 avge   9 for 103 best   68 5wi   18 10wm

Test Matches (1901–2 to 1913–14)

27 matches   189 wkts   16.43 avge   9 for 103 best   24 5wi   7 10wm

K. F. BARRINGTON

First-class Matches (1953 to 1968)

533 matches   31714 runs   45.63 avge   256 HS   76 hundreds

Test Matches (1955 to 1968)

82 matches   6806 runs   58.67 avge   256 HS   20 hundreds

A. V. BEDSER

First-class Matches (1939 to 1960)

485 matches   1924 wkts   20.41 avge   8 for 18 best   96 5wi   16 10wm

Test Matches (1946 to 1955)

51 matches   236 wkts   24.89 avge   7 for 44 best   15 5wi   5 10wm

I. T. BOTHAM

First-class Matches (1974 to 1993)

402 matches   19399 runs   33.97 avge   228 HS   38 hundreds
                1172 wkts   27.22 avge   8 for 34 best   59 5wi   8 10wm

Test Matches (1977 to 1992)

102 matches   5200 runs   33.54 avge   208 HS   14 hundreds
                383 wkts   28.40 avge   8 for 34 best   27 5wi   4 10wm

D. C. S. COMPTON

First-class Matches (1936 to 1964)

515 matches   38942 runs   51.85 avge   300 HS   123 hundreds
             622 wkts   32.27 avge   7 for 36 best   19 5wi   3 10wm

Test Matches (1937 to 1956–7)

78 matches   5807 runs   50.06 avge   278 HS   17 hundreds
            25 wkts   56.40 avge   5 for 70 best   1 5wi   0 10wm

W. G. GRACE

First-class Matches (1865 to 1908)

878 matches   54896 runs   39.55 avge   344 HS   126 hundreds
             2876 wkts   17.92 avge   10 for 49 best   246 5wi   66 10wm

Test Matches (1880 to 1899)

22 matches   1098 runs   32.39 avge   170 HS   2 hundreds
            9 wkts   26.22 avge   2 for 12 best   0 5wi   0 10wm

W. R. HAMMOND

First-class Matches (1920 to 1951)

634 matches   50551 runs   56.10 avge   336* HS   167 hundreds
             732 wkts   30.58 avge   9 for 23 best   22 5wi   3 10wm

Test Matches (1927–8 to 1946–7)

85 matches   7249 runs   58.45 avge   336* HS   22 hundreds
            83 wkts   37.80 avge   5 for 36 best   2 5wi   0 10wm

E. H. HENDREN

First-class Matches (1907 to 1938)

833 matches   57611 runs   50.80 avge   301* HS   170 hundreds

Test Matches (1920–1 to 1934–5)

51 matches   3525 runs   47.63 avge   205* HS   7 hundreds

J. B. HOBBS

First-class Matches (1905 to 1934)

825 matches   61237 runs   50.65 avge   316* HS   197 hundreds

Test Matches (1907–8 to 1930)

61 matches   5410 runs   56.94 avge   211 HS   15 hundreds

L. HUTTON

First-class Matches (1934 to 1960)

513 matches   40140 runs   55.51 avge   364 HS   129 hundreds

Test Matches (1937 to 1954–5)

79 matches   6971 runs   56.67 avge   364 HS   19 hundreds

A. P. E. KNOTT

First-class Matches (1964 to 1985)
511 matches   18106 runs   29.63 avge   156 HS   17 hundreds   1211 ct 133 st

Test Matches (1967 to 1981)
95 matches   4389 runs   32.75 avge   135 HS   5 hundreds   250 ct 19 st

J. C. LAKER

First-class Matches (1946 to 1964–5)
450 matches   1944 wkts 18.41 avge   10 for 53 best   127 5wi 32 10wm

Test Matches (1947–8 to 1958–9)
46 matches   193 wkts   21.24 avge   10 for 53 best   9 5wi   3 10wm

H. LARWOOD

First-class Matches (1924 to 1938)
361 matches   1427 wkts 17.51 avge   9 for 41 best   98 5wi   20 10wm

Test Matches (1926 to 1932–3)
21 matches   78 wkts   28.35 avge   6 for 32 best   4 5wi   1 10wm

G. A. R. LOCK

First-class Matches (1946 to 1970–1)
654 matches   2844 wkts 19.23 avge   10 for 54 best   196 5wi 50 10wm

Test Matches (1952 to 1967–8)
49 matches   174 wkts   25.58 avge   7 for 35 best   9 5wi   3 10wm

G. A. LOHMANN

First-class Matches (1884 to 1897–8)
293 matches   1841 wkts 13.73 avge   9 for 28 best   176 5wi 57 10wm

Test Matches (1886 to 1896)
18 matches   112 wkts   10.75 avge   9 for 28 best   9 5wi   5 10wm

W. RHODES

First-class Matches (1898 to 1930)
1107 matches 39802 runs   30.83 avge   267* HS 58 hundreds
              4187 wkts 16.71 avge   9 for 24 best   286 5wi 68 10wm

Test Matches (1899 to 1929–30)
58 matches   2325 runs   30.19 avge   179 HS   2 hundreds
              127 wkts   26.96 avge   8 for 68 best   6 5wi   1 10wm

J. B. STATHAM

First-class Matches (1950 to 1968)

559 matches   2260 wkts 16.37 avge   8 for 34 best   123 5wi 11 10wm

Test Matches (1950–1 to 1965)

70 matches   252 wkts   24.84 avge   7 for 39 best   9 5wi   1 10wm

H. SUTCLIFFE

First-class Matches (1919 to 1945)

747 matches   50138 runs   51.95 avge   313 HS   149 hundreds

Test Matches (1924 to 1935)

54 matches   4555 runs   60.73 avge   194 HS   16 hundreds

F. S. TRUEMAN

First-class Matches (1949 to 1969)

603 matches   2304 wkts 18.29 avge   8 for 28 best   126 5wi 25 10wm

Test Matches (1952 to 1965)

67 matches   307 wkts   21.57 avge   8 for 31 best   17 5wi   3 10wm

E. H. TYSON

First-class Matches (1952 to 1960)

244 matches   767 wkts   20.89 avge   8 for 60 best   34 5wi   5 10wm

Test Matches (1954 to 1958–9)

17 matches   76 wkts   18.56 avge   7 for 27 best   4 5wi   1 10wm

D. L. UNDERWOOD

First-class Matches (1963 to 1987)

676 matches   2465 wkts 20.28 avge   9 for 28 best   153 5wi 47 10wm

Test Matches (1966 to 1981–2)

86 matches   297 wkts   25.83 avge   8 for 51 best   17 5wi   6 10wm

H. VERITY

First-class Matches (1930 to 1939)

378 matches   1956 wkts 14.90 avge   10 for 10 best   164 5wi 54 10wm

Test Matches (1931 to 1939)

40 matches   144 wkts   24.37 avge   8 for 43 best   5 5wi   2 10wm

J. H. WARDLE

First-class Matches (1946 to 1967–8)

412 matches   1846 wkts   18.97 avge   9 for 25 best   134 5wi 29 10wm

Test Matches (1947–8 to 1957)

28 matches   102 wkts   20.39 avge   7 for 36 best   5 5wi   1 10wm

Note: There have been recent attempts to alter classification of some matches from that determined at the time they were played but many statisticians believe that, at this distance in time,
we cannot tamper with the figures that have been generally accepted for many years. The players affected in the above list are W. G. Grace, J. B. Hobbs, W. Rhodes and H. Sutcliffe and their
details given here are the 'traditional' ones and agree with Bill Frindall and *Wisden*.

As far as Hobbs and Sutcliffe are concerned, they were in no doubt as to the status of the
'disputed' matches. Both were adamant that the matches concerned were friendlies and got up
for the entertainment of the Maharajkumar of Vizianagram on a tour to India and Ceylon (now
Sri Lanka) in 1930–1 and were not to be regarded as first-class.

Australia

Note: Test Match details for A. C. Gilchrist, G. D. McGrath, R. T. Ponting and S. K. Warne *exclude* Australia v ICC World XI in 2005–6

D. G. BRADMAN

First-class Matches (1927–8 to 1948–9)
234 matches   28067 runs   95.14 avge   452* HS 117 hundreds

Test Matches (1928–9 to 1948)
52 matches   6996 runs   99.94 avge   334 HS   29 hundreds

G. S. CHAPPELL

First-class Matches (1966–7 to 1983–4)
321 matches   24535 runs   52.20 avge   247* HS 74 hundreds

Test Matches (1970–1 to 1983–4)
87 matches   7110 runs   53.96 avge   247* HS 24 hundreds

A. K. DAVIDSON

First-class Matches (1949–50 to 1962–3)
193 matches   6804 runs   32.86 avge   129 HS   9 hundreds
              672 wkts   20.90 avge   7 for 31 best   33 5wi 2 10wm

Test Matches (1953 to 1962–3)
44 matches   1328 runs   24.59 avge   80 HS   0 hundreds
             186 wkts   20.53 avge   7 for 93 best   14 5wi 2 10wm

A. C. GILCHRIST

First-class Matches (1992–3 to 2007–8)
190 matches   10334 runs   44.16 avge   204* HS 30 hundreds   756 ct 55 st

Test Matches (1999–2000 to 2007–8)
95 matches   5475 runs   47.60 avge   204* HS 17 hundreds   374 ct 35 st

C. V. GRIMMETT

First-class Matches (1911–12 to 1940–1)
248 matches   1424 wkts 22.28 avge   10 for 37 best   127 5wi 33 10wm

Test Matches (1924–5 to 1935–6)
37 matches   216 wkts   24.21 avge   7 for 40 best   21 5wi   7 10wm

R. N. HARVEY

First-class Matches (1946–7 to 1962–3)
306 matches   21699 runs   50.93 avge   231* HS 67 hundreds

Test Matches (1947–8 to 1962–3)
79 matches   6149 runs   48.41 avge   205 HS 21 hundreds

W. M. LAWRY

First-class Matches (1955–6 to 1971–2)
249 matches   18734 runs   50.90 avge   266 HS 50 hundreds

Test Matches (1961 to 1970–1)
67 matches   5234 runs   47.15 avge   210 HS 13 hundreds

D. K. LILLEE

First-class Matches (1969–70 to 1988)
198 matches   882 wkts   23.46 avge   8 for 29 best   50 5wi   13 10wm

Test Matches (1970–1 to 1983–4)
70 matches   355 wkts   23.92 avge   7 for 83 best   23 5wi   7 10wm

R. R. LINDWALL

First-class Matches (1941–2 to 1961–2)
228 matches   794 wkts   21.35 avge   7 for 20 best   34 5wi   2 10wm

Test Matches (1945–6 to 1959–60)
61 matches   228 wkts   23.03 avge   7 for 38 best   12 5wi   0 10wm

G. D. McGRATH

First-class Matches (1992–3 to 2006–7)
189 matches   835 wkts   20.85 avge   8 for 24 best   42 5wi   7 10wm

Test Matches (1993–4 to 2006–7)
123 matches   560 wkts   21.68 avge   8 for 24 best   29 5wi   3 10wm

K. R. MILLER

First-class Matches (1937–8 to 1959)
226 matches   14183 runs   48.90 avge   281* HS 41 hundreds
               497 wkts   22.30 avge   7 for 12 best   16 5wi   1 10wm

Test Matches (1945–6 to 1956–7)
55 matches   2958 runs   36.97 avge   147 HS   7 hundreds
              170 wkts   22.97 avge   7 for 60 best   7 5wi   1 10wm

A. R. MORRIS

First-class Matches (1940–1 to 1963–4)
162 matches   12614 runs   53.67 avge   290 HS   46 hundreds

Test Matches (1946–7 to 1954–5)
46 matches   3533 runs   46.48 avge   206 HS   12 hundreds

W. J. O'REILLY

First-class Matches (1927–8 to 1945–6)
135 matches   774 wkts   16.60 avge   9 for 38 best   63 5wi   17 10wm

Test Matches (1931–2 to 1945–6)
27 matches   144 wkts   22.59 avge   7 for 54 best   11 5wi   3 10wm

R. T. PONTING

First-class Matches (1992–3 to 2007–8)
212 matches   18378 runs   60.05 avge   257 HS   68 hundreds

Test Matches (1995–6 to 2007–8)
115 matches   9676 runs   58.64 avge   257 HS   34 hundreds

R. B. SIMPSON

First-class Matches (1952–3 to 1977–8)
257 matches   21029 runs   56.22 avge   359 HS   60 hundreds

Test Matches (1957–8 to 1977–8)
62 matches   4869 runs   46.81 avge   311 HS   10 hundreds

F. R. SPOFFORTH

First-class Matches (1874–5 to 1897)
155 matches   853 wkts   14.95 avge   9 for 18 best   84 5wi   32 10wm

Test Matches (1876–7 to 1886–7)
18 matches   94 wkts   18.41 avge   7 for 44 best   7 5wi   4 10wm

J. R. THOMSON

First-class Matches (1972–3 to 1985–6)
187 matches   675 wkts   26.46 avge   7 for 27 best   28 5wi   3 10wm

Test Matches (1972–3 to 1985)
51 matches   200 wkts   28.00 avge   6 for 46 best   8 5wi   0 10wm

V. T. TRUMPER

First-class Matches (1894–5 to 1913–14)

255 matches   16939 runs   44.57 avge   300* HS 42 hundreds

Test Matches (1899 to 1911–12)

48 matches   3163 runs   39.04 avge   214* HS 8 hundreds

S. K. WARNE

First-class Matches (1990–1 to 2007)

301 matches   1319 wkts 26.11 avge   8 for 71 best   69 5wi   12 10wm

Test Matches (1991–2 to 2006–7)

144 matches   702 wkts   25.53 avge   8 for 71 best   37 5wi   10 10wm

S. K. WARNE

versus India in India

By Season

Season	Matches	Overs	Maidens	Runs	Wickets	Avge	Best	5wi	10wm
1997–8	3	167	37	540	10	54.00	4 for 85	0	0
2000–1	3	152.1	31	505	10	50.50	4 for 47	0	0
2004–5	3	140	27	421	14	30.07	6 for 125	1	0
Totals	**9**	**459.1**	**95**	**1466**	**34**	**43.11**	**6 for 125**	**1**	**0**

By Ground

Ground	Matches	Overs	Maidens	Runs	Wickets	Avge	Best	5wi	10wm
Bangalore	2	120	27	379	9	42.11	3 for 106	0	0
Calcutta	2	96.1	10	364	3	121.33	2 for 65	0	0
Chennai	3	155.3	30	513	13	39.46	6 for 125	1	0
Mumbai	1	50	18	107	5	21.40	4 for 47	0	0
Nagpur	1	37.3	10	103	4	25.75	2 for 47	0	0
Totals	**9**	**459.1**	**95**	**1466**	**34**	**43.11**	**6 for 125**	**1**	**0**

Note: Warne's overall average versus India (home and away) is 14 matches, 43 wickets at 47.18 – by far his worst average against any Test team. His next worst is 65 wickets for 29.95 in 19 matches versus West Indies.

South Africa

Note: The Test Match details for M. V. Boucher and J. H. Kallis *exclude* Australia v. ICC World XI in 2005–6.

N. A. T. ADCOCK

First-class Matches (1952–3 to 1962–3)

99 matches   405 wkts   17.25 avge   8 for 39 best   19 5wi   4 10wm

Test Matches (1953–4 to 1961–2)

26 matches   104 wkts   21.10 avge   6 for 43 best   5 5wi   0 10wm

E. J. BARLOW

First-class Matches (1959–60 to 1982–3)

283 matches   18212 runs   39.16 avge   217 HS   43 hundreds

571 wkts   24.14 avge   7 for 24 best   16 5wi   2 10wm

Test Matches (1961–2 to 1969–70)

30 matches   2516 runs   45.74 avge   201 HS   6 hundreds

40 wkts   34.05 avge   5 for 85 best   1 5wi   0 10wm

K. C. BLAND

First-class Matches (1956–7 to 1973–4)

131 matches   7249 runs   37.95 avge   197 HS   13 hundreds

Test Matches (1961–2 to 1966–7)

21 matches   1669 runs   49.08 avge   144* HS   3 hundreds

M. V. BOUCHER

First-class Matches (1995–6 to 2007–8)

171 matches   7226 runs   33.60 avge   134 HS   8 hundreds   578 ct   33 st

Test Matches (1997–8 to 2007–8)

113 matches   4217 runs   30.33 avge   125 HS   4 hundreds   409 ct   20 st

A. A. DONALD

First-class Matches (1985–6 to 2003–4)

316 matches   1216 wkts   22.76 avge   8 for 37 best   68 5wi   9 10wm

Test Matches (1991–2 to 2001–2)

72 matches   330 wkts   22.25 avge   8 for 71 best   20 5wi   3 10wm

G. A. FAULKNER

First-class Matches (1902–3 to 1924)

118 matches   6366 runs   36.58 avge   204 HS   13 hundreds
449 wkts   17.42 avge   7 for 26 best   33 5wi   8 10wm

Test Matches (1905–6 to 1924)

25 matches   1754 runs   40.79 avge   204 HS   4 hundreds
82 wkts   26.58 avge   7 for 84 best   4 5wi   0 10wm

P. S. HEINE

First-class Matches (1951–2 to 1964–5)

61 matches   277 wkts   21.38 avge   8 for 92 best   20 5wi   4 10wm

Test Matches (1955 to 1961–2)

14 matches   58 wkts   25.08 avge   6 for 58 best   4 5wi   0 10wm

J. H. KALLIS

First-class Matches (1993–4 to 2007–8)

205 matches   15693 runs   54.30 avge   200 HS   46 hundreds
364 wkts   30.47 avge   6 for 54 best   8 5wi   0 10wm

Test Matches (1995–6 to 2007–8)

118 matches   9574 runs   56.98 avge   189* HS   30 hundreds
229 wkts   31.27 avge   6 for 54 best   5 5wi   0 10wm

G. S. LE ROUX

First-class Matches (1975–6 to 1988–9)

239 matches   5425 runs   25.71 avge   86 HS   0 hundreds
838 wkts   21.24 avge   8 for 107 best   35 5wi   3 10wm

Test Matches (none)

D. T. LINDSAY

First-class Matches (1958–9 to 1973–4)

124 matches   7074 runs   35.54 avge   216 HS   12 hundreds   292 ct   41 st

Test Matches (1963–4 to 1969–70)

19 matches   1130 runs   37.66 avge   182 HS   3 hundreds   57 ct   2 st

A. MELVILLE

First-class Matches (1928–9 to 1948–9)

190 matches   10598 runs   37.85 avge   189 HS   25 hundreds

Test Matches (1938–9 to 1948–9)

11 matches   894 runs   52.58 avge   189 HS   4 hundreds

B. MITCHELL

First-class Matches (1925–6 to 1949–50)
173 matches   11395 runs   45.39 avge   195 HS   30 hundreds

Test Matches (1929 to 1948–9)
42 matches   3471 runs   48.88 avge   189* HS   8 hundreds

A. D. NOURSE

First-class Matches (1932 to 1952–3)
175 matches   12472 runs   51.53 avge   260* HS   41 hundreds

Test Matches (1935 to 1951)
34 matches   2960 runs   53.81 avge   231 HS   9 hundreds

P. M. POLLOCK

First-class Matches (1958–9 to 1971–2)
127 matches   485 wkts   21.89 avge   7 for 19 best   27 5wi   2 10wm

Test Matches (1961–2 to 1969–70)
28 matches   116 wkts   24.18 avge   6 for 38 best   9 5wi   1 10wm

R. G. POLLOCK

First-class Matches (1960–1 to 1986–7)
262 matches   20940 runs   54.67 avge   274 HS   64 hundreds

Test Matches (1963–4 to 1969–70)
23 matches   2256 runs   60.97 avge   274 HS   7 hundreds

M. J. PROCTER

First-class Matches (1965 to 1988–9)
401 matches   21936 runs   36.01 avge   254 HS   48 hundreds
                1417 wkts   19.53 avge   9 for 71 best   70 5wi   15 10wm

Test Matches (1966–7 to 1969–70)
7 matches   226 runs   25.11 avge   48 HS   0 hundreds
              41 wkts   15.02 avge   6 for 73 best   1 5wi   0 10wm

B. A. RICHARDS

First-class Matches (1964–5 to 1982–3)
339 matches   28358 runs   54.74 avge   356 HS   80 hundreds

Test Matches (1969–70)
4 matches   508 runs   72.57 avge   140 HS   2 hundreds

H. J. TAYFIELD

First-class Matches (1945–6 to 1962–3)
187 matches   864 wkts   21.86 avge   9 for 113 best   67 5wi   16 10wm

Test Matches (1949–50 to 1960)
37 matches   170 wkts   25.91 avge   9 for 113 best   14 5wi   2 10wm

H. W. TAYLOR

First-class Matches (1909–10 to 1935–6)
206 matches   13105 runs   41.86 avge   250* HS 30 hundreds

Test Matches (1912 to 1931–2)
42 matches   2936 runs   40.77 avge   176 HS   7 hundreds

V. A. P. VAN DER BIJL

First-class Matches (1967–8 to 1982–3)
156 matches   767 wkts   16.54 avge   8 for 35 best   46 5wi   12 10wm

Test Matches (none)

J. H. B. WAITE

First-class Matches (1948–9 to 1965–6)
199 matches   9812 runs   35.04 avge   219 HS   23 hundreds   427 ct 84 st

Test Matches (1951 to 1964–5)
50 matches   2405 runs   30.44 avge   134 HS   4 hundreds   124 ct 17 st

West Indies

Note: Test Match details for B. C. Lara *exclude* Australia v. ICC World XI in 2005–6.

C. E. L. AMBROSE

First-class Matches (1985–6 to 2000)
239 matches   941 wkts   20.24 avge   8 for 45 best   50 5wi   8 10wm

Test Matches (1987–8 to 2000)
98 matches   405 wkts   20.99 avge   8 for 45 best   22 5wi   3 10wm

P. J. L. DUJON

First-class Matches (1974–5 to 1992–3)
200 matches   9763 runs   39.05 avge   163* HS 21 hundreds   447 ct 22 st

Test Matches (1981–2 to 1991)
81 matches   3322 runs   31.94 avge   139 HS 5 hundreds   267 ct 5 st

J. GARNER

First-class Matches (1975–6 to 1987–8)
214 matches   881 wkts   18.53 avge   8 for 31 best   48 5wi   7 10wm

Test Matches (1976–7 to 1986–7)
58 matches   259 wkts   20.97 avge   6 for 56 best   7 5wi   0 10wm

L. R. GIBBS

First-class Matches (1953–4 to 1975–6)
330 matches   1024 wkts 27.22 avge   8 for 37 best   50 5wi   10 10wm

Test Matches (1957–8 to 1975–6)
79 matches   309 wkts   29.09 avge   8 for 38 best   18 5wi   2 10wm

C. G. GREENIDGE

First-class Matches (1970 to 1992)
523 matches   37354 runs   45.88 avge   273* HS 92 hundreds

Test Matches (1974–5 to 1990–1)
108 matches   7558 runs   44.72 avge   226 HS 19 hundreds

C. C. GRIFFITH

First-class Matches (1959–60 to 1968–9)

96 matches   332 wkts   21.60 avge   8 for 23 best   17 5wi   1 10wm

Test Matches (1959–60 to 1968–9)

28 matches   94 wkts   28.54 avge   6 for 36 best   5 5wi   0 10wm

W. W. HALL

First-class Matches (1955–6 to 1970–1)

170 matches   546 wkts   26.14 avge   7 for 51 best   19 5wi   2 10wm

Test Matches (1958–9 to 1968–9)

48 matches   192 wkts   26.38 avge   7 for 69 best   9 5wi   1 10wm

D. L. HAYNES

First-class Matches (1976–7 to 1996–7)

376 matches   29030 runs   45.90 avge   255* HS   61 hundreds

Test Matches (1977–8 to 1993–4)

116 matches   7487 runs   42.29 avge   184 HS   18 hundreds

G. A. HEADLEY

First-class Matches (1927–8 to 1954)

103 matches   9921 runs   69.86 avge   344* HS   33 hundreds

Test Matches (1929–30 to 1953–4)

22 matches   2190 runs   60.83 avge   270* HS   10 hundreds

M. A. HOLDING

First-class Matches (1972–3 to 1989)

222 matches   778 wkts   23.43 avge   8 for 92 best   39 5wi   5 10wm

Test Matches (1975–6 to 1986–7)

60 matches   249 wkts   23.68 avge   8 for 92 best   13 5wi   2 10wm

C. C. HUNTE

First-class Matches (1950–1 to 1967)

132 matches   8916 runs   43.92 avge   263 HS   16 hundreds

Test Matches (1957–8 to 1966–7)

44 matches   3245 runs   45.06 avge   260 HS   8 hundreds

B. C. LARA

First-class Matches (1987–8 to 2006–7)
259 matches   21971 runs   51.57 avge   501* HS 64 hundreds

Test Matches (1990–1 to 2006–7)
130 matches   11912 runs   53.17 avge   400* HS 34 hundreds

M. D. MARSHALL

First-class Matches (1977–8 to 1995–6)
408 matches   11004 runs   24.83 avge   120* HS 7 hundreds
          1651 wkts 19.10 avge   8 for 71 best   85 5wi   13 10wm

Test Matches (1978–9 to 1991)
81 matches   1810 runs   18.85 avge   92 HS   0 hundreds
          376 wkts   20.94 avge   7 for 22 best   22 5wi   4 10wm

S. RAMADHIN

First-class Matches (1949–50 to 1965)
184 matches   758 wkts   20.24 avge   8 for 15 best   51 5wi   15 10wm

Test Matches (1950 to 1960–1)
43 matches   158 wkts   28.98 avge   7 for 49 best   10 5wi   1 10wm

I. V. A. RICHARDS

First-class Matches (1971–2 to 1993)
507 matches   36212 runs   49.40 avge   322 HS   114 hundreds

Test Matches (1974–5 to 1991)
121 matches   8540 runs   50.23 avge   291 HS   24 hundreds

A. M. E. ROBERTS

First-class Matches (1969–70 to 1984)
228 matches   889 wkts   21.01 avge   8 for 47 best   47 5wi   7 10wm

Test Matches (1973–4 to 1983–4)
47 matches   202 wkts   25.61 avge   7 for 54 best   11 5wi   2 10wm

G. ST A. SOBERS

First-class Matches (1952–3 to 1974)
383 matches   28314 runs   54.87 avge   365* HS 86 hundreds
          1043 wkts 27.74 avge   9 for 49 best   36 5wi   1 10wm

Test Matches (1952–3 to 1973–4)
93 matches   8032 runs   57.78 avge   365* HS 26 hundreds
          235 wkts   34.03 avge   6 for 73 best   6 5wi   0 10wm

C. L. WALCOTT

First-class Matches (1941–2 to 1963–4)

146 matches   11820 runs   56.55 avge   314* HS   40 hundreds

Test Matches (1947–8 to 1959–60)

44 matches   3798 runs   56.68 avge   220 HS   15 hundreds

E. DE C. WEEKES

First-class Matches (1944–5 to 1963–4)

152 matches   12010 runs   55.34 avge   304* HS   36 hundreds

Test Matches (1947–8 to 1957–8)

48 matches   4455 runs   58.61 avge   207 HS   15 hundreds

F. M. M. WORRELL

First-class Matches (1941–2 to 1964)

208 matches   15025 runs   54.24 avge   308* HS   39 hundreds

                349 wkts   28.98 avge   7 for 70 best   13 5wi   0 10wm

Test Matches (1947–8 to 1963)

51 matches   3860 runs   49.48 avge   261 HS   9 hundreds

                69 wkts   38.72 avge   7 for 70 best   2 5wi   0 10wm

New Zealand

Note: Test Match details for D. L. Vettori *exclude* Australia v. ICC World XI in 2005–6.

J. G. BRACEWELL

First-class Matches (1978–9 to 1990)

149 matches	4354 runs	25.91 avge	110 HS	4 hundreds
	522 wkts	26.66 avge	8 for 81 best	33 5wi	9 10wm

Test Matches (1980–1 to 1990)

41 matches	1001 runs	20.42 avge	110 HS	1 hundred
	102 wkts	35.81 avge	6 for 32 best	4 5wi	1 10wm

C. L. CAIRNS

First-class Matches (1988 to 2005–6)

217 matches	10702 runs	35.32 avge	158 HS	13 hundreds
	647 wkts	28.31 avge	8 for 47 best	30 5wi	6 10wm

Test Matches (1989–90 to 2004)

62 matches	3320 runs	33.53 avge	158 HS	5 hundreds
	218 wkts	29.40 avge	7 for 27 best	13 5wi	1 10wm

J. COWIE

First-class Matches (1932–3 to 1949–50)

86 matches	359 wkts	22.28 avge	6 for 3 best	20 5wi	1 10wm

Test Matches (1937 to 1949)

9 matches	45 wkts	21.53 avge	6 for 40 best	4 5wi	1 10wm

M. D. CROWE

First-class Matches (1979–80 to 1995–6)

247 matches	19608 runs	56.02 avge	299 HS	71 hundreds

Test Matches (1981–2 to 1995–6)

77 matches	5444 runs	45.36 avge	299 HS	17 hundreds

C. S. DEMPSTER

First-class Matches (1921–2 to 1947–8)

184 matches	12145 runs	44.98 avge	212 HS	35 hundreds

Test Matches (1929–30 to 1932–3)

10 matches	723 runs	65.72 avge	126 HS	2 hundreds

M. P. DONNELLY

First-class Matches (1936–7 to 1960–1)

131 matches   9250 runs   47.43 avge   208*HS   23 hundreds

Test Matches (1937 to 1949)

7 matches   582 runs   52.90 avge   206 HS   1 hundred

R. J. HADLEE

First-class Matches (1971–2 to 1990)

342 matches   12052 runs   31.71 avge   210* HS   14 hundreds

             1490 wkts   18.11 avge   9 for 52 best   102 5wi 18 10wm

Test Matches (1972–3 to 1990)

86 matches   3124 runs   27.16 avge   151* HS   2 hundreds

             431 wkts   22.29 avge   9 for 52 best   36 5wi   9 10wm

A. JONES

First-class Matches (1979–80 to 1995–6)

145 matches   9180 runs   41.53 avge   186 HS   16 hundreds

Test Matches (1986–7 to 1994–5)

39 matches   2922 runs   44.27 avge   186 HS   7 hundreds

B. B. McCULLUM

First-class Matches (1999–2000 to 2007–8)

68 matches   3548 runs   32.85   160 HS   6 hundreds   185 ct   13 st

Test Matches (2003–4 to 2007–8)

32 matches   1485 runs   30.93   143 HS   2 hundreds   95 ct   6 st

R. C. MOTZ

First-class Matches (1957–8 to 1969)

142 matches   518 wkts   22.71 avge   8 for 61 best   24 5wi   4 10wm

Test Matches (1961–2 to 1969)

32 matches   100 wkts   31.48 avge   6 for 63 best   5 5wi   0 10wm

A. C. PARORE

First-class Matches (1988–9 to 2001–2)

163 matches   6826 runs   32.66 avge   155* HS   10 hundreds   367 ct   24 st

Test Matches (1990 to 2001–2)

78 matches   2865 runs   26.28 avge   110 HS   2 hundreds   197 ct   7 st

J. R. REID

First-class Matches (1947–8 to 1965)

246 matches   16128 runs   41.35 avge   296 HS   39 hundreds
466 wkts   22.60 avge   7 for 20 best   15 5wi   1 10wm

Test Matches (1949 to 1965)

58 matches   3428 runs   33.28 avge   142 HS   6 hundreds
85 wkts   33.35 avge   6 for 60 best   1 5wi   0 10wm

I. D. S. SMITH

First-class Matches (1977–8 to 1991–2)

178 matches   5570 runs   26.77 avge   173 HS   6 hundreds   417 ct   36 st

Test Matches (1980–1 to 1991–2)

63 matches   1815 runs   25.56 avge   173 HS   2 hundreds   168 ct   8 st

B. SUTCLIFFE

First-class Matches (1941–2 to 1965–6)

233 matches   17447 runs   47.41 avge   385 HS   44 hundreds

Test Matches (1946–7 to 1965)

42 matches   2727 runs   40.10 avge   230* HS   5 hundreds

B. R. TAYLOR

First-class Matches (1963–4 to 1979–80)

141 matches   4579 runs   24.75 avge   173 HS   4 hundreds
422 wkts   25.13 avge   7 for 74 best   15 5wi   0 10wm

Test Matches (1964–5 to 1973)

30 matches   898 runs   20.40 avge   124 HS   2 hundreds
111 wkts   26.60 avge   7 for 74 best   4 5wi   0 10wm

G. M. TURNER

First-class Matches (1964–5 to 1982–3)

455 matches   34346 runs   49.70 avge   311* HS   103 hundreds

Test Matches (1968–9 to 1982–3)

41 matches   2991 runs   44.64 avge   259 HS   7 hundreds

D. L. VETTORI

First-class Matches (1996–7 to 2007–8)

128 matches   4305 runs   28.13 avge   137* HS   4 hundreds
407 wkts   32.28 avge   7 for 87 best   23 5wi   3 10wm

Test Matches (1996–7 to 2007–8)

79 matches   2676 runs   27.58 avge   137* HS   2 hundreds
244 wkts   34.49 avge   7 for 87 best   13 5wi   3 10wm

India

Note: The Test Match details for R. S. Dravid *exclude* Australia v. ICC World XI in 2005–6.

M. AZHARUDDIN

First-class Matches (1981–2 to 1999–2000)

229 matches   15855 runs   51.98 avge   226 HS   54 hundreds

Test Matches (1984–5 to 1999–2000)

99 matches   6215 runs   45.03 avge   199 HS   22 hundreds

B. S. BEDI

First-class Matches (1961–2 to 1981–2)

370 matches   1560 wkts   21.69 avge   7 for 5 best   106 5wi   20 10wm

Test Matches (1966–7 to 1979)

67 matches   266 wkts   28.71 avge   7 for 98 best   14 5wi   1 10wm

B. S. CHANDRASEKHAR

First-class Matches (1963–4 to 1979–80)

246 matches   1063 wkts   24.03 avge   9 for 72 best   75 5wi   19 10wm

Test Matches (1963–4 to 1979)

58 matches   242 wkts   29.74 avge   8 for 79 best   16 5wi   2 10wm

R. S. DRAVID

First-class Matches (1990–1 to 2007–8)

241 matches   19259 runs   56.81 avge   270 HS   52 hundreds

Test Matches (1996 to 2007–8)

121 matches   10075 runs   55.35 avge   270 HS   25 hundreds

F. M. ENGINEER

First-class Matches (1958–9 to 1976)

335 matches   13436 runs   29.52 avge   192 HS   13 hundreds   704 ct   120 st

Test Matches (1961–2 to 1974–5)

46 matches   2611 runs   31.08 avge   121 HS   2 hundreds   66 ct   16 st

S. M. GAVASKAR

First-class Matches (1966–7 to 1987)

348 matches   25834 runs   51.46 avge   340 HS   81 hundreds

Test Matches (1970–1 to 1986–7)

125 matches   10122 runs   51.12 avge   236* HS   34 hundreds

HARBHAJAN SINGH

First-class Matches (1997–8 to 2007–8)

129 matches   546 wkts   27.45 avge   8 for 84 best   35 5wi   6 10wm

Test Matches (1997–8 to 2007–8)

66 matches   275 wkts   31.03 avge   8 for 84 best   21 5wi   4 10wm

V. S. HAZARE

First-class Matches (1934–5 to 1966–7)

238 matches   18740 runs   58.38 avge   316* HS 60 hundreds

Test Matches (1946 to 1952–3)

30 matches   2192 runs   47.65 avge   164* HS 7 hundreds

KAPIL DEV

First-class Matches (1975–6 to 1993–4)

275 matches   11356 runs   39.21 avge   193 HS   18 hundreds
835 wkts   27.09 avge   9 for 83 best   39 5wi   3 10wm

Test Matches (1978–9 to 1993–4)

131 matches   5248 runs   31.05 avge   163 HS   8 hundreds
434 wkts   29.64 avge   9 for 83 best   23 5wi   2 10wm

S. M. H. KIRMANI

First-class Matches (1967–8 to 1993–4)

275 matches   9620 runs   30.15 avge   161 HS   13 hundreds   367 ct   112 st

Test Matches (1975–6 to 1985–6)

88 matches   2759 runs   27.04 avge   102 HS   2 hundreds   160 ct   38 st

A. KUMBLE

First-class Matches (1989–90 to 2007–8)

238 matches   1120 wkts   25.54 avge   10 for 74 best   72 5wi   19 10wm

Test Matches (1990 to 2007–8)

127 matches   608 wkts   29.06 avge   10 for 74 best   35 5wi   8 10wm

V. V. S. LAXMAN

First-class Matches (1992–3 to 2007–8)

206 matches   15235 runs   51.29 avge   353 HS   44 hundreds

Test Matches (1996–7 to 2007–8)

93 matches   5785 runs   43.82 avge   281 HS   12 hundreds

M. H. MANKAD

First-class Matches (1935–6 to 1963–4)

233 matches   11593 runs   34.60 avge   231 HS   26 hundreds
782 wkts   24.53 avge   8 for 35 best   38 5wi   9 10wm

Test Matches (1946 to 1958–9)

44 matches   2109 runs   31.47 avge   231 HS   5 hundreds
162 wkts   32.32 avge   8 for 52 best   8 5wi   2 10wm

V. M. MERCHANT

First-class Matches (1929–30 to 1951–2)

150 matches   13470 runs   71.64 avge   359* HS   45 hundreds

Test Matches (1933–4 to 1951–2)

10 matches   859 runs   47.72 avge   154 HS   3 hundreds

E. A. S. PRASANNA

First-class Matches (1961–2 to 1978–9)

235 matches   957 wkts   23.45 avge   8 for 50 best   56 5wi   9 10wm

Test Matches (1961–2 to 1978–9)

49 matches   189 wkts   30.38 avge   8 for 76 best   10 5wi   2 10wm

N. S. SIDHU

First-class Matches (1981–2 to 1999–2000)

157 matches   9571 runs   44.31 avge   286 HS   27 hundreds

Test Matches (1983–4 to 1998–9)

51 matches   3202 runs   42.13 avge   201 HS   9 hundreds

J. SRINATH

First-class Matches (1989–90 to 2003)

147 matches   533 wkts   26.31 avge   9 for 76 best   23 5wi   3 10wm

Test Matches (1991–2 to 2002–3)

??? matches   236 wkts   30.49 avge   8 for 86 best   10 5wi   1 10wm

S. R. TENDULKAR

First-class Matches (1988–9 to 2007–8)

247 matches   20545 runs   59.37 avge   248* HS   65 hundreds

Test Matches (1989–90 to 2007–8)

147 matches   11782 runs   55.31 avge   248* HS   39 hundreds

P. R. UMRIGAR

First-class Matches (1944–5 to 1967–8)

243 matches   16155 runs   52.28 avge   252* HS 49 hundreds

Test Matches (1948–9 to 1961–2)

59 matches   3631 runs   42.22 avge   223 HS   12 hundreds

D. B. VENGSARKAR

First-class Matches (1975–6 to 1991–2)

260 matches   17868 runs   52.86 avge   284 HS   55 hundreds

Test Matches (1975–6 to 1991–2)

116 matches   6868 runs   42.13 avge   166 HS   17 hundreds

S. VENKATARAGHAVAN

First-class Matches (1963–4 to 1984–5)

341 matches   6617 runs   17.73 avge   137 HS   1 hundred
              1390 wkts 24.14 avge   9 for 93 best   85 5wi   21 10wm

Test Matches (1964–5 to 1983–4)

57 matches   748 runs   11.68 avge   64 HS   0 hundreds
              156 wkts   36.11 avge   8 for 72 best   3 5wi   1 10wm

Pakistan

Note: Test Match details for Inzamam-ul-Haq *exclude* Australia v. ICC World XI in 2005–6.

ABDUL QADIR
First-class Matches (1975–6 to 1995–6)
209 matches   960 wkts   23.24 avge   9 for 49 best   75 5wi   21 10wm

Test Matches (1977–8 to 1990–1)
67 matches   236 wkts   32.80 avge   9 for 56 best   15 5wi   5 10wm

ASIF IQBAL
First-class Matches (1959–60 to 1982)
440 matches   23329 runs   37.26 avge   196 HS   45 hundreds

Test Matches (1964–5 to 1979–80)
58 matches   3575 runs   38.85 avge   175 HS   11 hundreds

FAZAL MAHMOOD
First-class Matches (1943–4 to 1963–4)
112 matches   466 wkts   18.96 avge   9 for 43 best   38 5wi   8 10wm

Test Matches (1952–3 to 1962)
34 matches   139 wkts   24.70 avge   7 for 42 best   13 5wi   4 10wm

HANIF MOHAMMAD
First-class Matches (1951–2 to 1975–6)
238 matches   17059 runs   52.32 avge   499 HS   55 hundreds

Test Matches (1952–3 to 1969–70)
55 matches   3915 runs   43.98 avge   337 HS   12 hundreds

IMRAN KHAN
First-class Matches (1969–70 to 1991–2)
382 matches   17771 runs   36.79 avge   170 HS   30 hundreds
       * 1287 wkts   22.32 avge   8 for 34 best   70 5wi   13 10wm

Test Matches (1971 to 1991–2)
88 matches   3807 runs   37.69 avge   136 HS   6 hundreds
       362 wkts   22.81 avge   8 for 58 best   23 5wi   6 10wm

INZAMAM-UL-HAQ

First-class Matches (1985–6 to 2007–8)

245 matches   16785 runs   50.10 avge   329 HS   45 hundreds

Test Matches (1992 to 2007–8)

119 matches   8829 runs   50.16 avge   329 HS   25 hundreds

JAVED MIANDAD

First-class Matches (1973–4 to 1993–4)

402 matches   28663 runs   53.37 avge   311 HS   80 hundreds

Test Matches (1976–7 to 1993–4)

124 matches   8832 runs   52.57 avge   280* HS   23 hundreds

MAJID KHAN

First-class Matches (1961–2 to 1984–5)

410 matches   27444 runs   43.01 avge   241 HS   73 hundreds

Test Matches (1964–5 to 1982–3)

63 matches   3931 runs   38.92 avge   167 HS   8 hundreds

MOHAMMAD YOUSUF

First-class Matches (1996–7 to 2007–8)

120 matches   9106 runs   50.58 avge   223 HS   27 hundreds

Test Matches (1997–8 to 2007–8)

79 matches   6770 runs   55.49 avge   223 HS   23 hundreds

MUSHTAQ MOHAMMAD

First-class Matches (1956–7 to 1985)

502 matches   31091 runs   42.07 avge   303* HS   72 hundreds
936 wkts   24.34 avge   7 for 18 best   39 5wi   2 10wm

Test Matches (1958–9 to 1978–9)

57 matches   3643 runs   39.17 avge   210 HS   10 hundreds
79 wkts   29.22 avge   5 for 28 best   3 5wi   0 10wm

SAEED ANWAR

First-class Matches (1986–7 to 2002–3)

146 matches   10169 runs   45.19 avge   221 HS   30 hundreds

Test Matches (1990–1 to 2001–2)

55 matches   4052 runs   45.52 avge   188* HS   11 hundreds

SHOAIB AKHTAR

First-class Matches (1994–5 to 2007–8)

128 matches 450 wkts 26.49 avge 6 for 11 best 28 5wi 2 10wm

Test Matches (1997–8 to 2007–8)

46 matches 178 wkts 25.69 avge 6 for 11 best 12 5wi 2 10wm

WAQAR YOUNIS

First-class Matches (1987–8 to 2003–4)

228 matches 956 wkts 22.23 avge 8 for 17 best 63 5wi 14 10wm

Test Matches (1989–90 to 2002–3)

87 matches 373 wkts 23.56 avge 7 for 76 best 22 5wi 5 10wm

WASIM AKRAM

First-class Matches (1984–5 to 2003)

257 matches 7161 runs 22.73 avge 257* HS 7 hundreds
1042 wkts 21.64 avge 8 for 30 best 70 5wi 16 10wm

Test Matches (1984–5 to 2001–2)

104 matches 2898 runs 22.64 avge 257* HS 3 hundreds
414 wkts 23.62 avge 7 for 119 best 25 5wi 5 10wm

WASIM BARI

First-class Matches (1964–5 to 1983–4)

286 matches 5751 runs 21.70 avge 177 HS 2 hundreds 684 ct 144 st

Test Matches (1967 to 1983–4)

81 matches 1366 runs 15.88 avge 85 HS 0 hundreds 201 ct 27 st

ZAHEER ABBAS

First-class Matches (1965–6 to 1986–7)

459 matches 34843 runs 51.54 avge 274 HS 108 hundreds

Test Matches (1969–70 to 1985–6)

78 matches 5062 runs 44.79 avge 274 HS 12 hundreds

Sri Lanka

Note: Test Match details for M Muralitharan EXCLUDE Australia v ICC World XI in 2005/06

M. S. ATAPATTU

First-class Matches (1989 to 2007–8)
228 matches   14591 runs   48.79 avge   253* HS   47 hundreds

Test Matches (1990–91 to 2007–8)
90 matches   5502 runs   39.02 avge   249 HS   16 hundreds

A. L. F. DE MEL

First-class Matches (1980–81 to 1986–7)
42 matches   109 wkts   37.90 avge   6 for 109 best   3 5wi   0 10wm

Test Matches (1981–2 to 1986–7)
17 matches   59 wkts   36.94 avge   6 for 109 best   3 5wi   0 10wm

P. A. DE SILVA

First-class Matches (1983–4 to 2002)
220 matches   15000 runs   48.38 avge   267 HS   43 hundreds

Test Matches (1984 to 2002)
93 matches   6361 runs   42.97 avge   267 HS   20 hundreds

R. L. DIAS

First-class Matches (1974–5 to 1991–2)
93 matches   4296 runs   32.05 avge   144 HS   5 hundreds

Test Matches (1981–2 to 1986–7)
20 matches   1285 runs   36.71 avge   109 HS   3 hundreds

T. M. DILSHAN

First-class Matches (1993–4 to 2007–8)
175 matches   9814 runs   37.03 avge   200* HS   22 hundreds

Test Matches (1999–00 to 2007–8)
45 matches   2347 runs   37.25 avge   168 HS   4 hundreds

A. P. GURUSINHA

First-class Matches (1984–5 to 1996)
124 matches   7169 runs   43.71 avge   162 HS   20 hundreds

Test Matches (1985–6 to 1996)
41 matches   2452 runs   38.92 avge   143 HS   7 hundreds

S. T. JAYASURIYA

First-class Matches (1988–9 to 2007–8)
261 matches   14742 runs   38.59 avge   340 HS   29 hundreds
   205 wkts   32.77 avge   5 for 34 best   2 5wi   0 10wm

Test Matches (1990–91 to 2007–8)
110 matches   6973 runs   40.07 avge   340 HS   14 hundreds
   98 wkts   34.34 avge   5 for 34 best   2 5wi   0 10wm

D. P. M. DE S. JAYAWARDENE

First-class Matches (1995 to 2007–8)
175 matches   13132 runs   51.49 avge   374 HS   39 hundreds

Test Matches (1997 to 2007–8)
95 matches   7478 runs   51.93 avge   374 HS   22 hundreds

M. F. MAHAROOF

First-class Matches (2001–2 to 2007–8)
41 matches   92 wkts   31.11 avge   7 for 73 best   1 5wi   0 10wm

Test Matches (2004 to 2007–8)
20 matches   24 wkts   60.75 avge   4 for 52 best   0 5wi   0 10wm

S. L. MALINGA

First-class Matches (2001–2 to 2007–8)
80 matches   242 wkts   30.66 avge   6 for 17 best   6 5wi   0 10wm

Test Matches (2004 to 2007–8)
28 matches   91 wkts   33.80 avge   5 for 68 best   2 5wi   0 10wm

M. MURALITHARAN

First-class Matches (1990 to 2007–8)
219 matches   1309 wkts   19.06 avge   9 for 51 best   115 5wi   32 10wm

Test Matches (1992 to 2007–8)
119 matches   730 wkts   21.89 avge   9 for 51 best   63 5wi   20 10wm

R. J. RATNAYAKE

First-class Matches (1982–3 to 1998–9)
59 matches   177 wkts   27.36 avge   6 for 57 best   11 5wi   0 10wm

Test Matches (1982–3 to 1991–2)
23 matches   73 wkts   35.10 avge   6 for 66 best   5 5wi   0 10wm

A. RANATUNGA

First-class Matches (1981–92 to 2000–1)
205 matches   11641 runs   44.26 avge   238* HS 25 hundreds

Test Matches (1981–2 to 2000)
93 matches   5105 runs   35.69 avge   135* HS 4 hundreds

K. C. SANGAKKARA

First-class Matches (1997–8 to 2007–8)
157 matches   10337 runs   45.13 avge   287 HS   23 hundreds   308 ct   33 st

Test Matches (2000 to 2007–8)
73 matches   6127 runs   55.19 avge   287 HS   16 hundreds   152 ct   20 st

W. P. U. J. C. VAAS

First-class Matches (1990–91 to 2007–8)
182 matches   643 wkts   24.80 avge   7 for 54 best   27 5wi   3 10wm

Test Matches (1994 to 2007–8)
104 matches   343 wkts   29.09 avge   7 for 71 best   12 5wi   2 10wm

Acknowledgements

I'm grateful to Martin Searby, Roy Wilkinson, Andrew Samson, Doug and Len Ettlinger, Don Neeley, Alec Bedser, Johnny Waite, Trevor Quirke and Jack Bannister for helping me to compile this book.

Index

He just wanted a decent book to read ...

Not too much to ask, is it? It was in 1935 when Allen Lane, Managing Director of Bodley Head Publishers, stood on a platform at Exeter railway station looking for something good to read on his journey back to London. His choice was limited to popular magazines and poor-quality paperbacks – the same choice faced every day by the vast majority of readers, few of whom could afford hardbacks. Lane's disappointment and subsequent anger at the range of books generally available led him to found a company – and change the world.

'We believed in the existence in this country of a vast reading public for intelligent books at a low price, and staked everything on it'
Sir Allen Lane, 1902–1970, founder of Penguin Books

The quality paperback had arrived – and not just in bookshops. Lane was adamant that his Penguins should appear in chain stores and tobacconists, and should cost no more than a packet of cigarettes.

Reading habits (and cigarette prices) have changed since 1935, but Penguin still believes in publishing the best books for everybody to enjoy. We still believe that good design costs no more than bad design, and we still believe that quality books published passionately and responsibly make the world a better place.

So wherever you see the little bird – whether it's on a piece of prize-winning literary fiction or a celebrity autobiography, political tour de force or historical masterpiece, a serial-killer thriller, reference book, world classic or a piece of pure escapism – you can bet that it represents the very best that the genre has to offer.

Whatever you like to read – trust Penguin.

read more
www.penguin.co.uk